Career Counseling
For African Americans

Career Counseling
For African Americans

Edited by

W. Bruce Walsh
The Ohio State University

Rosie P. Bingham
The University of Memphis

Michael T. Brown
University of California, Santa Barbara

Connie M. Ward
Private Practice, Jonesboro, Georgia

2001

LAWRENCE ERLBAUM ASSOCIATES, PUBLISHERS
Mahwah, New Jersey   London

Lawrence Erlbaum Associates, Inc., Publishers
10 Industrial Avenue
Mahwah, New Jersey 07430

Cover design by Kathryn Houghtaling Lacey

Library of Congress Cataloging-in-Publication Data

Career counseling for African Americans / edited by W. Bruce Walsh ... [et al.].
    p. cm.
Includes bibliographical references and index.
ISBN 0-8058-2715-3 (cloth : alk. paper) – ISBN 0-8058-2716-1 (pbk. : alk. paper)
    1.   Vocational guidance for minorities—United States. I. Walsh, W. Bruce, 1936-

HF5382.5.U5 C2563 2000
158.6'089'00973—dc21

                                                                00-057681

Contents

Preface

A significant question this volume attempts to answer is how counselors will help African Americans prepare for making career choices in the future. The models, strategies, methods, and information on career counseling described and elaborated in this volume attempt to show the way.

This text presents nine significant topics focusing on career counseling for African Americans: basic issues and concepts; career assessment; career counseling with African Americans; career counseling with dual-career African American couples; career transition issues; affirmative career counseling with African American women; career counseling in nontraditional career fields; the impact of the glass ceiling effect on the career development of African Americans; and future directions in career counseling theory, research, and practice with African Americans.

Each chapter takes a distinctive approach to the career-counseling needs of African Americans. These range from a focus on basic issues in career counseling for African Americans, issues related to career assessment, and the special needs of a broad range of African American diversity (e.g., special occupational factors, career transition issues, dual-career families, and future directions).

Chapter 1 by Brown and Pinterits discusses basic issues and concepts in career counseling for African Americans and sets the stage for the more specifically focused chapters to follow. Brown and Pinterits note that there has been little systematic study of career development counseling with African Americans. Most of what we do know is based on research whose participants were college-age students from relatively high economic status. Thus, there is very limited knowledge pertaining to factors affecting the career paths of African American youths from lower socioeconomic status (SES). In this context, Brown and Pinterits present general issues that must be considered in conducting career counseling with African Americans. Second, issues relevant to career intervention, content, process, and assessment are discussed.

Ward and Bingham in chapter 2 present some special challenges for career counselors, especially for those who are grounded in what may be called a traditional view of career assessment. These challenges include: the heterogeneity of African Americans in the United States; the practice of "one-size-fits-all" career services; the United States' ambivalence about its history of slavery; the impact of racism and segregation on the career development of African Americans; and internal and external structural barriers facing African Americans in relation to careers. In addition, Ward and Bingham present a broadened definition of career assessment in order to free the counselor from focusing the career assesment process too narrowly. The authors conclude by making a number of recommendations for career assessment with African Americans.

Chapter 3, by Bingham and Ward, on career counseling with African American males and females, first examines differences and similarities in the career-counseling issues of African American men and women. The authors then explore some of the major career theories to determine their relevance to African American career issues and review career theorists who include culture in their models. The authors go on to review and critique career-counseling models for African Americans. In response to questions raised, the authors make a number of recommendations for career counseling with African Americans. They recommend the following: learning and developing multicultural counseling skills; being aware that African Americans are not monolithic; being aware that African American males are unlikely to seek assistance and will need a more proactive outreach effort; evaluating rights of passage interventions; investigating and studying the role of self-efficacy in the career behavior of African Americans; exploring and studying the career development process for African Americans; and initiating more empirical studies on multicultural career-counseling assessment instruments.

Gilbert and Bingham, chapter 4, highlight issues important to understanding dual-career couples. The authors first identify areas that are unique to dual-career African American couples and thus crucial in any career-counseling process. They then propose a process for working with couples that combines career counseling with multicultural counseling and the research literature on dual-career families. Integrated into this review are responses from 10 dual-career African American couples that the authors interviewed in preparing this chapter. The intent in carrying out the interviews was to explore whether these couples' issues were consistent with those reported in the literature. Couples interviewed for the chapter were selected by identifying one couple and then asking members of the couple to recommend others. The partners in these 10 couples were asked about what they perceived to be problem areas in their dual-career lifestyle, what problems they considered unique to African American dual-career couples, and how they thought a career counselor could be helpful for a dual-career African American couple. In general, the authors note that partners uniformly voiced concerns about time constraints in all areas of their lives. In addition, they spoke of racism and the importance of instilling in the children a sense of pride in themselves and in their race.

In chapter 5, Constantine and Parker address the career transition issues of African American women and how these issues may vary based on voluntary and involuntary transition status. The authors further discuss the utility of social constructionist principles in working with African American women experiencing career transitions. Social constructionism posits that individuals actively construct the meanings of their perceptions and experiences, subsequently defining their own realities. According to social constructionism, there are multiple truths and realities that have been developed from people's belief systems, cultural group memberships, and previous experiences. Thus, Constantine and Parker suggest that constructivist principles would seem to be helpful to vocational counselors in aiding African American women to facilitate career transitions because of their ability to take into account cultural and systemic factors that impact women's career development. The authors conclude with a case example illustrating social constructionist vocational interventions.

Byars, in chapter 6, focuses on some of the issues relevant to the career development of African American women and the implications of these issues for career intervention. Variables like social class, racial salience, age, and ability status complexly interact with race and ethnicity, moderating these cultural influences on career-related behavior. One guiding assumption in this review is that the general context of discrimination and oppression is shared across all subgroups of African American women. The author notes that the chapter is divided into three sections. The first section highlights some of the typical experiences of African American women that significantly shape their orientation toward work. In the second section, social cognitive career theory is presented as a potential model for understanding African American women's experiences and cultural history and their consequential impact on career choice. The final section focuses on specific career-counseling strategies that might be utilized to promote and enhance African American women's career development.

In chapter 7, Hargrow and Hendricks examine the process of career counseling with African Americans in nontraditional occupations. The authors organized the chapter into four sections. The first section provides a brief historical overview of African American career choice and defines what it means to be an African American man or woman in a nontraditional career field. This section further explores factors that may impact nontraditional occupational choices. The second section reviews specific career-counseling issues that pertain to being an African American in a nontraditional field. The third section describes career-counseling strategies and interventions to consider when counseling African Americans in or for nontraditional career fields. The fourth section provides the reader with a list of resources and professional organizations that may be useful when working with African American clients in nontraditional occupations.

In chapter 8, Phelps and Constantine discuss the impact of the glass-ceiling effect on the career development of African Americans. The authors note that in regard to African Americans, literature based on the glass-ceiling concept is sparse compared to writings on White women. Of the literature available, most has focused on African American professional men in corporate America. In this context, this chapter presents a brief historical and contemporary overview of the glass-ceiling concept. The authors then discuss barriers to career development for African Americans. In addition, the authors address issues related to the glass ceiling's impact on African Americans employed in major occupational settings such as business and industry, higher education, and government. The authors also discuss both organizational interventions and career-counseling considerations to address the impact of the glass-ceiling effect on this workforce population.

The final chapter by Pope-Davis and Hargrove (chap. 9) discusses future directions in career counseling theory, research, and practice with African Americans. In this context, the chapter examines four potential theory-building directions. First, the authors recommend that vocational psychologists need to focus more attention on enhancing and testing traditional and emerging theoretical efforts for their cultural relevancy with African Americans. The authors note that the lack of applying these models with African Americans and failing to induce cultural variables into career-counseling models appear to be two significant barriers in deciding whether or not theorists should abandon previous theoretical foundations or begin developing alternate culturally relevant approaches. Second, the authors recommend that theorists should move away from simply comparing the career development of African Americans with Whites while using ethnocentric-based frameworks. Third, future directions in theory should be able to address the range of career needs motivating the vocational behaviors of African Americans across diverse educational backgrounds, gender groups, and social classes. Fourth, the authors recommend that vocational psychologists should begin to acknowledge and incorporate information about vocational behavior from multiple perspectives. In addition, a multidiscipline approach may further inspire a movement toward generating culturally relevant models of career development for African Americans.

In summary, this book will enhance the development of theory, research, and practice for the African American populations. In addition, it is our desire that this volume will lead to the specification of research that will reduce gaps in knowledge about theory, data, and practice in career counseling for African Americans.

W. B. Walsh
R. P. Bingham
M. T. Brown
C. M. Ward

Chapter 1

Basic Issues in the Career Counseling of African Americans

Michael T. Brown
E. Janie Pinterits
University of California–Santa Barbara

The status of persons of African descent in the United States is well known. Given their low status with respect to educational attainment, occupational prestige, unemployment rates, rates of underemployment, earning ratios, delinquency, and more, the quality of life for many African Americans warrants continued attention and vigorous intervention (Bingham & Ward, see chap. 3, this vol.; Brown, 1995). Effective career-development counseling constitutes a critically important element of the social, economic, political, and psychological emancipation of many African Americans (Brown, 1995; Parham & Austin, 1994). Immediate and culturally appropriate intervention into the vocational trajectories of persons of African American heritage is needed and needed early in their development (Brown, 1995; Fouad, 1995). For example, career intervention of some sort is needed, intervention that addresses the early and persistent bleeding of many African Americans from the educational pipeline (Brown, 1995; Fouad, 1995; Leung, 1995; Ogbu, 1991; Steele, 1997). Surveys show that African Americans want assistance with their educational and vocational problems (Carter & Wilson, 1992; Leong & Brown, 1995; Webster & Fretz, 1978) and are willing to use such counseling services (Stabb & Cogdal, 1992). Yet, there are important challenges facing those who wish to provide career services to African Americans.

What forms of career-counseling services do we provide to what types of persons of African American heritage under what specific circumstances to produce the needed outcomes? Although people of good will abound, professionals who recognize the career-development needs of

African Americans and wish to address them do not want to stumble around like Leong's (1993) "good-hearted bumblers." One of the purposes of this book is to help provide some guidance in providing efficacious counseling services to a population that could dearly profit from them. The purpose of this chapter is to present what appear to be the defining issues in providing the type of career counseling that would be helpful.

Models of career counseling exist that should significantly advance the practice of providing career services to African Americans (see Bingham & Ward, chap. 3, this vol.; Bowman, 1995; Cheatham, 1990; Fouad & Bingham, 1995; Leung, 1995). Furthermore, scholars already have written concerning the practice of conducting career assessments with African Americans (see Betz & Fitzgerald, 1995; Bowman, 1993, 1995; Fouad, 1993; Fouad & Bingham, 1995; Ward & Bingham, 1993). The specific focus of this chapter is to delineate critical issues in providing career services to African Americans.

First, general issues that must be considered in conducting career counseling with African Americans are presented. Then, issues relevant to career-intervention content, process, and assessment are presented.

GENERAL ISSUES

Pardon Our Speculations

A Familiar and Sad Refrain.   The various chapter writers in this volume make the same general observation that is repeated throughout the extant literature: There has been little systematic study of career-development counseling with African Americans. It is true that, even with more study, it is not possible to know everything relevant to the career counseling of any population (Betz & Fitzgerald, 1995). Nonetheless, it is also true that we need to know far more than we currently do (Betz & Fitzgerald, 1995; Bowman, 1995; Brown, 1995). Most of what we do know is based on research whose participants were college-age students from relatively high SES. Hence, we need to know more about factors affecting the career trajectories of African American youth from the lower SES.

Is African American Career Counseling and Development Unique? Despite years of study, we still lack knowledge about what is truly racial about the career behavior and counseling of African Americans (Brown, 1995; Smith, 1983). Researchers believe that social and economic experiences embedded in a history of ambivalent race relations circumscribe the career counseling and development of African Americans (Bowman, 1995; Cheatham, 1990; Murry & Mosidi, 1993). However, we do not understand how this circumscription works, nor do we know specifically how to incorporate this knowledge in crafting interventions. Thus, often expressed throughout the chapters in this book are speculations and untested assertions about what might be important to know about African Americans and how this information might be used to construct efficacious career interventions. Such a state of affairs is inescapable and even necessary until our research catches up with our theory.

Histo-Sociopolitical Explanations Are Incomplete. Available data show that African Americans appear to be oriented toward and enter low-paying and low-prestige occupations (Brown, 1995; Osipow & Fitzgerald, 1996; Smith, 1983), but we do not understand why. Social and economic status and racial and sex discrimination have been suggested as likely factors, but their effects and the mechanisms and processes by which their influence on career choice and adjustment are affected are not understood. Moreover, these factors are sociological in nature and do not help us understand how their influences are translated into individual career behavior.

Indeed, almost every chapter in this volume presents an argument that the legacy of slavery, the impacts of race and racial physiognomy, economic deprivations, low social standing, and the differential structure of opportunity are critically important features of the context of African Americans career choice and adjustment. Importantly, the influence of these features lies in their reality and perceived reality, in the minds of scientists and practitioners as well as clients and potential clients. Yet, it is reasoned that the influence is not ubiquitous and catholic; that is, the influences on African American career behavior appear to vary in effect in some yet to be specified ways from person to person, subpopulation to subpopulation, time to time, and situation to situation.

In order to account for the influence of context on behavior, many scholars (including the writers of chapters in this volume) believe that cultural specific or otherwise culturally valid variables account for the career behavior of African Americans (Betz & Fitzgerald, 1995; Carter, 1990; Cheatham, 1990; Kenney, 1994; Leong & Brown, 1995; Pope-Davis & Hargrove, chap. 9, this vol.). However, research exploring the role of such variables only now is beginning to appear in the published literature. Thus, even though the writers of the various chapters in this volume often offer speculations and tentative assertions regarding approaches to providing career counseling for African Americans, such was unavoidable, given the above and the pressing need to provide assistance to this population.

More Sophisticated Analyses Needed and Requested. Regarding the role of culture-specific or culturally valid variables, it is unreasonable to assert that African Americans differ from non-African Americans in cultural orientation and, simultaneously, maintain that the differences only work to the advantage of African Americans (cf., Gottfredson, 1986). For example, African Americans are often described as evidencing a collectivistic orientation, as opposed to an individualistic one (cf., Carter, 1990; Cheatham, 1990). It is reasonable that such an orientation may be advantageous for African Americans striving for survival under conditions of poverty and of legal social, economic, and political forms of systemic racism. However, a collectivistic orientation may be ineffective in managing behavior and people and negotiating situations in contemporary times. It is more tenable to assert that whatever differences exist between African Americans and other racial and ethnic groups, the differences have both positive and negative career-behavior consequences for African Americans. Parenthetically, orientations associated with non-African Americans likely work to both the advantage and disadvantage of those non-African Americans.

Culture, Race, and Ethnicity: Distinctions in Terms

It is important to understand what the present writers mean when they use the terms *culture*, *race* and *ethnicity*. As others noted (cf., Betancourt & Lopez, 1993), these terms are often confused. It is most useful to think of *culture* in psychological (hence, individual) rather than sociological (hence, group) terms. *Culture* is not a type of background, environment, or experience, but rather, is the network of meanings, behaviors, and relationships that an individual has learned from experiences in their environment (Axelson, 1985). As such:

1. Everyone has a culture and that culture constitutes what many persons refer to as *ethnicity*.
2. Culture is complex and multifaceted: People do not live and function as stereotypes.
3. Culture exists in a dynamic state of development.

It is probably best to consider race (i.e., ascription as an African American) as a social stratification construct predicated on mainly visible physical characteristics, but including historical, political features as well. It is a social grouping variable. Thus, participants in this and other societies have formed the belief that it is important to classify people based on certain visible physical characteristics (e.g., skin color, size and shape of nose and lips, texture and length of hair, etc.). Because of the assumed, presumed, and otherwise accepted importance of the classifications, social relationships and socially generated and provided personal information are stratified. As a consequence, the internal and external behavior of members of a society, over time and the histories of the society, are shaped, in part, by the racial context into which they are born. Those internal and external learned behaviors constitute one's *culture* or *ethnicity*. It is possible that individuals can be ascribed to a group on the basis of shared culture, forming cultural or ethnic groups; yet, it is very likely that people belong to many cultural groups. They are likely to belong to fewer races or racial groups.

Yet, race and culture are mutually deterministic. *Race* is a part of the social context that determines the aspects or qualities of culture or ethnicity we learn. Also, one's acquired learned cultural behaviors, in addition to one's perceived racial physiognomy, determine the *race* into which one assigns oneself or is assigned by others.

Sex Differences

The career-development and career-counseling issues of African American males and females appear to be different (Betz & Fitzgerald, 1995; Bowman, 1995; Gilbert & Bingham, chap. 4, this vol.; Subich & Billingsley, 1995). In part, the differences appear to stem from the joint effects of race and sex discrimination and the history of relations between males and females in African American life rooted in the days of slavery (Bingham & Ward, chap. 3; Gilbert & Bingham, chap. 4; Phelps & Constantine, chap. 8, this vol.). Although we are lacking an extensive and detailed picture of how and in what ways African American males and females differ, enough information exists to caution us in crafting treatment strategies.

Career Service Delivery

As indicated by Fouad and Bingham (1995) and Leong and Hartung (1997), to begin to understand the role of racial factors in career-service delivery, one must understand the impact of those factors on: the development and identification of career concerns, the help-seeking behaviors of clients, and the outcomes emanating from career service delivery.

What follows is a presentation of the issues that must be addressed in understanding the impact of race and culture on each of these three components of career-service delivery.

Development and Identification of Career Concerns. No attempt is made in this chapter to suggest that the career choice and adjustment processes and outcomes of African Americans lack commonality with those of other racial and ethnic groups. Research to date would indicate otherwise. Furthermore, even though the racial context into which one is born affects career choice and adjustment processes and outcomes, a given context does not dictate how an individual will respond to it. A challenge for the career-service deliverer, and the career client, is to describe an individual's racial context, how the individual is responding to it and how to evaluate the effectiveness of that responding. Yet, to the extent that race is salient in a society and in a person's life context, it will affect the nature and number of psychological variables that one develops and identifies over one's life. Some psychological variables emanating from a racially salient context would include racial salience, ethnic group identity, level of acculturation, cultural values (including but not limited to individualism and collectivism), occupational racial stereotypes, perceptions of occupational discrimination. Important questions for career service delivery providers and researchers need to be answered in the future: Do we know enough to say that certain responses to racial realities are problematic and do we know enough to prescribe context appropriate solutions?

Help-Seeking and Help-Provision.   Once an African American identifies that they have a problem, how do they go about seeking help in a race-salient society? Is it reasonable to expect such persons to use traditional career services? If so, what would increase their relevance to individuals for whom race is salient? In the provision of career services, what constitutes a culturally appropriate help source beyond the provision of accessible and available, language-fluent, and racially similar vocational therapists? These are many of the questions for which there are no clear answers, but which challenge individuals as they attempt to provide services to African Americans as well as non-African Americans. Consider how to design career services that are culturally appropriate for all.

Career Service Delivery Outcomes.   Given the racial context of our work, a critical issue for career-service professionals concerns outcomes: What should we reasonably expect to result from our endeavors? If racial differences in outcomes are due to race-based social and psychological differences, can differences in those outcomes be produced without eliminating the race-based social and psychological differences? Answers to such questions are urgently needed.

Supporting Nontraditional Career Trajectories

Any approach to the career counseling of African Americans must incorporate support of nontraditional career orientations, with respect to career choice and career adjustment (Phelps & Constantine, chap. 8; Pope-Davis & Hargrove, chap. 9, this vol.). Very few African Americans pursue, enter, and remain in science, mathematics, engineering, and technological fields (Betz,

1990; Hall & Post-Kammer, 1987), fields constituted of high-paying and high-prestige occupations. Among the career choice and decision-making issues associated with nontraditional career trajectories are: poor education and training (in terms of type, amount, and quality) and poor socialization to nontraditional educational and work fields (e.g., messages, experiences, mentors, and role models; Bowman, 1995; Fouad, 1995; Hall & Post-Kammer, 1987; Mc Daniels & Gysbers, 1992; Murry & Mosidi, 1993). The tracking away from such fields early in elementary school is also an issue (Betz, 1990; Fouad, 1995; Hackett & Byars, 1996; Hall & Post-Kammer, 1987). A number of factors are viewed as affecting the career adjustment of African Americans in nontraditional fields: biased hiring and promotion practices, tokenism, isolation and/or estrangement, and the stresses associated with being nontraditional (Pope-Davis & Hargrove, chap. 9, this vol.). It may be that cultural values held by many African Americans are desynchronous with the values associated with nontraditional career pursuits (see Kenney, 1994), but the area requires much more systematic study. Nonetheless, nontraditional career and educational pursuits in African Americans require active efforts to support and encourage them.

The Ams That I Am

Most scholars focusing on the career development and counseling of African Americans express the belief that African Americans (and, indeed, all persons in this country) must define themselves in a social context of race (and sex). As a consequence, their identities as racial beings represent some accommodation among diverse referents including self, various African American subpopulations, and the dominant culture (Cheatham, 1990; Gainor & Forrest, 1991; Helms & Piper, 1994). The resulting racial or cultural identities include conceptions of who one is and can be, what one can do and what one is capable of doing, and how one fits in the various social contexts that one can or will encounter (including the counseling context; see Parham & Austin, 1994). Although little research has investigated the possible career-counseling relevance of race-based identities, it appears clear that for some prospective clients and their counselors, race and race-based identities may be highly salient (Bowman, 1995; Cheatham, 1990; Evans & Herr, 1991; Gainor & Forrest, 1991; Gilbert & Bingham, chap. 4, this vol.; Hackett & Byars, 1996; Helms & Piper, 1994; Herring, 1990).

Dimensions of Differentiation. Furthermore, how an individual might view their relations with the dominant culture and other possible racial and cultural group referents appear to be important to consider. Although not systematically investigated by psychologists, it may prove to be very important in successful counseling for counselors and clients to consider how similar and how different clients perceive themselves with respect to various racial and cultural group referents (for a fuller discussion of the concept, see Fouad & Brown, 2000). In addition, clients need to consider how similar and how different they may be perceived by members and key representatives (viz., gate keepers) of the salient group referents (viz., middle-age, middle-class, White, American males). Indeed, such thinking has been previously advanced as helpful in explaining the career behavior of different racial and cultural group members (Brown & Voyle, 1997; Gottfredson, 1986; Leong & Brown, 1995; Lunneborg, 1997; Roe & Lunneborg, 1991). Social and psychological differentiation from the dominant culture and/or from one's ascribed social group(s) is viewed as directly and indirectly affecting career choice and adjustment behavior (Gilbert & Bingham, chap. 4, this vol.; Gottfredson, 1986; Leong & Brown, 1995; Pope-Davis & Hargrove, chap. 9, this vol.), but awaits systematic, empirical confirmation. There are, likely, a number of different psychological and social qualities on which people may be or may be perceived as different from various reference groups (cf., Leong & Brown, 1995).

African American Identity Is Not Monolithic. In considering race-based or cultural identities within the context of career counseling, it bears repeating that racial and cultural contexts are not unitary and static, but rather, multifaceted and dynamic (Brown, 1995; Parham & Austin, 1994). The forging of an identity within those contexts is a process that continually yields outcomes that are in many ways unique to individuals. Thus, racial or cultural stereotyping by scientists and practitioners as well as prospective clients for career counseling must inevitably be encountered and managed in and outside of counseling (Betz & Fitzgerald, 1995; Carter & Cook, 1992; Helms & Piper, 1994; Parham & Austin, 1994). There is not just one kind of African American and a one-size-fits-all approach to providing career services is untenable.

What follows are some likely intervention content issues followed by intervention process issues that a career-service provider should be prepared to address. Please note that other chapters in this volume address career-counseling issues that are relevant to specific African American subpopulations and contexts.

INTERVENTION: CONTENT ISSUES

In constructing career-counseling interventions, professionals interested in assisting Africans Americans must acknowledge the possibility that current forms of service provision (i.e., 50-minute, individual, talk-therapy sessions once a week at a clinic site) may not be an effective way of addressing the long-standing, society-sourced, group–family–community-shared, career-related problems of some African Americans. Although group, action-oriented, system-targeted meetings of unspecified duration at non-traditional sites around the community may need to be considered (Bowman, 1995; Gilbert & Bingham, chap. 4, this vol.; Hawks & Muha, 1991; Leung, 1995; Pope-Davis & Hargrove, chap. 9, this vol.; Bingham & Ward, chap. 3, this vol.), there is little in the way of empirically supported practice to guide the professional as to choices of intervention strategy. As strategy depends in part on the problem content, some content issues are presented, ones that a review of the extant literature indicates are important: coping with race and sex discrimination, increasing career-relevant expectations, and enhancing educational achievement and attainment.

Coping With Race and Sex Discrimination

Race and Sex Discrimination as Content. Virtually every writer addressing the career development and counseling of African Americans has pointed to the need to deal with racism and, at least with respect to African American women, sexism (Gilbert & Bingham, chap. 4, this vol.; Leung, 1995; Pope-Davis & Hargrove, chap. 9, this vol.). Although the salience of race (and probably sex) varies from person to person (cf., Helms & Piper, 1994), research has shown that counselors who address the possible role of race in counseling are viewed as more culturally competent and credible (cf., Atkinson & Lowe, 1995). In addition, both real and perceived forms of race and sex discrimination affect the lives of many African Americans. Thus, race and sex, however real and perceived, are important elements of stratification and differential treatment with which many African Americans must contend. Race and sex stratification affect identity and coping, with likely career counseling and development implications.

Race- and Sex-Based Identity. Contending with race and sex stratification and differential treatment clearly affects identity formation (Atkinson, Morten, & Sue, 1993; Fouad & Bingham, 1995; Helms, 1990; White & Parham, 1980). Given that African Americans may define themselves with respect to many different referents (Cheatham, 1990; Gainor & Forrest, 1991; White & Parham, 1980) and given that the salience or centrality of the various referents may differ (Gainor & Forrest, 1991; Helms & Piper, 1994), one of the major tasks of counselors will be to establish the relevance of race- and sex-based identity issues to the career choice and adjustment problems or challenges presented by African American clients. The ways counselors and clients define their race and sexual identities have implications for how they will relate together as well as how the client will relate to various other race and sex social contexts.

Social Isolation.   Given the aforementioned discussion, issues of real and perceived social isolation and alienation may need to be explored with respect to dominant culture contexts and various other racial, ethnic, and gender contexts (Gilbert & Bingham, chap. 4; Phelps & Constantine, chap. 8; Pope-Davis & Hargrove, chap. 9, this vol.). Historically, relations between the sexes and among the races have been problematic and it is reasonable to assert that problems associated with those relations might affect African American career behavior. Research relevant to the career adjustment of African Americans (cf., Pope-Davis & Hargrove, chap. 9, this vol.) and for women relevant to career choice and adjustment (cf., Betz & Fitzgerald, 1995) shows such effects. Consequently, issues of social support and social comfort are indicated as potential content issues whose salience depends on the individual African American and their various behavioral contexts.

Coping With "isms".   Of course, the identity and estrangement issues previously presented may either reflect or be exacerbated by the client's skill or skill confidence and/or efficacy deficits in managing racism and sexism (cf., Brown, 1995; Edwards & Polite, 1992; Hackett & Byars, 1996; Smith, 1983). Integrating the meaning of race and sex into one's vocational life and developing coping strategies to deal with the associated "isms" may represent important tasks to undertake in counseling (Bingham & Ward, chap. 3, this vol.; Brown, 1995). Racial context presents issues to which individuals develop (or fail to develop) coping strategies. Those developed strategies may be effective or not, depending on the context and on the one doing the evaluation. A challenge for career-delivery specialists is to determine the coping strategy being employed by a client and the method (or methods) of determining a strategy's effectiveness.

Assuming that the counselor and client determine that racism and sexism are salient counseling issues, what do we in counseling do about discrimination and the differential structure of opportunity? A client may need to work through feelings, beliefs, and behaviors associated with coping with the "isms". They may also need advocacy, coaching, and other forms of assistance in managing the "isms" effectively. At the very least, management of discrimination and the differential structure of opportunity need to be discussed with the client (Kiselica, 1995), perceived career choice and adjustment barriers must be identified (cf., McWhirter, 1997), and problem-solving activities (including problem inoculation) need to be accomplished (cf., Hawks & Muha, 1991).

Increasing Career-Relevant Expectations

Research is highly suggestive that level of career and educational expectations, not aspirations, determine prestige and income levels of career pursuits (Brown, 1995; McNair & Brown, 1983). It has been suggested that racism and sexism affect learning experiences in such a way as to decrease career-related expectations and reduce the range of occupations being considered by African Americans (Bowman, 1995; Brown, 1995; Dunn & Veltman, 1989; Fouad, 1995; Hackett & Byars, 1996; Lent, Brown, & Hackett, 1994; Murry & Mosidi, 1993; Ogbu, 1991; Steele, 1997). More research in this area is needed, but we venture that an important area of career intervention is on the career behavior relevant expectations.

One Approach. A social cognitive approach has been advocated as a means of increasing career-related expectations (Brown, 1995; Hackett & Byars, 1996; Lent et al., 1994; Leong & Brown, 1995). Utilizing such an approach, the expectations of African Americans can be modified by broadening their learning opportunities relevant to career-related experiences, teaching them how to effectively handle "isms," increasing the availability and accessibility of certain types of mentors and role models, providing more encouraging and empowering messages about success possibilities across the whole range of media, and reducing anxieties associated with succeeding in various social and behavioral contexts (Bowman, 1995; Hackett & Byars, 1996; Lent et al., 1994), especially with respect to math and science activities (Betz, 1990; Fouad, 1995; Hall & Post-Kammer, 1987; Murry & Mosidi, 1993).

It may be obvious that implementation of the social cognitive approach may require important changes in the society such that race and sex discrimination are eliminated (or at least reduced) and the structure of opportunity modified so as to be more equitable. Media images of African Americans need changes, and educational systems need significant alterations (Bowman, 1995; Dunn & Veltman, 1989; Hackett & Byars, 1996). Thus, a more expansive role for career counselors may be indicated (Leung, 1995).

Enhancing Educational Achievement and Attainment

No attempt to advance the career development of African Americans can be completely successful without attention being given to educational achievement and attainment (Betz & Fitzgerald, 1995; Bingham & Ward, chap. 3, this vol.; Brown, 1995; Dunn & Veltman, 1989; Fouad, 1995; Kunjufu, 1986; Leung, 1995; Ogbu, 1991; Pope-Davis & Hargrove, chap. 9, this vol.; White & Parham, 1980). Efforts need to be made to increase the real and perceived meaning and relevance of schooling among some African Americans (cf., Ogbu, 1991). The significance of schooling for African American clients must be examined and discussed within the context of their aspirations and expectations. Systemic interventions need to be directed toward improving the quality of educational experiences for African American children.

INTERVENTION: PROCESS ISSUES

Whereas content issues associated with the provision of culturally appropriate career services to African Americans concerns possible topics and problems that may be the focus of counseling, process issues concern how those issues might be most effectively addressed. The larger multicultural counseling literature is drawn upon because of its obvious relevance to career counseling and because very little appears in the empirical literature regarding multicultural issues in career counseling. Attention is devoted to the following issues: treating systemic problems; group approaches; racial and cultural counselor–client similarity; incorporating family, church, and community; active and directive counseling; sensitivities to the contextual realities of African American life; and patience.

Treating Systemic Problems

It would appear obvious that to the extent that context, the situations and circumstances in which African Americans develop and function, is the source of a persons problems, intervening in and on that context might become the target of counselor and client intervention (Leung, 1995). Such a counseling focus might be difficult to delimit within the confines of 50-minute, talk-therapy, clinic sessions. Indeed, it could involve group, family, and/or community mobilization to address significant career choice and adjustment issues of a client. Efforts like those of Cummins (1986) and Fouad (1995) reflect system-focused, career-intervention strategies.

Group Approaches

As Leung (1995) pointed out, group-oriented approaches have long been advocated for ethnic minorities such as African Americans (cf., Bowman, 1995; Shipp, 1983; Todisco & Salomone, 1991). One reason group approaches have been advocated is that they are viewed as congruent with the collectivist cultural orientation ascribed to African Americans (Bowman, 1995). Yet, we know almost nothing about the relative effectiveness of group and nongroup career interventions with African Americans (Leung, 1995). Furthermore, we know that not all African Americans exhibit or adhere to a collectivist orientation. Instead of a blanket endorsement of group approaches, we suggest that a group approach is indicated: (a) to the extent that the career issues of any African American are shared by others; (b) when the client exhibits and/or advocates a collectivist orientation; (c) when the issues of isolation and alienation present; and (d) when problem solving becomes the focus concerning issues of coping with racism and sexism.

Racial and Cultural Counselor–Client Similarity

Although more research into possible modifying variables is necessary, there is a documented preference among African Americans for racially and culturally similar counselors, with a strong likelihood that such counselors will be viewed as more credible and trustworthy (Atkinson & Lowe, 1995; Bowman, 1995; Kenney, 1994). Importantly, racial and cultural matching of counselor and client may be differentially important to clients as a function of the perceived salience of race (Atkinson & Lowe, 1995; Bowman, 1995; Helms & Carter, 1991). Thus, it may be that whenever possible, African American career clients ought to be offered the opportunity to select the race and, within broad parameters (including belief in the significance of racism and sexism), the culture of the counselor.

Trust. Recognizing that career counseling is embedded within a racial and cultural context (Fouad, 1993, 1995; Fouad & Bingham, 1995) where some degree of antipathy among the races exists, it is reasonable to suspect that trust might be an important career-counseling issue. The trust clients might have (or not) for counselors (Bowman, 1995; Jordan, 1991; Osipow & Fitzgerald, 1996) is an important process issue, but not often discussed is the importance of the trust–faith (or lack thereof) counselors have for or in clients. Thus, trust on both sides might present as content issues, the resolution of which has implications for the effectiveness of career counseling.

Tied to the issue of client trust of the counselor may be the issue of premature termination (Kenney, 1994). No data concerning racial factors involved in premature termination of career-counseling sessions is available at this time. Yet, given what we know for personal counseling sessions, trust appears to be a significant issue in premature termination (Atkinson & Lowe, 1995; Terrell & Terrell, 1984) and is facilitated by ethnic matching of counselors and clients.

Incorporating Family, Church, and Community

Given the often-asserted collectivist orientation of many African Americans, career counseling may need to take a form that best allows the client to consider and involve the input of important members of his or her life (Bowman, 1995; Carter & Cook, 1992; Hawks & Muha, 1991; Kenney, 1994; Parham & Austin, 1994). This assertion is echoed by other writers in this volume (Gilbert & Bingham, chap. 4; Bingham & Ward, chap. 3).

Active and Directive Counseling

There is some data that suggests that members of many ethnic groups seem to find directive forms of counseling more preferable and effective (cf., Atkinson & Lowe, 1995). There also appears to be reason for offering

African American clients an action-oriented, career-counseling approach (Griggs & Dunn, 1989). Perhaps because career counseling is perceived as inherently directive and action oriented, African Americans have expressed a greater preference for career counseling over other forms of counseling (Stabb & Cogdal, 1992). Until more research into the issue reveals otherwise, an active and directive career-counseling approach for African American clients is to be preferred.

Sensitivities to the Contextual Realities of African American Life

It may be tedious to read once more that a key to effective counseling with African Americans is a commitment and effort to understanding them and to understanding one's self (the counselor) within the context of individually experienced and fluid social, historical, economic, and political realities (Bingham & Ward, 1994; Fouad & Bingham, 1995; Todisco & Salomone, 1991). It may be especially tedious to repeatedly hear such recommendations in the absence of research data specifying the relation between such contextual realities and career behavior. Tedium notwithstanding, a counselor that is striving to function in a culturally appropriate manner must have or acquire as current an understanding as possible of the various meanings African Americans may attach to being an African American in this country (Bowman, 1995; Todisco & Salomone, 1991). They must be willing to help the client explore the broader social and economic implications of their constructions. Furthermore, a counselor must have some understanding of how clients' views of the world and their places in it are shaped by race, sex, and SES (Bingham & Ward, 1994; Bowman, 1995; Fouad, 1993, 1995; Fouad & Bingham, 1995; Leung, 1995).

Relatedly, counselors must recognize that they are racial and cultural beings, just as their clients are. Thus, their own views of the world, people, and behavior are shaped by a dynamic set of social, historical, economic, and political realities associated with race and sex (Bingham & Ward, 1994; Bowman, 1995; Fouad, 1993, 1995; Fouad & Bingham, 1995; Todisco & Salomone, 1991). Culturally competent counselors continually examine, evaluate, and strategically modify their cultural assumptions (Bingham & Ward, 1994; Bowman, 1995; Kimbrough & Salomone, 1993), especially before they expect to help African American clients to do so.

Patience

Brown (1996) observed that it may take time for racial and other psychocontextual issues to present themselves in counseling. The reason it may take time is due to the great sensitivity African Americans (and society in general) have regarding such issues. Thus, patience is urged in awaiting their emergence in career counseling as well as in dealing with them therapeutically.

INTERVENTION: ASSESSMENT ISSUES

Two goals of assessment are to know and understand another person and to acquire the information needed to help persons achieve their goals (cf., Walsh & Betz, 1995). Assessment is an important aspect of career counseling because counselors need: (a) to determine what domains of behavior are salient with respect to understanding a client and the client's career choice or adjustment concerns, (b) to determine how to meaningfully assess those domains, and (c) to make sense of the information once it is obtained. In this section of the chapter, the first two issues are the focus. To a large extent the latter issue, making sense of the information once it is obtained, is an intervention process issue. As such, it is an issue that is resolved in the process of helping a client engage and relate to the information obtained.

Scholars and practitioners are urged to keep in mind that testing constitutes one approach to assessment, but not the only approach (cf., Walsh & Betz, 1995). The reason for this reminder is because tests have not been constructed for many potentially important dimensions of African American life that are viewed as having career-related concomitants. Therefore, counselors have to use the counseling interview, life histories, and other information sources in order to assess some dimensions. What follows is a presentation of apparently salient variables to assess. Afterwards, a discussion of the meaningfulness of the information assessed is presented.

Salient Domains of Behavior

From what is currently known about the career development and counseling of African Americans, one can deduce that a number of either culturally specific or culturally salient variables impact them (Bowman, 1995; Carter, 1990; Cheatham, 1990; Fouad, 1993, 1995; Osipow & Fitzgerald, 1996; Subich & Billingsley, 1995). Consequently, it is important to assess them.

There are three major classes of variables that should have career salience for African Americans (cf., Gottfredson, 1986; Leong & Brown, 1995). The first class concerns variables measuring dimensions on which African Americans may differ from people in general (or the dominant culture group). The second class of variables concerns variables on which an individual African American may differ from other African Americans.

The third class includes variables concerning the degree to which a person is a primary caregiver and or a primary economic provider for others. In addition to these classes of variables, the importance of assessing language use and facility and expectations are discussed.

From a cursory reading of the African American psychology literature, many African Americans view themselves as very different from members of the general population (cf., White & Parham, 1980). The long, painful, and continuing history of race relations in the United States shows that many African Americans are viewed and treated as different from mainstream American society (cf., Hacker, 1992; Helms, 1990; Helms & Piper, 1994). Yet, true racial differences in career factors have been difficult to uncover (see Helms & Piper, 1994 for one important explanation of this state of affairs). However, the present conditions may be due to the fact that a number of potentially salient variables have not been operationalized and tested adequately with respect to the career choice and adjustment behavior of African Americans. Among such factors that might represent dimensions on which African Americans differ from majority culture persons or on which they may be unique and are expected to affect African American career development and counseling, reference group identity and cultural values orientation remain the focus.

Differences From the Dominant Culture Group.   The extant literature on African American career development and counseling is replete with references to importance of reference-group identity to career-relevant behavior, although many different terms are used (Bowman, 1995; Carter & Cook, 1992; Cheatham, 1990; Ogbu, 1991; Steele, 1997). *Acculturation* is one term and concept that is believed to have career-behavior significance (see also Pope-Davis & Hargrove, chap. 9, this vol.). Behavioral *acculturation* refers to the degree or extent to which a person of one race or nationality identifies with the dominant or host culture (Leong & Brown, 1995). *Values acculturation*, the degree of adherence to beliefs and practices that characterize cultural groups (cf., Kluckhohn & Strodtbeck 1961), is also expected to influence career trajectories (cf., Cheatham, 1990; Parham & Austin, 1994). *Racial salience* (Helms & Piper, 1994), as applied to career behavior, is another term; it refers to the extent to which a person perceives race to be a significant determinant of their work lives. (Racial and ethnic identity are other terms but these are discussed in the following section.) To the degree to which an African American is acculturated, lacks the perception of racial salience, and adheres to cultural values that are characteristic of the general population, the African American's career behavior is expected to be similar to that of members of the general population (see also Parham & Austin, 1994). To the extent that African Americans are not acculturated, see race as highly salient, and do not adhere to cultural values that are characteristic of the dominant culture, their career behavior is increasingly expected to be different from that of dominant culture persons. Therefore, *reference-group identity*, how variously termed or conceived, is expected to affect career-related choices, goals, performances and adjustments. It should be noted that to date, there exists one measure of racial salience (see Cardo, 1994) and no measure of African American acculturation to the mainstream. (The Ladrine and Klonoff, 1994, scale is best considered a measure of identification with one's ascribed social group.) Effective methods of assessment and measures of orientation of the cultural values of U.S. society exist (cf., Atkinson & Thompson, 1992; Singelis, Triandis, Bhawuk, & Gelfand, 1995; Triandis, McCusker, & Hui, 1990).

It is important to add here that although African Americans have their own perceptions of how they fit within the dominant culture group, members of the wider society relate with them on the basis of how they perceive that an individual African American fits within that society. Indeed, racism and sexism, the differential structure of opportunity, the lesser social value ascribed to many African American persons is a function of how members of the dominant social group perceive them. As Osipow and Fitzgerald (1996) expressed, race (and probably other social structural variables) is a sociophysical stimulus variable that effects how people in a society respond to an individual. As such, it is tied to the structural barrier of discrimination in a way that constrains career choice and adversely impacts career adjustment. Yet, we have not been able to subject how the general society relates to African Americans in our studies of African Americans counseling and development. It is critically important to find some means of doing so because societal perceptions and actions are expected to affect an individual's career behavior (cf., Lent et al., 1994). What may be useful in counseling is to determine how an individual believes the general society relates to him or her. Certainly, measures of such variables as cultural mistrust (Terrell & Terrell, 1981) and perceptions of occupational opportunities, barriers, and discrimination (cf., Bingham & Ward, 1994; Chung & Harmon, 1994; Hegarty & Dalton, 1995; Howell, Frese, & Sollie, 1984; Ladrine & Klonoff, 1996; Swanson, Daniels, & Tokar, 1996) offer promise as methods of doing so. Also, Yost and Corbishley (1987) offered a useful process for discovering career choice and decision-making barriers and evaluating their relative importance.

Differences From One's Ascribed Social Group. For many years now, most scholars and practitioners in the area have acknowledged that African Americans differ from one another in a variety of systematic ways (cf., Bingham & Ward, chap. 3, this vol.; Brown, 1995; Pope-Davis & Hargrove, chap. 9, this vol.) and that these within-group variations might help us better understand behavior of subgroups of and individual African Americans. Currently, scholars are searching for those important dimensions that might help us understand this within-group variation. *Racial identity, ethnic–cultural identity, culture-specific values* are terms referring to concepts that are conceived as capturing within-group variations among African Americans.

Racial identity refers to the processes by which persons develop (or not) racial collective identities in environments in which their socially ascribed racial group has differential access to sociopolitical power (Helms & Piper, 1994). Although an underinvestigated area, there are data that show that reference-group identity is associated with career decision-making behavior (cf., Helms & Piper, 1994). Erroneously, *ethnic identity* has been considered synonymous to racial identity by some professionals, but the term refers to the degree to which persons identify with the cultural beliefs and practices of their socially ascribed cultural group (cf., Leong & Brown, 1995). Ethnic identity is a concept that differs very little from the concept of *culture-specific values orientation* (sometimes termed *worldview orientation*), which refers to the degree to which a person endorses or adheres to values characteristic of their socially ascribed cultural group (cf., Leong & Brown, 1995).

Although not well explored, it is expected that African Americans, depending on the degree to which they hold positive or negative attitudes toward African Americans or European Americans, will exhibit behavior patterns consistent with such attitudes (including career choice and adjustment behaviors; Helms & Piper, 1994; Parham & Austin, 1994). The more an individual identifies with African Americans in general and endorses values characteristic of such persons, the more their career behavior is expected to be stereotypic of African Americans (Bingham & Ward, 1994; Bowman, 1995; Cheatham, 1990).

Scales exist to measure African American racial identity (Helms, 1990), African American acculturation (Baldwin & Bell, 1985; Landrine & Klonoff, 1994), and cultural values orientation (cf., Atkinson & Thompson, 1992), although the psychometric qualities of some of these instruments may need further evaluation and development.

Caregiver and Provider Role.   It is widely asserted that African Americans develop within a collectivist culture and as such exhibit a willingness to subordinate individuality for the sake of family and community (cf., White & Parham, 1990). Assuming such to be the case, one would expect issues of family and community support, care, and provision to be important factors affecting the career behavior of African Americans and important to consider in career counseling. Research has not generated strong evidence that those factors strongly affect African American career behavior, nor has it confirmed the importance of considering such factors in career counseling. In the absence of empirical findings indicating otherwise, many writers argued that family and community allegiances and responsibilities must be incorporated at some level in the career counseling (e.g., Bingham & Ward, 1994, chap. 3, this vol.; Gilbert & Bingham, chap. 4, this vol.; Pope-Davis & Hargrove, chap. 9, this vol.). Until the issue is shown not to be a significant feature of African American career development and given that such factors can significantly affect career trajectories (cf., Gottfredson, 1986), we support the practice of assessing the salient caregiver and provider obligations and constituents in the career counseling of African Americans.

Language Use and Facility. Although discussed by only a few scholars (Betz & Fitzgerald, 1995; Bingham & Ward, chap. 3, this vol.; Brown, 1995), it seems language use and facility determine the social circles in which an African American can negotiate and how successfully they can do so. To the extent that an African American can read, write, and speak standard English of the general society, the more effective they will be in reaching their career goals. The more capable they are at reading and communicating in the language of their communities, the more effective they will be at living, learning, and working in those social circles. Communication skills and facility with various social groups may be very important areas to assess with respect to African American career development.

Expectations. In light of the importance of career and educational expectations to African American career development (cf., Brown, 1995; Hackett & Byars, 1996; Lent et al., 1994; Thomas & Gordon, 1983), these expectations need to be the focus of career assessment (Lee, 1991). Of the various expectations that need to be examined, the following are considered to be of prime importance given the content issues presented earlier in this chapter: occupational prestige, educational attainment and achievement, coping with racism and sexism, and efficacy for math and science activities. Although measures of some of these expectations exist in the empirical literature (cf., Brown, 1995; Hackett & Byars, 1996; Lent et al., 1994; Thomas & Gordon, 1983), expectations are best assessed by engaging a client in a discussion about their expectations, the bases for them, and the possible consequences of holding them or changing them.

Meaningfulness of the Assessed Dimensions

The meaningfulness of the assessed dimensions lies in the reliability and validity of them for African American career development. If one considers reliability and validity as measurement concepts, few of the dimensions discussed earlier have been subjected to measurement. Of those that have, few have been normed or developed on representative samples of African Americans (cf., Eby, Johnson, & Russell, 1998; Fouad, 1993; Leong & Gim-Chung, 1995). From a research standpoint, such a state of affairs is disappointing to say the least.

However, from a counseling standpoint, the goal may be less the statistical meaningfulness of the various concepts and more their practical reliability and validity. Do we have reason to suspect that the identified concepts are relevant to African Americans and can exploration of such concepts yield information of practical utility? Until the current state of empirical affairs changes, it is believed that the identified concepts are likely to be relevant to a large number of African Americans and that engaging African American career clients in a discussion of some of the concepts will generate information highly relevant to enhancing their career development.

With respect to intervention content issues, all of the chapter authors in this volume discuss the impact of racism and sexism in the career lives of African Americans and how to address them. However, none of the chapter authors discuss how to develop skill and efficacy in African American career clients in dealing with "isms;" this issue awaits further treatment. Nonetheless, the chapters by Phelps and Constantine (chap. 8), Gilbert and Bingham (chap. 4), and Pope-Davis and Hargrove (chap. 9) discuss the importance of addressing the issue of social isolation, from other African Americans and from members of the dominant culture culture, as important to effective African American career counseling. Future writers might discuss particular treatment approaches and their efficacy for improving the career lives of African Americans. The chapters by Bingham and Ward (chap. 3) and Pope-Davis and Hargrove (chap. 9) discuss the importance of educational achievement and attainment for increasing the career prospects of African Americans. However, none of the chapter authors discuss intervention approaches to increasing them for this population. It is also unfortunate that none of the chapters contained in this volume specifically address the efficacy of the typical counseling context—that is, the efficiacy of the 50-minute session in a counseling clinic, hospital, or university for providing career services to African American clients.

With respect to intervention process issues, all of the chapters deal with the contextual realities of African American life and how to address them in the counseling process. In addition, the Bingham and Ward (chap. 3) and Pope-Davis and Hargrove (chap. 9) chapters directly discuss the issue of racial and cultural similarity for an effective vocational therapy process involving African American clients. It is also noteworthy that Gilbert and Bingham (chap. 4) and Bingham and Ward (chap. 3) discuss the involvement of family, church, and community in career counseling. Yet, we sense from reading those chapters that more remains to be said on the topic regarding how best to effect this involvement. In addition, much more could have been, and needs to be, written about how vocational therapists can treat systemic problems like racism. The chapter by Phelps and Constantine (chap. 8) is a bright spot in the literature, concerning the treatment of racisim in the career advancement and adjustment of African Americans. Notwithstanding, none of the volume's chapters address the process issues of group career counseling, active and directive career counseling, and patience in providing career counseling services to African Americans. Future scholarship in this area should directly address these issues.

Little in this volume bears on the broad issue of career assessment, and especially testing, for African Americans. All of the chapter authors more or less identify important domains of behavior to assess when counseling African American clients, although Bingham and Ward (chap. 3) and Pope-Davis and Hargrove (chap. 9) and this chapter deal with the issue in breadth. Also, Ward and Bingham (chap. 2), Gilbert and Bingham (chap. 4), and Pope-Davis and Hargrove (chap. 9) discuss the issues of primary caregiver and primary economic provider roles in African American career counseling; however, much more remains to be said on this issue. Similarly, future writers may wish to consider the issue of language facility and use in African American career counseling, although Bingham and Ward (chap. 3) present the issue. Except for the Pope-Davis and Hargrove chapter (chap. 9), little appears in this volume concerning the impact and treatment of career-related expectations among African Americans; more scholarship in this area is urged. Future writings might also devote more focus on the reliability and validity of career and career-relevant tests and measures for use in African American career counseling.

In conclusion, we believe that a number of important career-service delivery content, process, and assessment issues remain to be addressed with respect to providing career help to African Americans. Nonetheless, we believe that this volume fills an important void in the literature and represents an important step in guiding vocational therapists in the treatment of the career concerns of African Americans.

REFERENCES

Atkinson, D. R., & Lowe, S. M. (1995). The role of ethnicity, cultural knowledge, and conventional techniques in counseling and psychotherapy. In J. G. Ponterotto, J. M. Casas, L. A. Suzuki, & C. M. Alexander (Eds.), *Handbook multicultural counseling* (pp. 387–414). Thousand Oaks, CA: Sage.

Atkinson, D. R., Morten, G., & Sue, D. W. (1993). *Counseling American minorities* (4th ed.). Madison, WI: Brown & Benchmark/W. C. Brown Publishers.

Atkinson, D. R., & Thompson, C. E. (1992). Racial, ethnic, and cultural variables in counseling. In S. D. Brown & R. W. Lent (Eds.), *Handbook of counseling psychology* (2nd ed., pp. 349–382). New York: Wiley.

Axelson, J. A. (1985). *Counseling and development in a multicultural society.* Monterey, CA: Brooks/Cole.

Baldwin, J. A., & Bell, Y. R. (1985). The African self-consciousness scale: An Afrocentric personality questionnaire. *Western Journal of Black Studies, 9,* 61–68.

Betancourt, H., & Lopez, S. R. (1993). The study of culture, ethnicity, and race in American psychology. *American Psychologist, 48,* 629–637.

Betz, N. E. (1990). *What stops women and minorities from choosing and completing majors in science and engineering?* Washington, DC: Federation of Behavioral, Psychological, and Cognitive Sciences.

Betz, N. E., & Fitzgerald, L. F. (1995). Career assessment and intervention with racial and ethnic minorities. In F. T. L. Leong (Ed.), *Career development and vocational behavior of racial and ethnic minorities* (pp. 263–279). Mahwah, NJ: Lawrence Erlbaum Associates.

Bingham, R. P., & Ward, C. M. (1994). Career counseling with ethnic minority women. In W. B. Walsh & S. H. Osipow (Eds.), *Career counseling with women* (pp. 165–195). Mahwah, NJ: Lawrence Erlbaum Associates.

Bowman, S. L. (1993). Career intervention strategies for ethnic minorities. *Career Development Quarterly, 42,* 14–15.

Bowman, S. L. (1995). Career intervention strategies and assessment issues for African Americans. In F. T. L. Leong (Ed.), *Career development and vocational behavior of racial and ethnic minorities* (pp. 137–164). Hillsdale, NJ: Lawrence Erlbaum Associates.

Brown, M. T. (1995). The career development of African Americans: Theoretical and empirical issues. In F. T. L. Leong (Ed.), *Career development and vocational behavior of racial and ethnic minorities* (pp. 7–36). Hillsdale, NJ: Lawrence Erlbaum Associates.

Brown, M. T. (1996, August). Applying the Fouad and Bingham culturally appropriate career counseling model to African American clients. In Nadya A. Fouad (Chair), *Culturally appropriate career counseling model: Examining our roots and looking for a diverse future.* Symposium conducted at the annual convention of the American Psychological Association, Toronto, Canada.

Brown, M. T., & Voyle, K. M. (1997). Without Roe. *Journal of Vocational Behavior, 51,* 310–318.

Cardo, L. M. (1994). Development of an instrument measuring valence and ethnicity and perceptions of discrimination. *Journal of Multicultural Development and Counseling, 22,* 49–59.

Carter, D. J., & Wilson, R. (1992). *Minorities in higher education, 1991: Tenth annual status report.* Washington, DC: American Council on Education.

Carter, R. T. (1990). Cultural value differences between African-Americans and White Americans. *Journal of College Student Development, 31,* 71–79.

Carter, R. T., & Cook, D. A. (1992). A culturally relevant perspective for understanding the career paths of visible racial/ethnic group people. In H. D. Lea & Z. B. Leibowitz (Eds.), *Adult career development: Concepts, issues, and practices* (pp. 192–217). Alexandria, VA: The National Career Development Association.

Cheatham, H. E. (1990). Africentricity and career development of African Americans. *Career Development Quarterly, 38,* 334–346.

Chung, Y. B., & Harmon, L. W. (1994). The career interests and aspirations of gay men: How sex-role orientation is related. *Journal of Vocational Behavior, 45,* 223–239.

Cummins, J. (1986). Empowering minority students: A framework for intervention. *Harvard Educational Review, 56,* 18–36.

Dunn, C. W., & Veltman, G. C. (1989). Addressing the restrictive career maturity patterns of minority youth: A program evaluation. *Journal of Multicultural Counseling and Development, 17,* 156–164.

Eby, L. T., Johnson, C. D., & Russell, J. E. A. (1998). A psychometric review of career assessment tools for use with diverse individuals. *Journal of Career Assessment, 6,* 269–310.

Edwards, A., & Polite, C. (1992). *Children of the dream: The psychology of Black success.* New York: Bantam.

Evans, K. M., & Herr, E. L. (1991). The influence of racial identity and the perceptions of discrimination on the career aspirations of African American men and women. *Journal of Vocational Behavior, 44,* 173–184.

Fouad, N. A. (1993). Cross-cultural vocational assessment. *Career Development Quarterly, 42,* 4–13.

Fouad, N. A. (1995). Career linking: An intervention to promote math and science career awareness. *Journal of Counseling and Development, 73,* 527–534.

Fouad, N. A., & Bingham, R. P. (1995). Career counseling with racial and ethnic minorities. In W. B. Walsh & S. H. Osipow (Eds.), *Handbook of vocational psychology: Theory, research, and practice* (2nd ed., pp. 331–366). Mahwah, NJ: Lawrence Erlbaum Associates.

Gainor, K. A., & Forrest, L. (1991). African American women's self-concept: Implications for career decisions and career counseling. *Career Development Quarterly, 39,* 261–272.

Gottfredson, L. S. (1986). Special groups and the beneficial use of vocational interest inventories. In W. B. Walsh & S. H. Osipow (Eds.), *Advances in vocational psychology (vol. 1): Assessment of interests* (pp. 127–198). Hillsdale, NJ: Lawrence Erlbaum Associates.

Griggs, S. A., & Dunn, R. (1989). The learning styles of multicultural groups and counseling implications. *Journal of Multicultural Counseling and Development, 17,* 146–155.

Hacker, A. (1992). *Two nations.* New York: Scribner's.

Hackett, G., & Byars, A. (1996). Social cognitive theory and the career development of African American women. *Career Development Quarterly, 44,* 322–340.

Hall, E. R., & Post-Kammer, P. (1987). Black mathematics and science majors: Why so few? *Career Development Quarterly, 35,* 206–219.

Hawks, B. K., & Muha, D. (1991). Facilitating the career development of minorities: Doing it differently this time. *Career Development Quarterly, 39,* 251–260.

Hegarty, W. H., & Dalton, D. R. (1995). Development and psychometric properties of the Organizational Diversity Inventory (ODI). *Educational and Psychological Measurement, 55,* 1047–1052.

Helms, J. E. (1990). *Black and white racial identity: Theory, research and practice.* Westport, CT: Greenwood.

Helms, J. E., & Carter, R. T. (1991). Relationships of White and Black racial identity attitudes and demographic similarity to counselor preferences. *Journal of Counseling Psychology, 38,* 446–457.

Helms, J. E., & Piper, R. E. (1994). Implications of racial identity theory for vocational psychology. *Journal of Vocational Behavior, 44,* 124–138.

Herring, R. D. (1990). Attacking career myths among Native Americans: Implications for counseling. *School Counselor, 38,* 13–18.

Howell, F. M., Frese, W., & Sollie, C. R. (1984). The measurement of perceived opportunity for occupational attainment. *Journal of Vocational Behavior, 25,* 325–343.

Jordan, J. (1991). Counseling African American women: "Sister-friends." In C. C. Lee & B. L. Richardson (Eds.), *Multicultural issues in counseling: New approaches to diversity* (pp. 109–121). Alexandria, VA: American Counseling Associates.

Kenney, G. E. (1994). Multicultural investigation of counseling expectations and preferences. *Journal of College Student Psychotherapy, 9,* 21–39.

Kimbrough, V. D., & Salomone, P. R. (1993). African Americans: Diverse people, diverse career needs. *Journal of Career Development, 19,* 265–279.

Kiselica, M. S. (1995). *Multicultural counseling with teenage fathers: A practical guide.* Thousand Oaks, CA: Sage.

Kluckhohn, F. R., & Strodtbeck, F. L. (1961). *Variations in value-orientations.* Evanston, IL: Row, Peterson.

Kunjufu, J. (1986). *Motivating and preparing Black youth to work*. Chicago: African American Images.

Landrine, H., & Klonoff, E. (1994). The African American acculturation scale: Development, reliability, and validity. *Journal of Black Psychology, 20*, 104–127.

Landrine, H., & Klonoff, E. (1996). The schedule of racist events: A measure of racial discrimination and a study of its negative physical and mental health consequences. *Journal of Black Psychology, 22*, 144–168.

Lee, C. C. (1991). Counseling African Americans: From theory to practice. In R. L. Jones (Ed.), *Black psychology* (3rd ed., pp. 559–576). Berkeley: Cobb & Henry.

Lent, R. W., Brown, S. D., & Hackett, G. (1994). Toward a unifying social cognitive theory of career and academic interest, choice, and performance. *Journal of Vocational Behavior, 45*, 79–122.

Leong, F. T. L. (1993). The career counseling process with racial-ethnic minorities: The case of Asian Americans. *Career Development Quarterly, 42*, 26–40.

Leong, F. T. L., & Brown, M. T. (1995). Theoretical issues in cross-cultural career development: Cultural validity and cultural specificity. In W. B. Walsh & S. H. Osipow (Eds.), *Handbook of vocational psychology: Theory, research, and practice* (2nd ed., pp. 143–180). Mahwah, NJ: Lawrence Erlbaum Associates.

Leong, F. T. L., & Gim-Chung, R. H. (1995). Careeer assessment and intervention with Asian Americans. In F. T. L. Leong (Ed.), *Career development and vocational behavior of racial and ethnic minorities* (pp. 193–226). Mahwah, NJ: Lawrence Erlbaum Associates.

Leong, F. T. L., & Hartung, P. (1997). Career assessment with culturally different clients: Proposing an integrative-sequential conceptual framework for cross-cultural career counseling research and practice. *Journal of Career Assessment, 5*, 183–202.

Leung, S. A. (1995). Career development and counseling: A multicultural perspective. In J. G. Ponterotto, J. M. Casas, L. A. Suzuki, & C. M. Alexander (Eds.), *Handbook multicultural counseling* (pp. 549–566).Thousand Oaks, CA: Sage.

Lunneborg, P. W. (1997). Putting Roe in perspective. *Journal of Vocational Behavior, 51*, 301–305.

McDaniels, C., & Gysbers, N. C. (1992). *Counseling for career development: Theories, resources, and practice*. San Francisco: Jossey-Bass.

McWhirter, E. H. (1997). Perceived barriers to education and career: Ethnic and gender differences. *Journal of Vocational Behavior, 50*, 124–140.

Murry, E., & Mosidi, R. (1993). Career development counseling for African Americans: An appraisal of the obstacles and intervention strategies. *Journal of Negro Education, 62*, 441–447.

Ogbu, J. U. (1991). Minority coping responses and school experience. *Journal of Psychohistory, 18*, 433–456.

Osipow, S. H., & Fitzgerald, L. F. (1996). *Theories of career development* (4th ed.). Boston: Allyn & Bacon.

Parham, T. A., & Austin, N. L. (1994). Career development and African Americans: A contextual reappraisal using the nigrescence construct. *Journal of Vocational Behavior, 44*, 139–154.

Roe, A., & Lunneborg, P. W. (1991). Personality development and career choice. In D. Brown, L. Brooks, & Associates, *Career choice and development: Applying theories to practice* (2nd ed., pp. 68–101). San Francisco: Jossey-Bass.

Shipp, P. L. (1983). Counseling Blacks: A group approach. *Personnel and Guidance Journal, 62*, 108–111.

Singelis, T. M., Triandis, H. C., Bhawuk, D. P., & Gelfand, M. J. (1995). Horizontal and vertical dimensions of individualism and collectivism: A theoretical measurement and refinement. *Cross-cultural Research, 29*, 240–275.

Smith, E. J. (1983). Issues in racial minorities' career behavior. In W. B. Walsh & S. A. Osipow (Eds.), *Handbook of Vocational Psychology, Vol. 1: Foundations* (pp. 116–122). Hillsdale, NJ: Lawrence Erlbaum Associates.

Stabb, S. D., & Cogdal, P. A. (1992). Black college men in personal counseling: A five-year archival investigation. *Journal of College Student Psychotherapy, 7,* 73–86.

Steele, C. M. (1997). Race and schooling of Black Americans. In L. A. Peplau & S. E. Tatlor (Eds.), *Sociocultural perspectives in social psychology: Current readings* (pp. 359–371). Upper Saddle River, NJ: Prentice-Hall.

Subich, L. M., & Billingsley, K. D. (1995). Integrating career assessment into counseling. In W. B. Walsh & S. H. Osipow (Eds.), *Handbook of vocational psychology: Theory, research, and practice* (2nd ed., pp. 261–293). Mahwah, NJ: Lawrence Erlbaum Associates.

Swanson, J. L., Daniels, K. K., & Tokar, D. M. (1996). Assessing perceptions of career-related barriers: The Career Barriers Inventory. *Journal of Career Assessment, 4,* 219–244.

Terrell, F., & Terrell, S. (1984). Race of counselor, client sex, cultural mistrust level, and premature termination from counseling among Black clients. *Journal of Counseling Psychology, 31,* 371–375.

Terrell, F., & Terrell, S. L. (1981). An inventory to measure cultural mistrust among Blacks. *Western Journal of Black Studies, 5,* 180–184.

Thomas, G. E., & Gordon, S. A. (1983). Evaluating the payoffs of college investments for Black, White, and Hispanic students. *Center for Social Organization of Schools Report, Johns Hopkins University, 344,* 23.

Todisco, M., & Salomone, P. R. (1991). Facilitating effective cross-cultural relationships: The White counselor and the Black client. *Journal of Multicultural Counseling and Development, 19,* 147–157.

Triandis, H. C., McCusker, C., & Hui, C. H. (1990). Multimethod probes of individualsim and collectivism. *Journal of Personality and Social Psychology, 59,* 1006–1020.

Walsh, W. B., & Betz, N. E. (1995). *Tests and assessment* (3rd ed.). Englewood Cliffs, NJ: Prentice-Hall.

Ward, C. M., & Bingham, R. P. (1993). Career assessment of ethnic minority women. *Journal of Career Assessment, 1,* 246–257.

Webster, D. W., & Fretz, B. R. (1978). Asian American, Black, and White college students' preferences for help-giving sources. *Journal of Counseling Psychology, 25,* 124–130.

White, J. L., & Parham, T. A. (1980). *The psychology of Blacks: An African American perspective.* Englewood Cliffs, NJ: Prentice-Hall.

Yost, E. B., & Corbishley, M. A. (1987). *Career counseling: A psychological approach.* San Francisco: Jossey-Bass.

Chapter 2

Career Assessment for African Americans

Connie M. Ward
Private Practice

Rosie P. Bingham
The University of Memphis

Career assessment has been a large component of what constituted career counseling. In 1917, there was an early impetus for the development of the field of career counseling, and the need to assess large numbers of individuals for jobs in the armed services. Initially, the focus was on matching individuals with job characteristics and only later, in 1940, did some of the focus shift to the development of self-understanding. Career-assessment tools and instruments are based on career-development theories, which for the most part have originated with, been developed for, and normed on White middle-class, college-educated males (Myers, Haggin, & Speight, 1994; Subich, 1989; Ward & Bingham, 1993).

More recently, however, the career assessment of ethnic minority clients has received much attention (Bingham & Ward, 1994; Bowman, 1995; Brown, 1995; Foaud & Bingham, 1995; Leong, 1995; Ward & Bingham, 1993). Each of these authors presented frameworks, schemata, guidelines and/or instrumentation for use in career assessment of ethnic minority clients. Much of this work is still in the exploratory phase and is being presented to stimulate thoughts, generate areas of research, and spark debate and discussion within the career-counseling community.

The career assessment of African Americans demands a paradigm shift for career counselors. This change in thinking should include a focus on the counselor's preparation to work with African American clients, an emphasis on the counselor's understanding of the impact of his or her own racial identity development, cultural experiences, and worldview on the counseling interaction, and a shift from the over reliance on quantitative career assessment to an emphasis on the structure of the clinical assessment interview and the information gleaned from use of qualitative career assessments. Career counselors must suspend total reliance on the way they usually gather data or these counselors may miss valuable information about how their African American clients perceive the career development process. African Americans have a different history than do Euro-Americans, which effects the way in which they think about careers. In this chapter, the work of assessment in career counseling; the challenges to the career assessment of African Americans; reviews of career-assessment instruments, career-assessment models, frameworks, and structures and tools and their applicability to African Americans; current work on the Career Counseling Checklist for Clients (CCCC) quasiqualitative methods; and recommendations are discussed.

THE PURPOSE OF ASSESSMENT

Most writers agree that the general purpose of assessment is to gather information in order to understand the client's concerns. The purpose of assessment in career counseling has been seen as a way of helping the client gather and interpret information relevant to career decision making (Forrest & Brooks, 1993); serving as a source of feedback; providing new perspective; teaching or presenting new ideas; serving as stimulus for discussion (Campbell, 1990; Hackett & Lonborg, 1993) and facilitating expansion not only of knowledge of self and the work world, but also of actual abilities and interests, through relevant experiential learning (Betz, 1993).

Hansen, Stevic, and Warner (1986) identified several possible functions of tests that Forrest and Brooks (1993) believed to be just as relevant to career counseling as they are to other types of counseling. These functions are:

1. Identify the focus and the goals of counseling.
2. Identify the sources of the client's problem.
3. Identify the client's self-understanding.
4. Increase the counselor's understanding of the client.
5. Identify appropriate treatment strategies.

For the purposes of this chapter, *career assessment* includes standardized career-assessment tests and instruments as well as any tool the career counselor and client deem appropriate to increase the client's self understanding and the counselor's understanding of the information relevant to the African American client's career questions. This broadened definition may help free the counselor from focusing the career assessment process too narrowly.

CHALLENGES TO THE CAREER ASSESSMENT OF AFRICAN AMERICANS

The career assessment of African Americans may present some special challenges for career counselors, especially for those who are grounded in what may be called a traditional view of career assessment. These challenges may include: the heterogeneity of African Americans in the United States, the practice of one-size-fits-all career services, the United States' ambivalence about its history of slavery, the impact of racism and segregation on the career development of African Americans, and internal and external structural barriers facing African American in relation to their careers.

Heterogeneity

African Americans are not a monolithic group and African American culture is not unitary or static. Brown (1996) believed African Americans vary from the general society and from each other on a number of key dimensions, including SES, sex, gender, geographic region of origin, racial physiognomy, and history of immigration. Also included are the dimensions of educational attainment, marital status, family of origin mores, religious commitment, familial obligations and support, and geographic mobility because these are also factors that could influence African American career-assessment decision making. The career-assessment approaches used with African Americans should consider these key dimensions. One can already see that many of the traditional assessment tools do not consider these factors.

Brown (1996) urged individuals to think of culture beyond issues of race, ethnicity, gender, and so forth, to include all of an individual's past experiences that shape that individual's worldview. All of these learning experiences may affect an African American individual's career-assessment issues and experiences as well as how the individual may define and attach meaning to these issues.

Most of the research looking at the career assessment of African Americans focused largely on how African Americans as a group differs from other groups, especially White Americans (Myers et al., 1994). Other research has had such small samples of African Americans that there could not be within-group comparisons on even the majors dimensions, other than gender, such as age, educational attainment, SES, parental country of origin, ethnic affiliation, marital status, physical ability, or political affiliation. Studying these dimensions may tell us more about the heterogeneity of African Americans, about which factors have helped to shape individual African Americans levels of career aspirations and attainment, and how these dimensions may be important considerations when deciding the use of career assessment instruments and tools.

One Size Fits All

Bingham and Ward (1994) and Ward and Bingham (1993) urged that career counseling and career assessment be integrated with multicultural counseling. They realize this call may come into conflict with the one-size-fits-all, test-them-and-tell-them mentality, which has created a certain amount of comfort in the practice of career counseling. They believed, historically in the career-assessment process, that the primary emphasis has been on the manipulation and mastery of techniques and resources and less on the development of the individual and understanding the client's own particular assessment issues.

Cheatham (1990) introduced the concept of *"culture boundness"* in counseling by warning that helping professionals may be so culture-bound that their choice of helping interventions may come not from the client's cultural perspective and personal motives, but exclusively from that of the counselor's. Gordon, Miller, and Rollock (1990) warned of a *communicentric bias* that tends to make one's own community the center of the universe. These notions of culture-boundness and communicentric bias are extremely important to the career assessment process with African Americans where there is a danger of the counselor perfecting a technology and using it on all career clients regardless of the cultural, ethnic, racial, or gender needs. The one-size-fits-all mentality is essentially as dangerous as when the career counselor treats all their career clients like members of the counselor's own cultural group or when treating all clients from one cultural group as if they are all the same.

United States History of Slavery

The career assessment of African Americans challenges the career counselor because of the ambivalence the United States had about acknowledging, accepting, and integrating the existence of slavery into the history and development of this country. The United States had difficulty acknowledging the many different routes its citizens took, or were forced to take, on their way to pursuing full participation in this society. The message that everyone in this country has an equal opportunity to a decent education and productive career ignores the reality that African Americans were disenfranchised citizens until the legal barriers to an equal education came down in 1954 with the decision of *Brown v. Topeka Board of Education*, Kansas and the legal barriers to discrimination were addressed with the passage of the U. S. Civil Rights Act of 1964. This means African Americans have lived a little more than 30 years, of their over 300 years in this country, with equal opportunity and protection under the law. Even this legal opportunity and protection does not correct the social, economic, and educational segregation that still exists in this country today.

Most of the ancestors of African Americans started their participation in the U.S. workforce as Negro slaves. They were brought over as unwilling cargo to work the fields, clean the homes, raise the children, and cook the food of others and build the homes and infrastructure of this country, providing much of the craftsmanship that eventually made the United States so attractive to others. This labor was almost always unpaid. Although some African Americans were free men, the majority started their lives in the United States working through the cruel period of slavery, the short period of Reconstruction, the long period of segregation and Jim Crow laws, and the most recent short period of desegregation.

The history of slavery and segregation is important to the discussion of the career assessment of African Americans because most assessment instruments or tools look at factors the authors consider to be important to career success. In an Afrocentric worldview model, the will to survive and the resiliency of a people to not only survive, but to thrive under extreme circumstances would be factors to study and assess when looking at the career development of African Americans. It would also be important to look at why, in certain segments of the African American community, these same factors of survival and resiliency seem to be breaking down recently. What about this time in history make these same factors less than sufficient?

Impact of Racism and Segregation

The impact of this history of slavery and segregation has not been explored in the literature discussing career assessment, in general, or of African Americans, in particular. The career development of African Americans must be looked at within this unique social historical context (Osipow & Littlejohn, 1995). Osipow and Littlejohn (1995) suggested that when looking at the career development of African Americans, the effects of racism and discrimination on their historical, educational, social, political, and economic development must be accounted for because African Americans were subjected to external forces that have not been conducive to the development of self. African Americans have had to cope with the external and/or structural barriers of racism and discrimination when completing important developmental tasks. Several authors have looked at the negative and/or adaptive internal impact of these external forces on the self concept of African Americans (Cross, 1985; Fannon, 1967; Grier & Cobb, 1968). This awareness of the issues reflecting the self-concept of African Americans should be considered when developing and implementing career-assessment tools. More recently, Highland and Sudarsky-Gleiser (1994) looked at the impact of internalized racism on the extended self and found "internalized racism has a major impact on self-efficacy (a person's perception of his or her ability to successfully perform a particular task or behavior)" (pp. 306–307).

It is believed that career assessment must take place in a cultural context. The career counselor should look at the African American client within that client's own social historical or social political context. It is important for the career counselor to recognize and acknowledge the social, political, and economic realities of the nation at a given time in history. In the past, career counselors have not been able and/or comfortable applying this to African American clients as well as they have to Euro-Americans clients. Forthright acknowledgment of these realities allows the client to voice his or her own fears or beliefs, which may be powerful inhibitors or motivators. This will essentially give the counselor more information about how the African American client views his or her opportunities in the world of work and which assessment tools may be useful and relevant (Bingham & Ward, 1994).

Internal and External Barriers to Careers for African Americans

Bowman (1995) differentiated the prevailing message of the Protestant work ethic from secondary messages that African Americans may also hear on a daily basis. These messages can be powerful inhibitors or motivators and can have an impact on whether an African American career client seeks outside career help or resources and on the ability of the client to benefit from various career-assessment tools. These secondary messages may include the following: (a) because of their ethnicity, there are only certain careers open to African Americans; (b) African Americans seeking same-race role models and/or mentors in various careers may find few or none; (c) African Americans may receive negative or discouraging feedback about careers that their peers, or their elders, do not perceive are possible for their ethnic group; (d) African Americans entering a career where there are few ethnic minorities may receive the message that their hiring occurred because of their race instead of their qualifications; and (e) some African Americans are in positions that force them to interact in a system that is alien and hostile in order to achieve certain status (Bowman, 1995). All of these secondary messages may serve to confound the task of choosing a relevant and effective career assessment tool.

These messages are rarely explored in the traditional process of career assessment because most authors of career theories, tests, and other assessment techniques have done little to acknowledge that racial, ethnic, gender, and other diversity issues in the general population have ignored these issues in the development and norming of their tests and instruments. This practice led to the use of theories, tests, and assessment techniques normed on one population, generalized to all others, and presented as generic standard (Myers et al., 1994). Myers et al. (1994) argued that the theories and assessments developed on White middle-class males are specific to their own culture rather than a generic standard for all of us. These authors question whether the dominance—control and imposition through means of enslavement, colonization, and imperialism—gives European American males the right to determine a generic standard by which all others should be compared. Because most models and methods of career assessment were developed on White middle-class, college-educated men, their use with African Americans presents another challenge for career counselors.

This challenge is similar to that presented by researchers (Betz, 1992, 1993; Hackett & Lonborg, 1993) in the career assessment for women who believe that effective career counseling with women must first assess the internal and external barriers on women's careers. Similarly, counselors working with African Americans should assess the internal and external barriers on the careers of African Americans. African American males confront the issues of racism and discrimination, whereas African American females confront these issues in addition to sexism. Betz (1993), Farmer (1976), and Gottfredson (1986) suggested that women, racial and/or ethnic minorities, and others confront structural and cultural barriers to career development, barriers that often restrict the likelihood of making and implementing congruent career choices. Again, these structural barriers might be covert or overt racism and discrimination and/or sexism and the cultural barriers may be socialization, opinions of others, social isolation, a push toward assimilation and conflicts with the client's own worldviews.

Cheatham (1990) believed that because career decisions are based on perceived opportunities, African Americans perceive more obstacles to occupational goals than do Whites, despite similar levels of aspirations. It is important for career counselors working with African American clients to assess their client's perception of obstacles. Cheatham's warning suggests that only assessing level of aspiration does not tell the whole story. The perception of one's self-efficacy taps the confidence felt about the ability to succeed (Hackett & Betz, 1992).

Subich (1989) proposed that career counselors and career clients concentrate on barriers such as low self-efficacy or self-limiting expectations. She encouraged individual practioners to focus on helping clients overcome those internal constraints they have acquired during the socialization process. Subich (1989) recommended the career counselor and client concentrate on how the low self-esteem or self-defeating expectations could impair career clients from competing successfully in an aggressive job market. We suggest that the task for the career counselor is to work with the African American career client to identify or assess these self-limiting expectations and then develop interventions to replace them with more adaptive skills and attitudes. Then, the client is free to decide whether to compete in the aggressive job market or to pursue part-time or full-time work in the home, working in the community, or working for family and friends. African American clients with more adaptive skills would likely experience more success. This may be true as long as the counselor allows the African American to define what constitutes career success for him or her. The career counselor should take caution to understand the historical, sociopolitical, and cultural foundation for the development of the self-limiting behaviors lest the counselor err by unwittingly blaming the African American client for this adaptive reaction to history and experiences.

CAREER ASSESSMENT INSTRUMENTS

It is not the intention of this chapter to provide a review of career assessment instruments and tests because so many other authors have already written excellent reviews. For comprehensive reviews on traditional career assessment tools, the reader is referred to Swanson (1995) and Walsh and Betz (1995). Other reviews focused on the use of career assessment with women (Betz, 1993; Hackett & Lonborg, 1993), African Americans (Swanson & Bowman, 1994), the lack of applicability of the traditional career-assessment tools based on worldview (Myers et al., 1994), racial identity development and career assessment (Helms, 1984), and career assessment related to one's "calling" (Highland & Sudarksky-Gleiser, 1994). These authors provided excellent descriptions, discussions, and critiques of career-assessment tests, instruments, and tools.

Those reviews also suggest what has already been stated regarding the development of career-counseling theories and career-assessment instruments. Because the instruments were normed on a White, middle-class, college-educated male standard, their use with other populations, although widespread, has recently been called into question. It is suggested that the counselor proceed with caution when using these instruments with African American clients. Counselors should also use the frameworks presented by Bingham and Ward (1994), Highland and Sudarsky-Gleiser (1994), Myers et al. (1994), Swanson and Bowman (1994), and Ward and Bingham (1993), spend some time creating their own, or at least challenge themselves to think about the impact of racial and/or sexual discrimination when counseling an African American career client.

Myers et al. (1994) discussed the lack of research that shows career-assessment tests and instruments as highly applicable to most African Americans. They pointed to the fact that many African Americans are disenfranchised economically and educationally because they are members of the so-called underclass, the unemployed, and those that are not in school or training programs and are not looking for a job. They also believed that many African Americans who are employed are underemployed or not in full-time jobs that provide for career advancement or mobility. Probably, more and more of these individuals will be seen in the job market as Welfare Reform is put into place. How are career-assessment tools to help these individuals? How do counselors serve these individuals if they do not seek help in traditional places?

Models and Frameworks

Ward and Bingham (1993) presented a structure or framework for the career assessment of ethnic minority women using the clinical interview as the primary assessment instrument. Their focus was on learning the essential information brought to the career-counseling process by both the career counselor and the client. They contended that although the career counselor has spent many years preparing for his or her career, the counselor must do additional preparation when encountering an ethnic minority client because he or she must provide an atmosphere that respects that the career-counseling client brings the most important information to the process. This framework has merit for use with African American career clients because of its focus on counselor preparation.

Ward and Bingham (1993) suggested that initially establishing rapport is important in the framework developed for the career assessment of ethnic minority women. The framework provides a Decision Tree model to help with determining if the client is coming for career and/or personal counseling. Stabb and Cogdal (1990) contended that it is more acceptable for African Americans clients to seek career counseling rather than personal counseling. Ward and Bingham (1993) suggested that the career counselor may want to assess the impact of the client's culture, family influences, racial and/or ethnic issues, and finances on the client's concerns. The exploration of racial and/or ethnic issues' may clear up the career client's questions, but if questions remain, then the career counselor may want to explore more traditional career questions, possibly using assessment instruments or approaches that are appropriate for the career client.

Although Ward and Bingham (1993) initially subscribed to a Decision Tree model that forced a choice between whether the counselor would be conducting career or personal counseling, such a dichotomy rarely exists. When working with African American clients, the counselor should be prepared to provide all the services the client needs or actively make efforts to insure a good referral is made. Although African American clients are more likely than other ethnic groups to express the need for career counseling (Wilson & Brown, 1992). Stabb and Cogdal (1990) reminded us that African Americans seeking career counseling may also have other issues. Because it is known that it is sometimes very difficult for African Americans, especially African American males, to seek help, the counselor does not want to risk discouraging the client by fragmenting the help. This recognition is in line with Highland and Sudarsky-Gleiser (1994), Swanson (1995), and Yost and Corbishley (1987) as well as our own experiences with clients who present with career concerns.

The Multicultural Career Counseling Checklist for Counselors (MCCCC) was designed to aid counselors in determining how to assess if the client needed special consideration in career assessment. This check-list was divided into three sections: counselor preparation, exploration and assessment, and negotiation and working consensus.

The counselor preparation section of the process focuses on things the counselor should do before the client enters the room. Ward and Bingham (1993) suggested the following:

1. The counselor develop the minimum multicultural competencies (Sue, Arredondo, & McDavis, 1992).
2. The counselor should determine his or her familiarity or comfort with different racial and/or ethnic groups.
3. The counselor should be open to learning from the client.
4. The counselor should be aware of where he or she is in his or her racial identity development and how this stage might impact an ethnic minority client.
5. The counselor should be open to the racial identity development of the client.

The exploration and assessment section of the checklist was designed to help the career counselor make appropriate decisions about the assessment tool(s) to be used with the client. Career counselors must determine the role and impact of racial, ethnic, or gender issues on the questions the career client brings. Various areas of focus, such as the client's perception of limitations and obstacles, familial ethnocultural identification, family support and obligations, the impact of role models and past educational experiences, should be scrutinized. Ward and Bingham (1993) believed the career counselor should exercise a great deal of flexibility because this assessment is performed as a clinical interview.

The section on negotiation and working consensus helps the counselor and client determine the type of help the client wants. Ward and Bingham (1993) suggested the counselor focus on: the role of women in the client's chosen career; career commitment and questions related to balancing work and family; and the client's perceptions on the impact of the interaction of racism and sexism. Although very little attention has been given to how to choose instruments or approaches to be used, it is hoped that with increased emphasis on racial and/or ethnic information, the counselor will be better prepared to look at traditional tools of assessment in a different light.

The final assessment tool is the CCCC. This assessment tool was developed to help the career client frame their expectations, illustrate the complexity of the career counseling process, and help the client to see there are many issues relevant to the career assessment process. The CCCC was designed as structure for the initial interview. It focuses on issues related to self efficacy, understanding of self and the world of work, personal or sociopolitical obstacles, decision-making skills, and self-confidence.

One of the main values of the CCCC is its emphasis on the clinical interview as an appropriate assessment tool. Much of the information the career client seeks can be uncovered with the help of the career counselor by refining this clinical interview and starting with adequate preparation, as outlined in the MCCCC and CCCC, by both the counselor and client for the career-counseling process.

Although the Ward and Bingham (1993) model focused on ethnic minority women, the framework has value for working with African American males and females because of its emphasis on structuring the clinical interview as the initial assessment tool. The particular value provided by the framework is its focus on providing the career client with an environment where the discussion of whatever issues the client deems important is allowed and the counselor is asked to look at the world of work through the client's experiences. The career counselor's skill is needed to help the African American client avoid premature foreclosure on possibilities, while also helping the client with the delicate balance between aspirations and the realities of the present U.S. job market and work environment.

Swanson and Bowman (1994) also developed a four-step outline for tasks and decisions for the career assessment of African Americans. They suggested the following:

1. Initial emphasis on establishing rapport.
2. Determining the decision rules used to decide a formal assessment process.
3. Additional decision rules to determine the type of assessment and the type of assessment instrument.
4. Emphasis on the counselor's expertise to provide an effective test interpretation.

At each stage in the model, the authors provide stimulus questions for the counselor related to race or racial identity development, which assessment tools are chosen at which point in the process, and how to introduce the assessment tool and gauge client response.

RECENT CAREER ASSESSMENT RESEARCH
WITH AFRICAN AMERICANS

Most recently, Richie et al. (1997) have undertaken a major qualitative study of the career development of prominent, high-achieving African American and White women. The authors studied 18 women in eight fields. The authors were motivated by the difficulty of applying the existing career-development theories and models to the career experiences of African American women because so little is known about the effects of the interaction of both sexism and racism. They also focused their study on women who had already achieved prominence in their fields instead of college students. Interest in this study is due to the fact that they used the clinical interview as a relevant assessment tool.

Using a qualitative rather than a quantitative approach, Richie et al. (1997) sought to explore the following variables: background influences, including family, SES, education, and gender role socialization; stress, coping, and resiliency; self-efficacy and attributional factors; community and social support; external challenges and obstacles such as sexism and racism; and factors related to individual personality and temperament.

Richie et al. (1997) presented an emergent theoretical model for understanding the career development of high-achieving African American and White women. This model is illustrated by five major components, a *core story* that is surrounded by *sociocultural, personal background,* and *current contextual conditions* with *actions and consequences* resulting and cycling back to exert influence on the contextual conditions.

The *core story* looks at how the women see themselves and who they are in relation to the world, to others, and to their work. The core story is characterized by these women's "strength and perseverance in facing challenges, their reliance on internal standards and judgment, their strong passion for work, and a relational orientation that focuses in interconnectedness with others and the balancing of tasks and relationships" (Richie et al., 1997, pp. 138–139). The authors found that the African American women in their sample persevered in the face of barriers such as sexism, racism, low SES, or personal life situations; valued their work and its intrinsic rewards more than the extrinsic; displayed a passion, commitment, and investment in their careers; had a vision of how they and their work fit into the big picture; expressed a connectedness to other women and other African Americans in and out of their fields; and tended to think from a collective, rather than an individualistic, perspective about work and personal life (Richie et al., 1997).

In this emergent model, Richie et al. (1997) presented three layers or wraps that surround or filter through the core. In the outermost wrap, *sociocultural conditions*, the impact of sexism and racism are questioned. These authors found differences in the African American and the White sample, with African American women responding to both the barriers of racism and sexism. The authors reported finding the African American women describing the effects of racism and sexism to be very similar to that of the White sample descriptions of the effects of sexism alone; the coping strategies used were very similar. Richie et al. (1997) found that the African American sample outlined difficulties that were due to the interactive oppressions of racism and sexism; described the importance of both oppressions in their development; and noted that racism and sexism were linked. They found that African American women faced obstacles, such as lack of opportunities, outright discrimination, prejudice from others, and personal and professional isolation, and these women reported relying on their communities and other African Americans for support.

In the personal conditions layer, the authors (Richie et al., 1997) looked at messages and expectations of families, teachers, and others; early interests and experiences in the career field; influences of mentors and role models; and formal and informal preparation and training for the career. Although the African American women in their sample reported the importance of support and encouragement from their parents, teachers, and partners or spouses, few reported having role models or mentors. The African American women in the sample could identify the positive and negative impact of racism and being African American had on their career development and personal lives. The positive effects included opportunities provided by the Civil Rights Movement, exposure to African Americans as leaders and role models in segregated communities, and the strong positive racial identity messages from their families. On the negative side, there were concerns about the impact of racism and being considered as a token professionally.

Richie et al.'s (1997) innermost wrap is *current contextual conditions* such as stress, pain, and internal or external difficulty; the coping strategies used to handle difficulties and stress; and levels of support from families, partners or spouses, colleagues, friends, and community. The African American women in the sample reported general solid support from others in their personal lives and encouragement and support of the African American community, while again reporting work-related stressors of racism and sexism in their daily lives and at work.

The actions and consequences portion of the model look at specific ways these women lead their work lives. The African American women in the sample spoke of their connectedness with and valuing of people, the struggle to balance their personal and professional lives, the desire to make a difference in the world, and the desire to make changes in their particular field for others (Richie et al., 1997).

This study is useful because although assessing very high-achieving African American women, the authors allow a glimpse into the complex struggles confronting the African American women with the most resources, such as high-educational attainment, strong family support, above-average feelings of self-efficacy, positive self-concepts and rich external rewards, and yet they did not perceive themselves as escaping the impact of racism and sexism. This study has implications for African American women who will achieve less, have fewer resources and support, and still face racism and sexism and for the career counselors who will have to determine appropriate assessment tools for them.

CURRENT WORK ON CCCC

A shortcoming of the work of Ward and Bingham (1993) is the lack of empirical validation of the assessment tools presented. To date, only one study has looked at the value of the CCCC: Prigoff (1996) used the CCCC as a research tool. The reader is referred to Ward and Bingham (1993) for additional information on the CCCC. The CCCC (adapted from Ward & Tate, 1990) is designed to do the following: identify the variables that might influence clients in their decision making; gain a more comprehensive view of the client's career-related concerns; and help determine the client's readiness to focus on career-related concerns rather than personal, familial, or societal factors. The 42 questions on the CCCC are also designed to assess the possible influence of cultural and sociopolitical variables, such as race, ethnicity, gender, age, religious beliefs, and physical ability, on career decision making.

This instrument has been primarily used, in clinical settings, as a way to identify potential areas for exploration in the career counseling and assessment process. However, no empirical study has specifically examined whether racial minority students report greater career concerns with decision making and sociopolitical factors than do White students. Prigoff (1996) proposed exploring differences between African American and White students on career variables as indicated by the CCCC. Although she looked at differences related to age, gender, marital status, and academic year, Prigoff primarily focused on racial group differences.

Prigoff (1996) studied the responses of 89 White and 38 African American students, for a total of 127 undergraduate participants, 49% of whom were underclassmen and 26% of whom were upperclassmen, with the remaining participants being classified as special or nonstudent status. The majority of the sample was single. Prigoff divided the 42 items of the CCCC into the three following scales: *Understanding of Self*, *Decision Making*, and *Personal, Familial, and Sociopolitical Factors*.

Prigoff (1996) found significant differences between the African American and White students on the *Understanding Self* scale. African American students reported a better understanding of themselves in relation to the world of work, vocational interests, skills, needs, and education than did the White students. African American and White students were not found to be significantly different based on their racial group membership on the *Personal, Familial, and Sociopolitical Factors*.

Prigoff (1996) offered the following possible explanations for her results of no significant differences between African American and White students on their perception of sociopolitical obstacles to their career decision making:

- Younger students may be less likely to perceive ethnic barriers and stereotypes in the world of work due to youth, limited work experience, and general lack of knowledge about the world of work (Arbona & Novy, 1991).
- The youth of the sample may make these students more likely to be at the pre-encounter stage of their racial identity development (Helms, 1984).
- Students who perceive definite sociopolitical barriers to their career decision making might be less likely to seek the assistance of a counseling center that they may regard as not being supportive of their beliefs and/or their race.

Prigoff (1996) believed that because the African American students reported a better understanding of themselves in relation to the world of work, vocational interests, skills, needs, and education, this may explain why they also reported that sociopolitical factors would not impact their vocational decisions.

FUTURE STUDY

Prigoff's (1996) research is the first study using the CCCC. The limited sample size of 38 African American students makes it difficult to generalize from these results. The instrument was developed as a tool of preparation for the clinical interview for career counselors and clients. Additional work will have to be done to make the CCCC an assessment that differentiates from between- or within-groups.

Ward and Bingham (1993) adapted the CCCC from Ward and Tate (1990) to be part of a career-assessment process for use with ethnic minority women. This career assessment process involved: preparing the career counselor to work with ethnic minority clients before they arrive for counseling by using the MCCCC; using the CCCC to stimulate the client to think more thoroughly about their career concerns and as a guide for conducting the initial career-counseling interview; and the Career Decision Tree model that was developed to help the counselor and client determine the route of the career-counseling process.

Although the CCCC is not really an assessment instrument, Prigoff's (1996) efforts are to be appreciated. Replication of the study with a larger sample size and focusing on within-group differences for African Americans is suggested. Future studies might compare the responses of African American freshmen and sophomores with those of juniors and seniors because underclassmen may be more focused on choosing a major to satisfy parents and advisors and upperclassmen may be more focused on how their major relates to a career. It would also be interesting to compare the responses of African American college students to working adults in the workforce for 1–5, 6–10, and over 10 years. There is some reason to suspect that many of the possible barriers outlined by the CCCC may not become apparent or real until the individual is actually in the workforce. There could be comparisons made of the responses of African American males and females to determine if there are special forces, for the counseling, unique to that gender. The CCCC should be updated to include mores items related to client's perception of self-efficacy, perception of structural barriers, and items that could focus on client premature foreclosure related to some careers.

Prigoff's (1996) study suggested that additional information on the subject's racial identity development may be useful interpreting the results.

The CCCC continues to be a useful clinical assessment tool for career counselors and clients and the client's ability to relate to the questions may be affected by the client's age, gender, work experience, feelings of self-efficacy, and stage of racial identity development.

Integrating Existing Models With New Ideas

Assessments used in career counseling may range from the traditional standardized tests and inventories to qualitative assessments such as vocational card sorts, lifelines, observations, work samples, and value-clarification exercises (Goldman, 1990), fantasy exercises (Spokane, 1991), to genograms and vocational autobiographies (Brown & Brooks, 1991), and informational interviewing (Yost & Corbishley, 1987). Foaud and Bingham (1995) believed it was very important that crossculturally competent counselors match their assessments and interventions with the career issues defined by the client, while incorporating the relevant cultural variables. Then, the assessments and interventions are tailored to meet their client's needs. Interests, values, functional skills, abilities, personality, career decision making, and adjustment, as well as racial, ethnic, cultural, and gender issues may be explored using qualitative assessment techniques.

Goldman (1990) saw several advantages to using qualitative assessment in career counseling of women, such as encouraging the active participation of the client in assessment; promoting a holistic and integrated view of career concerns; and making it easier to incorporate cultural and gender issues at a very fundamental level. These reasons would also be relevant for the use of qualitative assessment with African Americans. Yet, qualitative assessment is not a panecea and cultural, racial, ethnicity, and gender bias can be present in the administration and interpretation of these tools. The counselor would have to make sure cultural, racial, ethnicity, and gender issues were accurately used with these and any assessment instruments. Hackett and Lonborg (1993) suggested that although qualitative assessment methods can be used by themselves, they may be more effective when used in combination with standardized instruments and tests. In this case, the information generated from the standardized tests may be used to validate and reinforce the information gathered through the qualitative assessment. It must be noted that much of the information generated by the qualitative assessments would not have been generated by traditional standardized tests. This combination of quantitative and qualitative assessment should be called a *quasiqualitative method*. This quasiqualitative model is fashioned into a triangle with qualitative career-assessment methods, such as the clinical interview, on one side of the base and quantitative career-assessment methods, such as standardized tests, on the other side of the base. At the peak of the triangle is life stories and experiential information that could be used to confirm the information gathered from the other two methods. In this method, one assessment may provide some answers but may lead to the need for a follow-up assessment (see Fig. 2.1).

Recommendations

1. In order to adequately provide career counseling and assessment to clients other than White, middle-class males, the career counselor should be prepared to review the literature on multicultural counseling, racial identity development, and gender issues.

2. Career counselors must acknowledge the reality of racism so that the counselor can help the clients increase their ability to master the situation by providing cognitive and behavioral coping skills to combat the impact of racism.

3. There needs to be more within-group research to exploit the differences in African Americans on the key dimensions discussed earlier, such as SES status, gender, geographic region of origin, marital status, educational attainment, familial obligations and support, and history of immigration. This research may provide information on why some African Americans seemingly compete successfully in the dominant aggressive job market and some never compete. It may also inform individuals about the prices each of these groups pay.

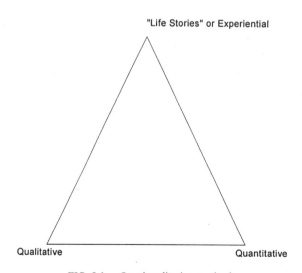

FIG. 2.1.   Quasiqualitative methods.

4. Research on what is considered to be career success for African Americans is needed. Answers to this question may be multidimensional and complex. Will more acculturated African Americans consider factors more like the dominant culture? What value will be given to overcoming structural barriers?

5. Career counselors should acknowledge that structural barriers such as racial and/or sexual discrimination still exist and although these are barriers that can be confronted, this confrontation may take an emotional and physical toll on African Americans on a daily basis. Research is needed to understand this toll. It is still rare when African Americans are asked in counseling about the nature of their environmental constraints.

6. Career counselors must realize that traditional career theories and career-assessment instruments were developed for the career clients with the most internal and external resources. So, for a large portion of the working population who are not college educated, who do not see their job as a manifestation of their personality, and who are not pursuing full-time, continuous employment with an emphasis on upward mobility, these assessment tools will prove to be less than useful. This is important because a large portion of the African American population will fall into these categories. Assessment tools and theories must be developed to address these individuals.

SUMMARY

The work of career assessment with African Americans is at once challenging and complex. The work originates within theories, tools, and frameworks developed for and by others in this society, those who, by the nature of their experiences and privileges, share a very different worldview. At best, this particular European worldview constitutes a portion of the worldview of most African Americans. The challenges previously outlined suggest areas that the counselor should consider before working with an African American client. The focus is on the counselor having enough self-knowledge to recognize his or her own worldview and how it might contribute to any culture boundness (Cheatham, 1990) or communicentric bias (Gordon et al., 1990), which then might unwittingly serve as a structural barrier for that African American client.

Because most career-development theories and/or assessment tools and instrumentation were developed by and for White, middle-class, college-educated males, it is suggested that the counselor must do the initial preparation work on self and then prepare for an African American client by challenging himself or herself to allow the client to reveal what assessments are needed. The counselor would guide this process by establishing a rapport with the client, asking the appropriate questions, broadening the discussion to include cultural, racial identity development, worldview, family, and gender-related issues, as well as being open to discussion to any internal and structural barriers that might exist and could include racial and sexual discrimination. It is noted in the Richie et al. (1997) study that even the high-achieving African American women document these issues as having significant impact on their career development.

It is noteworthy that Bingham and Ward (1994), Fouad and Bingham (1995), Swanson and Bowman (1994), and Ward and Bingham (1993) all presented models or frameworks related to the career assessment of African Americans and/or people of color that rely heavily on the clinical interview as a primary career-assessment tool. It is believed that the structure of the clinical interview is very important when working with African American career clients. This clinical interview should provide the framework for choosing career-assessment instruments. It is also believed that African American clients may benefit from the culturally skillful use of qualitative career-assessment tools in concert with standardized tests and instruments, a quasiqualitative approach. We look forward to continued research on the aforementioned models and others as well as the continued generation of new culturally appropriate assessment tools and additional information on how to use the already existing standardized instruments in more culturally appropriate ways, if applicable.

REFERENCES

Arbona, C., & Novy, D. M. (1991). Career aspirations and expectation of Black, Mexican-American and White students. *The Career Development Quarterly, 39*, 231–239.

Betz, N. E. (1992). Career Assessment: A review of critical issues. In S. D. Brown & R. W. Lent (Eds.), *Handbook of Counseling Psychology* (2nd ed., pp. 453–484). New York: Wiley.

Betz, N. E. (1993). Issues in the use of ability and interest measures with women, *Journal of Career Assessment, 1*(3), 217–232.

Bingham, R. P., & Ward, C. M. (1994). Career counseling with ethnic minority women. In W. B. Walsh & S. H. Osipow (Eds.), *Career counseling for women* (pp. 165–195). Hillsdale, NJ: Lawrence Erlbaum Associates.

Bowman, S. L. (1995). Career interventions strategies and assessment issues for African Americans. In F. T. L. Leong (Ed.), *Career development and vocational behavior of racial and ethnic minorities* (pp. 137–164). Mahwah, NJ: Lawrence Erlbaum Associates.

Brown v. Topeka Board of Education (D. Kan. 1954).

Brown, D., & Brooks, L. (1991). *Career counseling techniques*. Boston: Allyn & Bacon.

Brown, M. T. (1995). The career development of African Americans: Theoretical and empirical issues. In F. T. L. Leong (Ed.), *Career development and vocational behavior of racial and ethnic minorities* (pp. 7–36). Mahwah, NJ: Lawrence Erlbaum Associates.

Brown, M. T. (1996, August). *Applying the Fouad and Bingham culturally appropriate career counseling model to African American clients*. Symposium conducted at convention of the American Psychological Association, Toronto, Canada.

Campbell, V. L. (1990). A model for using tests in counseling. In C. F. Watkins, Jr. & V. L. Campbell (Eds.), *Testing counseling practice* (pp. 1–7). Hillsdale, NJ: Lawrence Erlbaum Associates.

Cheatham, H. E. (1990). Africentricity and career development of African Americans. *The Career Development Quarterly, 38*, 334–346.

Cross, W. (1985). Black identity: Rediscovering the link between personal identity and reference group orientation. In M. B. Spencer, G. K. Brookins, & W. R. Allen (Eds.), *Beginnings: The social and affective development of Black children* (pp. 93–122). Hillsdale, NJ: Lawrence Erlbaum Associates.

Fannon, F. (1967). *Black skin, White masks.* New York: Grove Press.

Farmer, H. S. (1976). What inhibits achievement and career motivation in women? *The Counseling Psychologist, 6*, 12–14.

Forrest, L., & Brooks., L. (1993). Feminism and career assessment. *Journal of Career Assessment, 1*(3), 233–245.

Fouad, N. A., & Bingham, R. P. (1995). Career counseling with racial/ethnic minorities. In W. B. Walsh & S. H. Osipow (Eds.), *Handbook of vocational psychology* (2nd ed., pp. 331–366). Hillsdale, NJ: Lawrence Erlbaum Associates.

Goldman, L. (1990). Qualitative assessment. *The Counseling Psychologist, 18*, 205–213.

Gordon, E. W., Miller, F., & Rollock, D. (1990). Coping with communicentric bias in knowledge production in the social sciences. *Educational Researcher, 19*(3), 14–19.

Gottfredson, L. S. (1986). Special groups and the beneficial use of vocational interests inventories. In W. B. Walsh & S. H. Osipow (Eds.), *Advances in vocational psychology: Vol. 1, The assessment of interests* (pp. 127–198). Hillsdale, NJ: Lawrence Erlbaum Associates.

Grier, W., & Cobb, P. (1986). *Black rage.* New York: Bantam.

Hackett, G., & Betz, N. E. (1992). Self-efficacy perceptions and the career-related choices of college students. In D. H. Schunk & J. L. Meece (Eds.), *Student perception in the classroom: Causes and consequences* (pp. 229–246). Hillsdale, NJ: Lawrence Erlbaum Asssociates.

Hackett, G., & Lonborg, S. D. (1993). Career assessment for women: Trends and issues. *Journal of Career Assessment, 1*(3), 197–216.

Hansen, J., Stevic, R., & Waner, R. (1986). *Counseling theory and process.* Boston: Allyn & Bacon.

Helms, J. E. (1984). Toward a theoretical explanation of the effects of race on counseling: Black/White interactional model. *The Counseling Psychologist, 46*, 186–193.

Highland, P. S., & Sudarsky-Gleiser, C. (1994). Co-essence model of vocational assessment for racial/ethnic minorities (CEMVA-REM): An existential approach. *Journal of Career Assessment, 2*(3), 304–329.

Leong, F. T. L. (Ed). (1995). *Career development and vocational behavior of racial and ethnic minorities.* Mahwah, NJ: Lawrence Erlbaum Associates.

Myers, L. J., Haggins, K. L., & Speight, S. L. (1994). The optimal theory and career assessment: Towards an inclusive, global perspectives. *Journal of Career Assessment, 2*(3), 289–303.

Osipow, S. H., & Littlejohn, E. (1995). Toward a multicultural theory of career development: Prospects and dilemmas. In F. T. L. Leong (Ed.), *Career development and vocational behavior of racial and ethnic minorities* (pp. 251–262). Mahwah, NJ: Lawrence Erlbaum Associates.

Prigoff, G. L. (1996). *A comparison of African American and Caucasian-American college students' responses on the career checklist for clients.* Paper presented at the annual meeting of the Tennessee Psychological Association, Glatlinburg, TN.

Richie, B. S., Fassinger, R. E., Linn, S. G., Johnson J., Robinson, S., & Prosser, J. (1997). Persistence, connection, and passion: A qualitative study of the career development of highly achieving African American-Black and White women. *Journal of Counseling Psychology, 44*(2), 133–148.

Spokane, A. R. (1991). *Career intervention.* Englewood Cliffs, NJ: Prentice-Hall.

Stabb, S., & Cogdal, P. (1990). *Needs assessment and the perception of help in a multicultural college population.* Paper presented at the ACPA Convention, St. Louis, MO.

Subich, L. (1989). A challenge to grow: A reaction to Hoyt's article. *Career Development Quarterly, 37*, 213–217.

Sue, D. W., Arredondo, P., & McDavis, R. J. (1992). Multicultural counseling competencies and standards: A call to the profession. *Journal of Multicultural Counseling and Development, 20*, 64–88.

Swanson, J. L. (1995). The process of outcome career counseling. In W. B. Walsh & S. H. Osipow (Eds.), *Handbook of vocational psychology* (2nd ed., pp. 217–260). Hillsdale, NJ: Lawrence Erlbaum Associates.

Swanson, J. L., & Bowman, S. L. (1994). Career assessment with African-American clients. *Journal of Career Assessment, 2*(3), 210–225.

Walsh, W. B., & Betz, N. E. (1995). *Tests and assessment*. Englewood Cliffs, NJ: Prentice-Hall.

Ward, C. M., & Bingham, R. P. (1993). Career assessment of ethnic minority women. *Journal of Career Assessment, 1*(3), 246–257.

Ward, C. M., & Tate, G. (1990). *The career checklist*. Georgia State University Counseling Center. Also *Journal of Career Assessment, 1*(3), 246–257, Summer, 1993.

Wilson, R., & Brown, D. (1992). African Americans and career development: Focus on education. In D. Brown & C. W. Minor (Eds.), *Career needs in a diverse workplace: Implications of the NCDA Gallup survey* (pp. 11–26). Alexandria, VA: National Career Development Association.

Yost, E. B., & Corbishley, M. A. (1987). *Career counseling: A psychological approach*. San Francisco: Jossey-Bass.

Chapter 3

Career Counseling With African American Males and Females

Rosie P. Bingham
The University of Memphis

Connie M. Ward
Private Practice

African American men and women have not had the same social and economic advantages as Whites in the United States. It almost seems too obvious to remind readers that Blacks and Whites have journeys in this country that mainly begin from different vantage points. The majority of Whites started their journey free; whereas the large majority of Blacks began their journey in slavery. So, the career development and career interests of the two groups have necessarily been different. African Americans have spent 300 years fighting for the right to have careers free and clear. One must now ask, "Have we taken African Americans into account as career theories and interventions have been created and implemented?" It is assumed that most major career theories were formulated on middle-class, college-educated, White males and that group is the only one that has had such specific attention. Additionally, one assumes that since the inclusion of the dimension of culture into the theoretical discourse on career counseling, racial and ethnic groups have generally gained more prominence and exploration. Yet, it is likely that career counseling with African American men and women in this country still needs special consideration.

The popular press recently reported data that suggests it is urgent that special attention is given to the career needs of African Americans. For example, it has been reported that the average, young male child in this country stands a 1 in 20 chance of being involved in the criminal justice system. Yet, for African American males that figure is 1 in 4. This country

49

cannot afford to have such a large number of Black males involved in the criminal justice system without serious and detrimental consequences to the family and the very fabric of life and culture of the United States.

The high school drop-out rates suggest that the involvement of African American males in the criminal justice system will not change without substantive interventions. In 1990, the drop-out rate for all African Americans was 13.2% compared to 9% for Whites. Under 20% of Blacks complete college (U.S. Department of Labor, 1992). Nevertheless, the work force is changing rapidly and without a substantial number of Blacks in the job market. What will happen to the economy? The data suggest that career counseling may be essential if change is to occur.

Even when African Americans complete college, they still face discrimination. The data indicate that Black men earn 80¢ for every $1 made by White individuals and Black women earn about 62¢ (Woody, 1992). There are even important within-group differences. When all factors are held constant, light-skinned African American males will earn $6,000 more annually than their darker skinned counterparts. The situation for dark-skinned Black women is even worse. On average, other factors being equal, darker colored women will earn $9,000 less than lighter colored Black women. These data indicate a significant need to understand the career issues that face African American men and women. They also suggest a profound necessity to find effective career intervention models.

In this chapter, the differences and similarities in the career counseling issues of African American men and women are examined; second, some of the major career theories to determine their relevance to African American career issues are explored; third, career theorists who include culture in their models are reviewed; and last, career-counseling models for African Americans are reviewed and critiqued. The Culturally Appropriate Career Counseling model (CACCM), which seems to hold some promise for usefulness with this population, is applied. Finally, a series of recommendations for career-counseling interventions is proposed.

DIFFERENCES AND SIMILARITIES

Some of the issues facing African American men may be very different from those facing African American women. Evidence from counseling agencies indicates that African American men are far less likely to seek counseling services than are African American women. For example, in the annual reports of the various agencies in which the authors have been employed, Black women generally sought counseling at a rate 50% greater than that of African American men (Chando et al., 1997). Even though Stabb and Cogdal (1990) reported that Blacks were more likely to seek career counseling than psychological counseling, the ratio remained the same. Because Black men are less likely to seek career counseling than Black women, one of the first issues to address is the counselor's access to Black men.

The next difference may be in the individual concerns of the two groups. Although African American men and women believe that their career paths are affected by race and ethnicity (Gainor & Forrest, 1991; Harris, 1995; Stoltz-Loike, 1996; Wilson, Tienda, & Wu, 1995), African American women also perceive gender as a barrier to their advancement. Simpson (1996) examined a study on the career progress of Black women who had become lawyers between 1973 and 1983. Although these women often had degrees from the most prestigious law schools, their careers had not resulted in the same level of achievement as White lawyers. In Neely's (1990) survey of the top 250 law firms in the United States, all had at least one female partner. Although the firms had an average of eight women partners, they averaged less than one minority partner. Black women lawyers could most often be found practicing in government or very small private groups. Nevertheless, these women perceived gender and race to be barriers. Burlew and Johnson (1992) indicated that Black women in nontraditional careers generally perceived gender and racial discrimination as stumbling blocks to their career advancement.

Black men are more likely to only report race as a discriminating factor in their career success. Slaney and Brown (1983) found an interaction of race and socioeconomic levels as perceived barriers to career advancement for Black men. Ten years later, Luzzo (1993) asserted that African American men viewed ethnicity as a barrier to their future success. Interestingly, Wilson et al. (1995) indicated that employment gaps, including unemployment and underemployment are greatest for college-educated African American men. African American men are generally likely to face more layoffs and firings than their Euro-American counterparts (Wilson et al., 1995).

The role of family may play different roles in the career development of Black men and women. In the Black community, there has been a common tradition of protecting the African American male. The practice appears to have developed as a result of the history of lynching and imprisonment of African American men. Perhaps that history helps to account for the finding in Harris' (1995) study assessing the factors that influence career counseling among African American male adolescents; it revealed that the young men needed help with emancipation from their families. They also needed help with developing a sense of self and deciding on a career. It is known that African American males are more prone to join a gang at an earlier age than are White males (Delaney, 1995). It appears that career interventions with African American males need to start very early and include the family.

Generally, African Americans believe that race is a barrier to career success. The employment data suggests a correlation among race and earnings, layoffs, firings, and promotions (Woody, 1992). It is easy to see that there are between- and within-group differences that the career counselor must consider when working with African American men and women.

MAJOR THEORIES

There have been numerous critiques of the major theories and their lack of attention to ethnic minorities. (Bowman, 1995; Brown, 1995; Leong & Brown, 1995) Therefore, a long review will not be provided in this chapter. However, general findings specific to African Americans are reported. Theories such as trait factor, person environment, self concept and development were not conceptualized with Black Americans in mind. Nevertheless, there has been research on some of these theories that include or even focused on African Americans.

Perhaps the most widely researched of the theories is Holland's (1985) Person Environment theory. Walsh and his associates (Bingham & Walsh, 1978; O'Brien & Walsh, 1976; Sheffey, Bingham, & Walsh, 1986; Walsh, Hildebrand, Ward, & Mathews, 1983; Ward & Walsh, 1981) began exploring the validity of Holland's Self-Directed Search and Vocational Preference Inventory for Blacks over 20 years ago. Holland (1985) maintained that a choice of occupation is an expression of personality. He asserted that personality and environments could be described by six types: realistic, artistic, investigative, social, enterprising, and conventional. Holland further indicated that the most satisfied workers would be those who are in environments congruent with their personalities; therefore, an individual with a realistic personality would be most satisfied and productive in a realistic environment. Numerous studies of African Americans (Bingham & Walsh, 1978; O'Brien & Walsh, 1976; Sheffey et al., 1986; Walsh et al., 1983; Ward & Walsh, 1981) have provided support for the validity of the vocational interest patterns espoused by Holland.

An interesting pattern that occurred relative to Holland's hexagonal model is the tendency for African Americans to be overrepresented in social occupations. In fact, the Social-personal/vocational descriptor is often a part of the vocational orientation of African Americans regardless of occupational choice (Bingham & Walsh, 1978). Miller, Springer, and Wells (1988) confirmed that trend when they found that most African Americans in their study had Social as the highest or second highest code in their personality types. The next logical question to be raised is, "what is the role of worldview and racial identity in the development of vocational personality types?"

Holland's theory generally fits best in the category of trait-factor conceptualizations and no other of the major vocational theories has generated as much research with African American subjects. Parsons (1909) began theorizing about trait factor as goodness-of-fit between the qualities needed in a job and the qualities, interests, and abilities of individuals. Parsons postulated that if one could find individuals with traits that match the factors needed for a job, then those individuals were likely to be happy and satisfied in those jobs. So, very early in the vocational literature, the proposition of congruence between person and job was suggested, but the impact of race and gender was overlooked. Consequently, it is difficult to know what factors lead to congruence for African Americans and the work environments in which they find themselves.

Brown's (1995) review of the research literature revealed that for the most part, very few studies exist in which African Americans are subjects in the trait-factor research. More specially, Brown reported no studies using Roe's theory, especially her psychologically based classification system of occupations. Regardless, there may be one facet of Roe's (1956) theory that may have special relevance for understanding the career choice process of African Americans. Roe proposed that individuals have genetic endowments that combine with family background and childrearing practices, which in turn, effect occupational choice. Later, in this chapter, the culturally appropriate model as described by Fouad and Bingham (1995), in which they suggest a similar process, is discussed. Their model purports that people of color are born with genetic traits that influence career choice. Like Roe, however, there is no research to support the Fouad and Bingham contentions.

On the other hand, there is research support for application of Super's (1990) career development theory with people of color. The research needs to be more systematic in order to determine its relevance for African Americans (Brown, 1995). Super (1990) proposed developmental stages in the career-choice process. He maintained that occupational choice is determined by the self-concept. The self-concept and its implementation varies as a function of stage development. Some of the questions raised by Super's theory could directly center on the role of poverty and racism in the development of self-concept in African Americans. Further questions targeted the confounding of SES and race in studies examining career maturity in African Americans. (The reader is referred to Leong and Brown, 1995 for an extensive discussion in this area.)

It has been concluded that each of the previous theories listed may shed light on the career development of African Americans, however, one can only speculate in some areas because the call for substantive research has not been adequately answered, except for the empirical studies on Holland's theory.

THEORISTS WITH A SPECIFIC CULTURAL FOCUS

For years, many authors have known that diverse groups of people must be included in career or vocational psychology theories. Walsh and his associates conducted numerous studies that sought to validate Holland's operational definitions of his theories (Bingham & Walsh, 1978; O'Brien & Walsh, 1976; Sheffey et al., 1986; Ward & Walsh, 1981). Others commented on the relevance to ethnic minorities of the theories of Super (1990), Roe (1956), and others (Brown, 1995; Fouad & Arbona, 1994; June & Pringle, 1977). Smith (1975) was one of the early critics of the relevance of vocational theories to Black individuals. Richardson (1993) and Subich (1993) discussed ways to expand the focus of the career theories to meet the needs of African Americans.

Yost and Corbishley (1987) described an eight-stage model that integrates career and psychological concepts. These authors discussed the need to broaden the career process to include work and nonwork variables, attention to the client–counselor relationship and inclusion of psychological concepts such as client resistance and nonverbal behavior. Yost and Corbishley (1987) emphasized the possible need to consider cultural variables for some ethnic minority clients; however, they did not offer suggestions about when it is appropriate to consider those variables.

Brown and Brooks (1991) and Peterson, Sampson, and Reardon (1991) provided a more extensive discussion of culture in their cognitive approaches to career theories. Peterson et al. (1991) noted that culture is important in identity formation. They also indicated that no one culture is superior to another and that all cultures provide meaning for their members. Peterson et al. pointed out the necessity of understanding differences in communication styles across cultures. The discussion stopped short of incorporating much of the work on worldviews and racial identity development.

Like Peterson et al., Brown and Brooks (1991) included a discussion of cultural variables that examined the sociopolitical nature of counseling. They provided an extensive discussion of the relevance of culture to career counseling. They even offered some specific data on various ethnic groups. Brown and Brooks recommended that counselors become multiculturally skilled, using competencies like those described by Sue, Arrendondo, and McDavis (1992).

Fouad and Bingham (1995) provided an extensive discussion of a culturally appropriate model for career counseling with ethnic minorities. Although we provide only a cursory overview of that model here, we discuss, in greater detail, its relevance to career counseling with African Americans. The Fouad–Bingham model is an extension of the work proposed by Ward and Bingham (1993). Ward and Bingham described a practice-based intervention for working with ethnic minority women. They proposed a two-phased process that required preliminary work by the counselor and the client. In the first phase, before the counselor sees the client, Ward and Bingham suggested that the counselor complete the MCCC. The MCCC begins by asking the counselor to identify his or her racial and/or ethnic identity and the client's racial and/or ethnic identity. The MCCC is then divided into three parts: *Counselor Preparation, Exploration and Assessment*, and, *Negotiation and Working Consensus*. In the *Counselor Preparation* section, there are 13 statements that require the counselor to consider concepts ranging from familiarity with multicultural counseling competencies to awareness of the importance of the interaction of gender and race in the client's life. In the *Exploration and Assessment* section, the 13 statements require that the counselor review various levels of understanding and awareness in areas such as the client's career question and the client's perception of his or her competence, ability, and self-efficacy. The final section has 20 statements that help the client and counselor to develop a planned intervention in the career-counseling endeavor.

The second phase of preparation involves the client. Clients are asked to complete the CCCC before seeing the counselor. This checklist has 42 statements that ask the client to assess concerns that might impact the career exploration and decision-making process. Sample items include the role of ethnicity, age, fear of making mistakes, and the role of the family in the decision process. Ward and Bingham (1993) reported that these two checklists grew out of their clinical work with ethnic minority clients. Although the documents seemed to have served a practical function for the authors, there has only been one quantitative research study on any portion of the process.

Prigoff (1996) administered the CCCC to 127 students at a large southern university. The sample included 89 European Americans and 38 African Americans. In order to analyze the data in a more efficient manner, Prigoff created three categories: *Understanding Self, Decision Making*, and *Personal, Familial, and Sociopolitical*. Each of the 42 items on the checklist was assigned to one of the three groupings. The results indicated significant differences in only one category, *Understanding Self*. African American students indicated more understanding of themselves in relation to the world than did European American students.

From this two-phase preliminary starting place, Fouad and Bingham (1995) developed a model for the actual counseling-intervention process. They proposed a seven-step culturally appropriate career-counseling model. The steps included establishing rapport, identification of career issues, assessment of cultural variables, setting culturally appropriate processes and goals, designing culturally appropriate interventions, making appropriate decisions, and implementing the career plan with follow-up.

Although the Fouad–Bingham model is the most extensive model that we are currently aware of, it is not specific to African American clients. However, because the model has not yet been subjected to any quantitative research, it is not possible to speak to its validity. Nonetheless, it holds some logical promise and it is more closely examined later in this chapter to explore its possible utility in career counseling with African American men and women.

MODELS FOR AFRICAN AMERICANS

We found no career-counseling theories that were specifically relevant to African Americans. Primarily, authors reported on and critiqued major traditional theories. Generally, the theories did not take race into consideration in their development. Most researchers have spent time exploring the generalizability of the theories to the African American population. Parts of some of the theories can be generalized to African Americans, however, as Osipow and Littlejohn (1995) stated, career-counseling theories need to take into consideration the role and importance of history, economics, politics, education, and social environments along with the impact of discriminatory practices. They concluded that most vocational development theories have not done that.

There are some writers (Bowman, 1995; Brown, 1995) who discussed in depth career-counseling intervention techniques with African Americans or the state of the career literature with African Americans. Accordingly, the work of Cheatham (1990) and Thomas and Alderfer (1989) are highlighted in the following text.

The work of Cheatham (1990) is particularly relevant because it provides a model for incorporating a Eurocentric with an Africentric social order that helps counselors more adequately understand the career behavior of African American clients. Cheatham based his model on the earlier work of Nobles (1976), who maintained that one's worldview is important to the entire development of individuals in given societies. Nobles described a European worldview that emphasizes survival of the fittest, competition, control over nature, and a focus on the individual. The African worldview, on the other hand, concentrates on survival of the group, harmony with nature and cooperation. Cheatham (1990) reported that African Americans could have some combination of these two worldviews because of the legacy of the African heritage and dominant European heritage evident in the United States. Cheatham indicated that there is an interplay between the two worldviews that influences the career behavior of African Americans. He cautioned counselors to understand that African Americans are not a monolithic group, therefore, one should not assume that the acculturation, adaptation of values, and social interplay are identical for each member of the group. However, Cheatham did suggest that the influence of Africentrism may explain the overrepresentation of African Americans in social and behavioral careers.

Figure 3.1 is Cheatham's (1990) Heuristic Model of African American Students' Career Development. The model demonstrates that the counselor must take into consideration the sociopolitical and sociohistorical context of African American career development. Noteworthy, the model does not cast as negative or positive the impact of the Africentric or the Eurocentric social order. In fact, Cheatham maintained that what might be disabling in the Eurocentric social order for one African American might be enabling for another. The same would be true for the enabling and disabling features of the Africentric social order. In part, the impact of the social order on individuals is determined by their level of acculturation.

Interestingly, Cheatham (1990) asserted that the Eurocentric social order has a "direct and predominant effect on the career development process" (p. 341). Conversely, the effect of the Africentric social order is indirect and tentative. Cheatham (1990) indicated that it is more useful for African American development if the components of each social order are reciprocal and complimentary. One assumes that the Eurocentric social order is more direct and predominant because of the historical structure of career choice, career awareness, and occupational development in the United States.

The strength of Cheatham's model is that it incorporates the traditional theories and adds specifics about the African American culture. It, therefore, provides a more wholistic lens through which to view the careerdevelopment process. It would be useful for Cheatham to explain the model in greater detail and perhaps to include an example of the model's application.

Although Cheatham's model provides insight about the career-development process that leads to the selection of a career or occupation, Thomas and Alderfer (1989) offered a model that explicates the career development of African Americans after they have entered the labor market. In their *Model of Black Career Development*, which is adapted from Dickens and Dickens (1982), Thomas and Alderfer described a four-stage career-development process that includes *entry, adjustment, planned growth,* and *success.* During the *entry phase,* the African American individual is pleased to have a job and feels a sense of false security that results in containment of anger and ignoring race issues. The individual's behavior is very reserved. During the *adjustment phase,* the individual begins to notice White peer advancement, while being aware of his or her own lack of advancement. Anger now is more apparent and interpersonal relationships are more strained. Black colleagues are more aggressively and purposefully sought out for support.

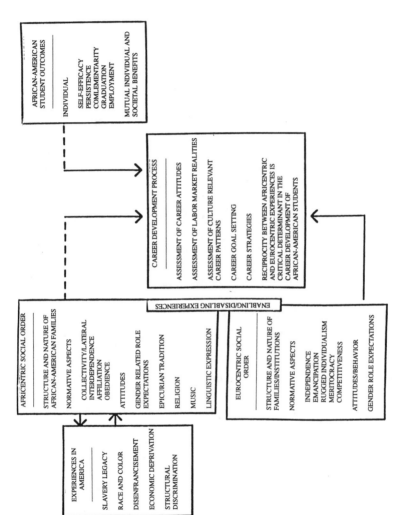

FIG. 3.1. Heuristic model. *Note.* Heuristic Model of African American Students' Career Development on p. 38 in Africentricity and Career Development of African Americans by Harold E. Cheatham, *Career Development Quarterly*, June, 1990, Vol. 38, p. 334–345. Reprinted with permission.

Thomas and Alderfer reported that job effectiveness begins to decline, which is evidence of severe emotional strain.

Thomas and Alderfer (1989) stated that in order to advance, the individual eventually realizes that he or she must do more work more effectively and efficiently than his or her White counterpart. More personal goal setting is initiated; personal style is developed along with self-confidence. The final stage, *success*, is marked by a greater awareness of Blackness and racism. Communication is used more effectively, goals are continually set, and interpersonal relationships are more appropriate.

Although Thomas and Alderfer (1989) did not develop a model that helps to understand the career decision-making and selection process, they effectively demonstrated how issues of race influence the job or career development of African Americans. Even though the model has not been quantitatively studied, its readers can, at least, increase their awareness of the necessity of understanding that race and the perception of racism is generally present in the day-to-day work environment of African Americans and effects the career-development processes.

There are other authors (Bowman, 1995; Brown, 1995; Parham, 1993; Smith, 1983) who have written extensively about the need for career counseling with African Americans. Their work has mainly focused on critiques of major theories as they relate to Black people. The authors tended to call for more research on traditional vocational theories with Black populations. It is believed that if the theories were not conceptualized with African American people in mind, they will always fall short of a full explanation of Black career decision-making behavior. On the other hand, because we believe that all people have some behaviors in common, the theories will always have some revelance to African American career behavior. Furthermore, it is useful to design models for career interventions that are more fully descriptive of the career behavior of Black Americans. The next logical step is to design research programs to validate or invalidate the models.

Culturally Appropriate Career Counseling Model

The results of review of the career literature suggested that the CACCM can be effectively used as an intervention process with African American men and women.

The CACCM has seven steps:

1. Establishment of a culturally appropriate relationship
2. Identification of career issues
3. Assessment of cultural variables

4. Establishment of culturally appropriate goals
5. Selection of culturally appropriate interventions
6. Facilitation of decision making and clarification
7. Implementation

As indicated earlier, the CACCM (Fouad & Bingham, 1995) is an extension of the work of Ward and Bingham (1993), who were very careful to emphasize the necessity for counselors to prepare for work with their clients. If a counselor uses the MCCCC as part of that preparation, the statements should prompt an exploration of the sociocultural and sociohistorical context of African American people. Parham and Austin (1994) cautioned, however, that categorical data about African Americans will not effectively provide the information about Black people. It is important to have a general sense of the history and culture of African Americans. According to Parham and Austin (1994), it is even more important to understand how Black people have adapted to sets of circumstances and how they feel about themselves, other African Americans, and European Americans. Bingham and Guinyard (1982) reported that African American women believe that White people have very negative notions about Black women. It may prove valuable for White counselors to be aware of that, especially if the client is an African American woman. Certainly, it is also important for the counselor to understand his or her own views about Black people.

Bingham and Ward (1994) described three instruments that appear to be quite useful in working with African Americans, the Career Decision Tree, the MCCCC, and the CCCC. The *Decision Tree* describes a process that reminds counselors to make an initial determination about the client's interest in career counseling versus personal counseling. As reported elsewhere, Stabb and Cogdal (1990) indicated that African Americans are more likely to seek career counseling than psychological counseling. It is important to note that sometimes the client is actually in need of psychological help, but finds it more acceptable to seek career help.

In the Astin (1990) study on entering college freshmen, results from one local university indicated that African Americans were far less likely to seek psychological help than their White counterparts. Utilization data from university and college counseling centers (Chando et al., 1997) supports the evidence that African Americans use career counseling much more readily than personal counseling. The data indicated that African American women sought counseling at nearly triple the rate of African American men. Therefore, the career counselors must first understand that African American men in need of career help are not likely to seek that help. If counselors really want to deliver services to this group, they must be creative and proactive. When African American men and women seek career counseling, they may be masking a greater need for psychological help. In light of this information, counselors are nonetheless advised to not assume that the client is avoiding psychological services when he or she is seeking the aid of a career counselor.

The counselor can use the MCCCC to help with counselor preparation and the CCCC to facilitate client preparation. A complete description of these instruments can be found in Ward and Bingham (1993).

Engaging in the aforementioned steps will lay the foundation for the first step of the CACCM, the establishment of a culturally appropriate relationship (Fouad & Bingham, 1995). Obviously, African Americans are not a homogeneous group, and therefore, there is no cookbook definition of what a culturally appropriate relationship encompasses. It is clear, however, that programs that succeed with this population are those in which strong positive relationships develop between the primary parties. The authors observed that when African American clients interact with African American counselors, it seems important to the client to have a slightly informal and friendly relationship. During the early 1970s, a most popular notion abounded—that a successful counseling relationship with a Black client had to be one of friendship. It has been the authors' experience, however, that if the counselor is too much like a friend, the counseling relationship is not effective. Ethically, it is important for counselors to keep boundaries clear in any therapeutic relationship. African Americans seem to expect a somewhat more formal initial relationship with White counselors. Such needs may derive from the long history of racial strife in the United States. Even so, those relationships that seem to be the most effective generally evolve into a less formal relationship.

One can see that both types of ethnic combinations (Black client–Black counselor and Black client–White counselor) come with unique sets of concerns. One of the first concerns is for the type and effectiveness of relationship the client is seeking, given that the client and counselor may be considerably different. Comas-Diaz and Jacobson (1987) described an ethnocultural assessment that the authors found useful in helping to establish an appropriate relationship. The ethnocultural assessment is a five-step process that attempts to understand the client's cultural heritage, including the ethnocultural backgrounds of the client's father and mother. The last step in the assessment asks the counselor to evaluate the relationship the client might be anticipating with the counselor. The counselor must look for possible transference and counter transference points in the relationship. Such an assessment is useful because the counselor can be very deliberate about the role of ethnicity as he or she begins to work on establishing rapport with the client.

Central to establishing any multicultural relationship are the *core conditions of empathy, warmth, respect, trust, concreteness, and positive regard.* In this context Bingham and Ward (1994) suggested that the counselor allow the client to serve as a cultural teacher. It is important to listen to the needs of the client and respond openly and forthrightly to the client's cues and statements. It is especially important for the counselor to pay attention to clients' cues, given the potential differences between African American males and females. We are aware that Black males are not as likely to seek counseling; therefore, when they do seek it, the counselor must be very curious about their motivation. If the counselor does not understand Black male counseling agency utilzation patterns very early in the process, it may be much more difficult to establish rapport with the client and the client will leave counseling prematurely.

The second step in the CACCM is the *identification of career issues*. Fouad and Bingham (1995) divided the issues into five areas: cognitive, social emotional, environmental, behavioral, and external barriers. The counselor must determine the focus of the career counseling session, what propelled the client into career counseling. The very essence of *counseling* is that the client wants some relief from something and thinks the counselor can help with alleviation of the problem. This definition is quite salient for African American men, given that they are not likely to engage in career counseling. If a man has decided to seek help, the counselor can assume that he is either highly acculturated or in great need of services. Some African American psychologists believe that African Americans have learned to put up with high levels of distress before being willing to talk to a stranger (Gilleylen, personal communication, October 3, 1997). The authors also noted an interesting phenomenon among African American men that is a combination of a concept more often associated with Asian cultures—saving face—and one more associated with White men—control. In Black society, the phenomenon is sometimes labeled *playing it cool*. In order to understand the concept, the reader is invited to observe the social interaction (i.e., play) of a group of adolescent African Americans. There appears to be a game of one-upsmanship in the verbal interchanges. Deconstruction of the language reveals the saving face and control aspects of the play. How does one play it cool and ask for help simultaneously?

Adding to the problem is the social history that comes from the role of the welfare worker (i.e., counselor) in the lives of so many African Americans. For the economic survival of the family, it was important that the man not interact or be anywhere visible when the counselor came around. The women were left to hide the male's involvement with the family and to hide any material things of significance from the welfare worker, less the family suffer the loss of whatever they had gained from the system.

Given the aforementioned and the earlier caveat that the client could really be seeking psychological help, the counselor must be very diligent about identifying the career issues. It is easy to understand that the career concerns could differ dramatically from client to client. The client could be struggling with issues such as loss of confidence, racism, sexism, cognitive dissonance, or a simple lack of information about the world of work. The reader is referred to Brown and Brooks (1991) for a listing of other cognitive categories that might prove useful in designing intake interview questions.

In determining the career issues, the counselor has already begun Step 3, *assessing the impact of cultural variables on career issues*. Fouad and Bingham (1995) depicted spheres of influence consisting of a biological or genetic core, gender, family, racial and/or ethnic group and majority group, and their impact on career choice (see Fig. 3.2). Although the concept is essentially sound, it is hypothesized that the influence model is more realistical-

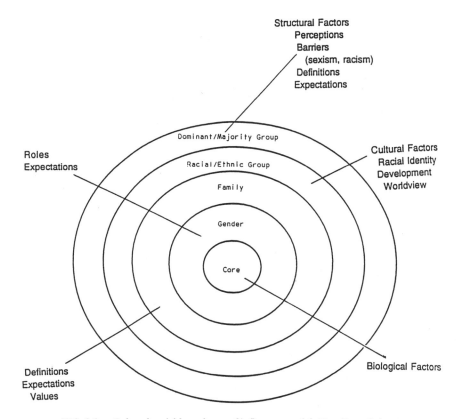

FIG. 3.2. Cultural variables spheres of influence model. *Note.* From Spheres of influence of cultural variables, on p. 351 in Fouad, N. and Bingham, R. P. (1995). Career Counseling with racial and ethnic minorities. In W. B. Walsh & S. H. Osipow (Eds.), *Handbook of Vocational Psychology* (pp. 331–366). Mahwah, NJ: Lawrence Erlbaum Associates. Printed with permission.

ly depicted as a spiral of influence because the variables are dynamic and interactional (see Fig. 3.3). There is much movement and different levels of power that each variable holds at various stages in the client's career-development process. We support the notion that the spheres of influence can be larger or smaller depending on the client's life circumstances. They are, however, never discrete and self contained. The gender differences are likely to be substantial, given the previous discussion.

There is ample evidence of gender differences in the world of work (Cook, 1993). Men receive higher pay. Most Fortune 500 companies are headed by men. Men far outdistance women in employment in occupations related to science and math. Most of these differences are proportionally similar for African American men and women. Bridges (1993) noted that the gender differences begin appearing from the time of birth. She noted the differences in colors associated with the sex of babies, blue

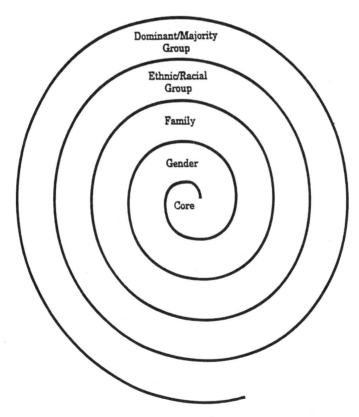

FIG. 3.3.   Spiral of influence of cultural variables. Copyright 1997 by Rosie P. Bingham, printed with permission.

for boys, pink for girls. In addition to traditional sex role differences, the African American community often overlays those with ones that are embedded in the social history and fabric of Black life. For example, the history of the lynching and jailing of African American men and boys has lead the family to be especially protective of the males. There are now more African American males involved in the criminal justice system than there are in higher education. The Black family is faced with the complicated process of helping African American males know where the boundaries of their freedom may be and what the expansion of their limits can be so that they are better able to gain a strong sense of self efficacy. The Black male is given messages that instruct him to find a career that allows him to take care of a family while being all that he can be, but is simultaneously encouraged to not risk the angering of the majority society so that his life or freedom is taken away. Interestingly, the threat is perceived by Black Americans to exist whether or not the boys and men are engaged in positive or negative behavior.

Smith (1983) found that on Super's Career Maturity scale (CMS), the scores of adolescent African Americans were lower than those for their White counterparts. It behooves the counselor to be cognizant of the effect of behaviors on the development of maturity and how career maturity is assessed by an instrument designed for a different cultural group. It may be that it is the subtlety of such messages that powerfully impacts the career decision making of African American men (Osipow & Littlejohn, 1995).

Such subtlety may also be present for Black women. The labor force data (Federal Glass Ceiling Commission, 1995) consistently shows different employment and salary patterns for men and women. Although the overall salaries of African American women are less than that of African American men, employment for Black men has been decreasing, whereas it has been increasing for Black women (Woody, 1992). Clearly, there are many environmental factors associated with this trend. The data signal to the career counselor that there may be a need to explore the trend when the clients present themselves for career-counseling intervention. It may be that Black women are receiving messages about the role of work in their lives from family and society that may be very positive and could help to shape the quality of the intervention the counselor may find effective.

Labor force statistics also show that women are far less evident in careers that involve math and science (Woody, 1992). When boys and girls begin elementary school, they perform equally well in the science and math (Bernstein, 1992). A drop off in interest and achievement in the areas begins to appear during the middle-school years, so that by the time of high school graduation, girls lag far behind boys in interest in and selection of occupations involving science, math, and now technology.

This pattern is true for African American males and females. Some writers (Hackett & Betz, 1981) speculated that there are societal cues that give messages that effect the self-efficacy of girls and women in this area. Gainor and Forrest (1991) indicated that Black women will sometimes limit their career choices and aspirations because of perceptions of sexism and racism in the workplace.

Fouad and Bingham (1995) identified the family as the next source of greatest influence on the career-development process. A core belief in the field of psychology is that family plays a major role in shaping and defining individuals' personalities, mate selection, career choice, and so forth (Akbar, 1991; Denga, 1988; Evansoki & Wu Tse, 1989; Wehrly, 1988). Indeed, the family is a strong source of reinforcement of the career aims of Black boys and girls. Family members help to define the role of work in the lives of other family members. Woody (1992) described the personal work history of four African American females. In each, the woman discussed the reinforcement to work that she received from her family. One woman said her mother insisted that she and her siblings had to work as teenagers. Another reported that her role model was her grandmother, who worked during the entire time the woman was exposed to her. The woman therefore decided very early in life that she would also work all of her life. The idea of not working was never entertained as a possiblity. Although in African American families the notion of work is preeminent, there seems to be less push for particular occupations. McGoldrick, Pearce, and Giordano (1982) suggested that particular ethnic groups can be significantly overrepresented in particular occupations. It also seems clear that oftentimes families dictate the occupational choices of the children. It may be that the social history of Black Americans influences their tendency to not push their children into particular careers. It could be that the reality of the employment market and the exposure of Blacks to specific careers, dictate a more measured and restricted view of what is available as career options (Bowman & Tinsley, 1991).

The values and expectations of the family are greatly influenced by the worldview of the ethnic and/or racial group. *Worldview* includes the values, beliefs, attitudes, and perceptions one holds about the world. One's worldview may influence career choices. For example, Nobles (1976) and Nobles and Goddard (1993) described an African worldview that valued the needs of the group over those of the individual. An individual with such a worldview might need to consider the impact of his or her career choice on an entire race or cultural group. Akbar (1991) maintained that group affiliation is very important in the lives of African Americans. It could be that the prominent role of the group in the lives of African Americans explains some of their career and work behavior. Figure 3.4 is representative of an African worldview versus a European worldview, which Nobles (1976) maintained

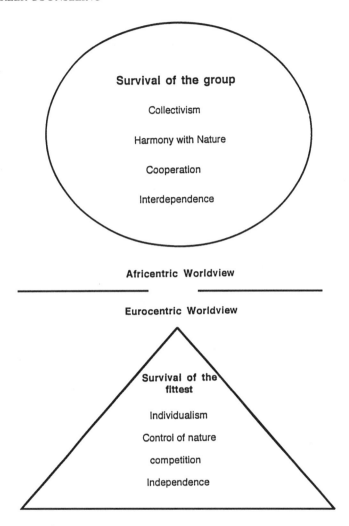

FIG. 3.4.   Two worldviews. Copyright 1997 by Rosie P. Bingham, printed with permission.

focuses on the individual and survival of the fittest. The African worldview has been depicted as a circle with members enclosed and generally of equal standing. Groups like these will sometimes produce a spokesperson for the group, but the group values demand that the leader regularly return to the circle. In this model, in order for the individual to advance, the entire group must advance. Likewise, when the group progresses, the individual progresses. On the other hand, the European worldview was represented as a pyramid. It is hierarchical and has an expectation that some individuals will eventually rise to the top. Some members must necessarily remain on the bottom to support the individual rise to the top. The career choice can merely be the means to personal gain (Cheatham, 1990).

The circle could also be labeled as an Africentric view of career behavior, whereas the pyramid might be labeled Eurocentric. According to Cheatham (1990), in order for a career counselor to be effective, both models need to be taken into account when working with African Americans. Cheatham asserted that there is a distinct African American self that is supported by empirical evidence (Boykin, 1983; Dillard, 1972; Grambs, 1972; Silverstein & Krate, 1975; Sims, 1979). The career counselor must consider such things as the African American's need for an effective expression, affiliation, collectivity, orality, and so forth. They must also consider the Eurocentric values of independence, time orientation, competition, and so forth. Counselors must understand that their clients are not likely to be aware that all of these factors influence their career development. Because African Americans are not a monolithic group, it is essential to understand the role of acculturation. An individual's race and color do not necessarily define his or her worldview. Therefore, one African American could be aptly described by an African worldview and another epitomizes a European worldview. The recommendation is that the career counselor include knowledge and understanding about both.

In addition to the role of worldview, Helms and Piper (1994) and Parham and Austin (1994) suggested that racial identity is an important aspect of career development. A description of the steps of racial identity are not included in this chapter because the theory is described in numerous places (Cross, 1971; Helms, 1990; Ponterotto, 1988). Parham and Austin (1994) contended that the stage of one's racial identity development might influence the career-decision process. They further indicated that the nigrescence construct provides a useful framework for helping counselors and clients understand the career-development process of African Americans. Bingham and Ward (1994) speculated that the racial identity stage of the counselor and of the client influence the quality and effectiveness of the actual counseling intervention session, especially if the client and counselor are at conflicting stages of development.

The last layer of the spiral is the dominant or majority group. It seems reasonable to assume that the cultural values of the majority group shape and define the society. The values of that society also influence the career-development process of the minority group members. Katz (1985) defined the components of the White culture in the United States. Her definition embodies a Eurocentric worldview. The foregoing discussion addresses some of the issues with which career counselors must be concerned. Along with those issues, counselors must also take note of what Fitzgerald and Betz (1992) labeled as *structural barriers*. Discrimination, sexism, and racism are examples of structural barriers that might impact the career process of African Americans.

Boykin (1983) maintained that "Racial stratification operates principally through the imposition of vocational barriers that have historically denied African American people assess to higher status occupations" (p. 331). Labor market data indicates that as the status of the occupation goes up, the number of Blacks in those occupations decreases (Woody, 1992). There had been a gap in the narrowing of academic proficiency between Blacks and Whites during the 1980s; however, now the gap may no longer be narrowing. It may be that the incidence of poverty is a continuing problem in successful career changes for African Americans. Poverty and discrimination play a part in the opportunity for exposure to career role models and information about the world of work. Gottfredson (1982) maintained that as access to careers is blocked due to a lack of ability, discrimination, or other barriers, individuals move down the list of possible career options until they find options that are realizable for them. It may be that some Black individuals foreclose on their career options as a result of societal barriers long before they complete developmental tasks that may be important to career growth and maturity.

As suggested by Fouad and Bingham (1995), the importance and impact of the cultural variables differ from one individual to the next. What does not change, however, is the need for the career counselor to pay close attention to these cultural components in the assessment and intervention phases of career counseling with African Americans.

The next step in the CACCM is *setting culturally appropriate process and goals*. Appropriate goals and process are determined by the client's culture. It is reasonable to assume the if a career counselor is to be effective in facilitating the vocational decision-making process of African Americans, he or she must understand the extent to which the clients have an Africentric or Eurocentric worldview. Step 3 of this model should have helped the client clarify issues that could be associated with any confusion the client might have resulting from a conflict with these two worldviews. If the client has an Africentric worldview, then he is likely to want to consider the impact his career decision will have on his ethnic group, family, and/or community. On the other hand, a client with primarily a Eurocentric orientation may want his or her career goal centered around self-actualization only. An example of a culturally appropriate process for African Americans might include a counseling style that is more personal and affective versus one that is more distant and rational. African Americans tend to have strong affiliation needs even in counseling relationships. Sue and Sue (1990) encouraged counselors to be aware that he or she can have one of four conditions when working in a therapeutic environment: (a) culturally appropriate process and culturally appropriate goals, (b) culturally appropriate process and culturally inappropriate goals, (c) culturally inappropriate process and culturally appropriate goals, or (d) culturally inappropriate process and culturally inappropriate goals. The career counselor who does not work from the same cultural orientation as the African American client can easily use inappropriate process or set inappropriate goals. Appropriateness along both of these dimensions can be enhanced by remembering to use the client as cultural teacher and partner in counseling.

Culturally appropriate process and goals should guide the counselor and client in selection of *culturally appropriate interventions*, the fifth step of the Fouad–Bingham model. Bowman (1993) suggested that group interventions are effective with African Americans. Rather than a traditional group counseling intervention, it may be necessary to use outreach to and through a peer group. Given the fact that such a small number of Black males seek traditional counseling, the intervention may need to be in the form of a workshop or presentation to an intact group with which the male is affiliated. For example, on a college campus a vocational presentation to a fraternity may be the initial contact for the career intervention. During the group presentation, it will be important for the counselor to demonstrate and connect with the cultural values related to career exploration that are held by the group members. At that session the group members will have an opportunity to begin to establish a relationship with the career counselor. The counselor can begin making arrangements for follow-up appointments as needed.

Although African American women are more likely to actively seek counseling, the counselor must still remember to be responsive to cultural values and beliefs and design interventions that are reflective of those values and beliefs. It is important to remember that African Americans generally value intimacy and a sense of belonging. Also, counselors should be aware of issues surrounding self efficacy. Each of these concerns can influence the intervention strategy.

The last two steps of the model—*decision making and implementation and follow-up*—must be consistent with the approach described throughout this chapter. The counselor must be willing to go outside traditional counseling if culture is to be integrated into the process.

Just as this model is not static, neither are clients. They will change and may need to cycle through steps as their self-understanding increases and as they gain more knowledge about the world of work. Their racial identity stage may change and their perspectives on work and the majority culture may undergo transformation. The typical number of career-counseling sessions seldom will allow the therapist to witness such changes, therefore, it is important for the counselor to make sure that the client knows that he or she can return for counseling as needed and as is appropriate.

RECOMMENDATIONS

By now it should be clear that culture is inextricably linked to vocational behavior. Counseling takes place in a cultural context. Any effective vocational theory building, career counseling, and interventions about and for African Americans must include the social, historical, political, and economic realities of Black life. In order to add more depth and breadth to the discourse, counselors must include notions of worldview and racial identity development. It may be important to seek ways to integrate the Afrocentric worldview and the Eurocentric worldview as new career-development theories and interventions are created. These factors are basic to developing an understanding about counseling interventions with this population.

The following are also recommended:

1. Learn about and develop multicultural counseling skills.
2. Be aware that African Americans are not monolithic. There are numerous within-group differences, perhaps most notably are the gender distinctions.
3. Because African American males are so unlikely to seek help, a more proactive outreach effort is required.
4. Evaluate rites of passage interventions. Such programs may hold great promise for those individuals interested in devising immediate interventions (Delaney, 1995).
5. The role of self-efficacy in the career behavior of African Americans needs to be studied.
6. Develop other research areas to include factors that lead to congruence for African Americans and the differential impact of the family on the career development process of Black men and women.
7. Initiate empirical studies on multicultural career counseling instruments like the CCCC.

These recommendations will necessitate changes in the academic and training missions and objectives of educational and clinical service institutions. Given the expected workforce changes expected for the 21st century the changes are vitally necessary if we expect to fully utilize all members of the society.

REFERENCES

Akbar, N. (1991). *Chains and Images of Psychological Slavery*. Jersey City, NJ: New Mind Productions.

Astin, A. W. (1990). *The Black undergraduate: Current status and trends in the characteristics of freshmen*. Los Angeles: Higher Education Research Institute, University of California.

Bernstein, J. D. (1992). *Barriers to women entering the workforce: Math anxiety*. (New Jersey Research Bulletin No. 3). Upper Montclair, NJ: Montclair State College Life Skills Center. (ERIC Document Reproduction Service No. ED 359 381)

Bingham, R. P., & Guinyard, J. (1982). *Counseling Black women: Recognizing societal scripts*. Paper presented at the Southeastern Psychological Association, Atlanta, GA.

Bingham, R. P., & Walsh, W. B. (1978). Concurrent validity of Holland's theory for college-degreed black women. *Journal of Vocational Behavior, 13*, 242–250.

Bingham, R. P., & Ward, C. M. (1994). Career counseling with ethnic minority women. In W. B. Walsh & S. H. Osipow (Eds.), *Career counseling for women* (pp. 165–196). Hillsdale, NJ: Lawrence Erlbaum Associates.

Bowman, S., & Tinsley, H. (1991). The development of vocational realism in Black American college students. *Career Development Quarterly, 39*, 240–249.

Bowman, S. L. (1993). Career intervention strategies for ethnic minorities. *Career Development Quarterly, 42*, 14–25.

Bowman, S. L. (1995). Career intervention strategies and assessment issues for African Americans. In F. T. L. Leong (Ed.), *Career development and vocational behavior of racial and ethnic minorities* (pp. 137–164). Mahwah, NJ: Lawrence Erlbaum Associates.

Boykin, A. W. (1983). The academic performance of Afro-American children. In J. T. Spence (Ed.), *Achievement and achievement motives: Psychological and sociological approaches* (pp. 321–371). San Francisco: Freeman.

Bridges, J. S. (1993). Pink or blue: Gender-stereotypic perceptions of infants as conveyed by birth congratulations cards. *Psychology of Women Quarterly, 17*, 193–205.

Brown, D., & Brooks, L. (1991). *Career counseling techniques*. Boston: Allyn & Bacon.

Brown, M. T. (1995). The career development of African Americans: Theoretical and empirical issues. In F. T. L. Leong (Ed.), *Career development and vocational behavior of racial and ethnic minorities* (pp. 7–36). Mahwah, NJ: Lawrence Erlbaum Associates.

Burlew, A. K., & Johnson, J. L. (1992). Role conflict and career advancement among African American women in nontraditional professions. *The Career Development Quarterly, 40*, 302–312.

Chando, C. M., Bekis, B., Cogdal, P. A., Gilleylen, C. E., Hurley, F. W., & Kenney, G. E. (1997). *Center for Student Development Annual Report 1996*. The University of Memphis, a Tennessee Board of Regents University, Memphis, TN.

Cheatham, H. (1990). Africentricity and career development of African Americans. *The Career Development Quarterly, 38*, 334–346.

Comas-Diaz, L., & Jacobson, F. M. (1987). Ethnocultural identification in psychotherapy. *Psychiatry, 50*, 232–241.

Cook, P. E. (1993). The gendered context of life: Implications for women's and men's career-life plans. *The Career Development Quarterly, 41*, 227–237.

Cross, W. E. (1971). The Negro-to-Black conversion experience: Toward a psychology of Black liberation. *Black World, 20*, 13–27.

Delaney, C. H. (1995). Rites of passage in adolescence. *Adolescence, 30*(120), 891–897.

Denga, D. I. (1988). Influence of traditional factors on career choice among Nigerian secondary school youth. *Journal of Multicultural Counseling and Development, 16*, 1–15.

Dickens, F., & Dickens, J. B. (1982). *The Black manager*. New York: Amacom.

Dillard, J. L. (1972). *Black English: Its history and usage in the United States*. New York: Vintage Books.

Evansoki, P. D., & Wu Tse, F. (1989). Career awareness program for Chinese and Korean American parents. *Journal of Counseling and Development, 67*, 472–474.

Federal Glass Ceiling Commission. (1995). *Good for business: Making full use of the nations's human capital: The environmental scan: A fact finding report of the Federal Glass Ceiling Commission*. Washington, DC: U.S. Government Printing Office.

Fitzgerald, L., & Betz, N. E. (1992, April). *Career development in cultural context: The role of gender, race, class, and sexual orientation*. Paper presented at the conference on Theories Convergence in Vocational Psychology, East Lansing, MI.

Fouad, N. A., & Arbona, C. (1994). Careers in a cultural context. *Career Development Quarterly, 43*(1), 96–104.

Fouad, N. A., & Bingham, R. P. (1995). Career counseling with racial and ethnic minorities. In W. B. Walsh & S. H. Osipow (Eds.), *Handbook of vocational psychology: Theory, research and practice* (2nd ed., pp. 331–366). Mahwah, NJ: Lawrence Erlbaum Associates.

Gainor, K. A., & Forrest, L. (1991). African American women's self-concept: Implications for career decisions and career counseling. *Career Development Quarterly, 39*, 261–272.

Gottfredson, L. (1982). Circumscription and compromise: A developmental theory of occupational aspirations. *Journal of Counseling Psychology, 28*, 545–579.

Grambs, J. D. (1972). Negro self-concept reappraised. In J. A. Banks & J. D. Grambs (Eds.), *Black self-concept: Implications for education and social science* (pp. 171–220). New York: McGraw-Hill.

Hackett, N. E., & Betz, N. (1981). A self-efficacy approach to the career development of women. *Journal of Vocational Behavior, 18*, 326–339.

Harris, S. M. (1995). Psychological development and Black male masculinity: Implications for counseling economically disadvantaged African American male adolescents. *Journal of Counseling and Development, 73*, 279–287.

Helms, J. E. (1990). *Black and White racial identity: Theory, research and practice*. Eastport, CT: Greenwood.

Helms, J. E., & Piper, R. E. (1994). Implications of racial identity theory for vocational psychology. *Journal of Vocational Behavior, 44*, 124–138.

Holland, J. L. (1985). *Making vocational choices* (2nd ed.). Englewood Cliffs, NJ: Prentice-Hall.

June, L. N., & Pringle, G. D. (1977). The concept of race in the career development theories of Roe, Super, and Holland. *Journal of Non-White Concerns in Personnel and guidance, 6*(1), 17–24.

Katz, J. H. (1985). The sociopolitical nature of counseling. *The Counseling Psychologist, 13*, 615–624.

Leong, F. T. L., & Brown, M. (1995). Theoretical issues in cross-cultural career development: Cultural validity and cultural specificity. In W. B. Walsh & S. H. Osipow (Eds.), *Handbook of vocational psychology: Theory, Research, and Practice* (2nd ed., pp. 143–180). Mahwah, NJ: Lawrence Erlbaum Associates.

Luzzo, D. A. (1993). Value of career-decision-making self-efficacy in predicting career-decision-making attitudes and skills. *Journal of Counseling Psychology, 40*, 194–199.

McGoldrick, M., Pearce, J. K., & Giordano, J. (Eds.). (1982). *Ethnicity and family therapy*. New York: Guilford.

Miller, M. J., Springer, T., & Wells, D. (1988). Which occupational environments do Black youths prefer? Extending Holland's topology. *School Counselor, 36*, 103–106.

Neely, D. E. (1990). Inroads for women, few for minorities: A survey and comparison of leading law firms in the tri-state area. *New York Law Journal*, 21.

Nobles, W. W. (1976). Extended self: Rethinking the Negro self-concept. *Journal of Black Psychology, 2*, 15–24.

Nobles, W. W., & Goddard, L. L. (1993). An African-centered model of prevention for African-American youth at high risk. In L. L. Goddard (Ed.), *An African-centered model of prevention for African-American youth at high risk* (Center for Substance Abuse Prevention Rep. No. 6, pp. 115–128). Rockville, MD: U. S. Dept. of Health and Human Services.

O'Brien, W. F., & Walsh, W. B. (1976). Concurrent validity of Holland's theory for non-college degreed Black working men. *Journal of Vocational Behavior, 8*, 239–246.

Osipow, S. H. (1975). The relevance of theories of career development to special groups. In J. S. Piocou & R. E. Campbell (Eds.), *Career behavior of special groups: Theory, research, and practice* (pp. 9–22). Columbus, OH: Merrill.

Osipow, S. H., & Littlejohn, E. M. (1995). Toward a multicultural theory of career development: Prospects and dilemmas. In F. T. L. Leong (Ed.), *Career development and vocational behavior of racial and ethnic minorities* (pp. 251–261). Mahwah, NJ: Lawrence Erlbaum Associates.

Parham, T. (1993, August). *Discussant in cultural contexts of identify formation—some international perspectives*. Paper presented at the 101st convention of the American Psychological Association, Toronto, Canada.

Parham, T. A., & Austin, N. L. (1994). Career development and African Americans: A contextual reappraisal using the Nigrescence construct. *Journal of Vocational Behavior, 44*, 139–154.

Parsons, F. (1909). *Choosing a vocation*. Boston: Houghton Mifflin.

Peterson, G. W., Sampson, J. P., & Reardon, R. C. (1991). *Career development and services: A cognitive approach*. Pacific Grove, CA: Brooks/Cole.

Ponterotto, J. G. (1988). Racial consciousness development among white counselor trainees: A stage model. *Journal of Multicultural Counseling and Development, 16*, 146–156.

Prigoff, G. L. (1996, October). *A comparison of African American and Caucasian-American college students' responses to the career checklist for clients*. Paper presented at the annual convention of the Tennessee Psychological Association, Gatlinburg, TN.

Richardson, M. S. (1993). Work in people's lives: A location for counseling psychologists. *Journal of Counseling Psychology, 40*, 425–433.

Roe, A. (1956). *The psychology of occupations*. New York: Wiley.

Sheffey, M. A., Bingham, R. P., & Walsh, W. B. (1986). Concurrent validity of Holland's theory for college educated black men. *Journal of Multicultural Counseling and Development, 64*(7), 437–439.

Silverstein, B., & Krate, R. (1975). *Children of the dark ghetto: A developmental psychology*. New York: Praeger.

Simpson, G. (1996). The plexiglass ceiling: The careers of Black women lawyers. *The Career Development Quarterly, 45*, 173–188.

Sims, S. (1979). Sharing in Black children: The impact of reference group appeals and other developmental factors. In A. W. Boykin, A. J. Franklin, & J. F. Yates (Eds.), *Research directions of Black psychology* (pp. 146–148). New York: Russell Sage.

Slaney, R. B., & Brown, M. T. (1983). Effects of race and socioeconomic status on career choice variables among college men. *Journal of Vocational Behavior, 23*, 257–269.

Smith, E. J. (1975). Profile of the Black individual in vocational literature. *Journal of Vocational Behavior, 6*, 41–59.

Smith, E. J. (1983). Issues in racial minorities' career behavior. In W. B. Walsh & S. H. Osipow (Eds.), *Handbook of vocational psychology: Vol. 1, Foundations* (pp. 161–222). Hillsdale, NJ: Lawrence Erlbaum Associates.

Stabb, S., & Cogdal, P. (1990, April). *Needs assessment and the perception of help in a multicultural college population*. Paper presented at the ACPA Convention, St. Louis, MO.

Stoltz-Loike, M. (1996, December). Annual review: Practice and research in career development and counseling—1995. *The Career Development Quarterly, 45*, 99–140.

Subich, L. M. (Ed.). (1993). How personal is career counseling? [Special Issue]. *Career Development Quarterly, 42*(2), 129–131.

Sue, D. W., Arredondo, P., & McDavis, R. J. (1992). Multicultural counseling competencies and standards: A call to the profession. *Journal of Multicultural Counseling and Development, 20*, 64–88.

Sue, D. W., & Sue, D. (1990). *Counseling the culturally different: Theory and practice*. New York: Wiley.

Super, D. E. (1990). A life-span, life-space approach to career development. In D. Brown & L. Brooks (Eds.), *Career choice and development* (2nd ed., pp. 197–261). San Francisco: Jossey-Bass.

Thomas, D. A., & Alderfer, C. P. (1989). The influence of race on career dynamics: Theory and research on minority career experiences. In M. B. Arthur, D. T. Hall, & B. S. Lawrence (Eds.), *Handbook of career theory* (pp. 133–158). Cambridge, England: Cambridge University Press.

U.S. Department of Labor. (1992). *Occupational outlook handbook*. Washington, DC: U.S. Government Printing Office.

Walsh, W. B., Hildebrand, J. O., Ward, C. M., & Matthews, D. F. (1983). Holland's theory and non-college degreed working Black and White women. *Journal of Vocational Behavior, 22*, 182–190.

Ward, C. M., & Bingham, R. P. (1993). Career assessment of ethnic minority women. *Journal of Career Assessment, 1*, 246–257.

Ward, C. M., & Walsh, W. B. (1981). Concurrent validity of Holland's theory for non-college-degreed black women. *Journal of Vocational Behavior, 18*, 356–361.

Wehrly, B. (1988). Influence of traditional factors on career choice among Nigerian secondary school youth. *Journal of Multicultural Counseling and Development, 16*, 3–5.

Wilson, F. D., Tienda, M., & Wu, L. (1995). Race and unemployment: Labor market experience of Black and White men, 1968–1988. *Work and Occupations, 22*, 245–270.

Woody, B. (1992). *Black women in the workplace: Impacts of structural change in the economy*. Westport, CT: Greenwood.

Yost, E. B., & Corbishley, M. A. (1987). *Career counseling: A psychological approach*. San Francisco: Jossey-Bass.

Chapter 4

Career Counseling With Dual-Career Heterosexual African American Couples*

Lucia Albino Gilbert
University of Texas at Austin

Rosie P. Bingham
The University of Memphis

Career counseling for heterosexual African American dual-career couples may present some interesting challenges for a career counselor. Herr and Cramer (1992) stated that the career counseling process between a client and a counselor helps to "bring about self understanding and . . . decision-making in the counselee, who has responsibility for his or her own actions." (p. 538). This description becomes much more complicated when the "counselee" is a dual-career couple.

This chapter highlights issues important to understanding dual-career couples. First, areas that are unique to dual-career African American couples and thus crucial in any career counseling with them are identified. Then, a process for working with couples that combines career counseling with multicultural counseling and the research literature on dual-career families is proposed.

AFRICAN AMERICAN DUAL-CAREER FAMILIES IN PERSPECTIVE

Rapoport and Rapoport (1969) described a *dual-career couple* as two people in a marriage who pursue continuous, independent, and professional careers and also maintain a family life together. The idea seemed revolu-

---

*The terms *Black* and *African American* are used interchangeably in this chapter as are the terms *White* and *Euro-American*.

tionary in the late 1960s because women, even those who prepared for lifelong careers, were expected at the time to put careers secondary to marriage and children. Today, some 30 years later, dual-career marriages are quite prevalent, and dual-earner families are the norm.

The research concerning dual-career families falls into the following three main areas:

1. Studies on the relation among women's employment and their husbands' and children's well-being, gender-role attitudes, and behaviors, as well as women's own well-being.
2. Comparisons of women and men in such areas as family role involvement, participation in household work, marital and parenting satisfaction, coping strategies, and stress.
3. Investigations of dual-career family life in the context of societal norms and practices such as child care availability and quality, employer policies and practices, institutional racism and sexism, and the definitions of what makes for successful careers (Barnett & Rivers, 1996; Gilbert, 1993).

To date, much less research has focused on African American dual-career couples than on Euro-American dual-career couples. Moreover, although these three areas of research are as important for African American couples as for Euro-American couples, the assumptions underlying research in these areas are by necessity quite different for each group. In studies of Euro-American dual-career couples, a valid assumption was that life roles were gendered and did not overlap, with men best suited for employment roles and women best suited for home and caretaking roles. As Euro-American women moved into the workplace and sought full-time career roles rather than lower paying jobs, there was concern for harm to the family as well as to the woman herself. This concern centered around views of women as primary caregivers and nurturers to men and children and as unsuited "by nature" to workplace and career demands. Implicit also was the view that women's roles were changing and expanding, but men's were not, and that women made any necessary accommodations.

The dual-career situation manifested itself quite differently for African American women and men. Two differences appear particularly crucial in understanding African American dual-career couples. First, the context of African American women's and men's employment differs from that of Euro-American women and men. Second, partners in African American dual-career families are faced with issues of both race and gender.

The Context of Women's and Men's Employment

African American women have a long history of expecting to work outside the home and being significant financial contributors to the household. Indeed, employment is normative for the African American woman; African American women have traditionally had a higher labor force participation rate than European American women, both prior to marriage and during marriage (Staples & Johnson, 1993; Vaz, 1995). Slave women worked long and grueling hours just like the slave men and were expected to put their family's needs after the needs of others (Jones, 1987). After slavery, it was often safer for African American women (rather than men) to be employed because of threats of the lynching of African American men (hooks, 1981).

Thus, the relatively recent norm of working outside the home for European women, especially among Euro-American middle-class women with husbands to support them, is a long-established norm for African American women. The research literature clearly indicates that African American husbands hold more favorable attitudes toward their spouses' job or career participation than do Euro-American husbands and that African American husbands' well-being is positively associated with their spouses' income (Blee & Tickamyer, 1995; Orbuch & Custer, 1995). Similar findings occur in studies of high school and college-aged women and men. A study by Thomas (1986), examining the views of Black female eighth to twelfth graders about their career goals, reported that all the participants indicated that they planned to work after completing their education. Moreover, a majority of the respondents had identical ideal and real work aspirations. In a study comparing African American and Euro-American college students' expectations, Ganong et al. (1996) reported higher expected professional success and higher levels of desired education for African American students, regardless of sex, than for Euro-American students. In addition, the absolute level of career commitment was quite high. These studies support the long-standing clear cultural expectation held by both women and men that African American women will be employed regardless of their marital status.

Also important in understanding the context of African American women's employment are the limitations placed historically on Black men's employment opportunities and status, which contrasts markedly with the privileged position accorded to White men. Black men have encountered persistent discrimination and limited educational and career opportunities. Unlike White men, societal views of male economic success and power have not extended to the Black male. Hunter and Davis (1992), for example, concluded from their study of African American man's concept of manhood that African American men equate masculinity less with success, wealth, ambition, and power, and more with self-determination and accountability. There is also some indication that African American men are less likely to associate marriage with a necessary part of the adult masculine role (Fossett & Kiecolt, 1993). Thus, both African American women and men developed concepts of self and family life that differ markedly from their Euro-Ameican counterparts.

Issues of Race and Gender

Despite this greater flexibility in employment roles of women and men among African Americans as a group, there is also research to indicate the presence of traditional role expectations and behavior. However, here again, the context differs dramatically. Partners in African American dual-career families are faced with issues of both race and gender. Prejudicial attitudes and societal structures and practices associated with racism are normative to their lives and to the lives of their children. Because of the ongoing and unpredictable nature of racist comments, reactions, and behaviors in one's daily life, dealing with racism can be a major source of stress that needs constant managing.

The pervasiveness of racism may also intensify the effects of sexism for African American women (Greene, 1994; Wyche, 1993). In the essay, "Sexism: An American Disease in Blackface," Lorde (1984) asked:

> If this society ascribes roles to Black men which they are not allowed to fulfill, is it Black women who must bend and alter our lives to compensate, or is it society that needs changing? And why should Black men accept these roles as correct ones, or anything other that a narcotic promise encouraging acceptance of other facts of their own oppression. . . . As Black women and men, we cannot hope to begin dialogue by denying the oppressive nature of male privilege. (p. 62)

Similar to partners in heterosexual Euro-American dual-career families, as Lorde poignantly described, African American partners also struggle with women's and men's views of gender roles and male power, privilege, and superiority vis-à-vis women. Ganong et al.'s (1996) study of college students provides a case in point. Despite the lack of differences in expectations for career success and achieving career goals between women and men, both African American and Euro-American women expected their future partners to be more intelligent, more successful professionally, and to make more money, and males of both races expected their future partners to do more parenting than they would do.

A number of writers described African American women's socialization as caretakers of children, men, and extended family. A prevalent stereo-

typed image of African American women is that they are innately independent, strong, and assertive, and because of this, they can take care of
men as well as children. Yet, as hooks (1994) noted, Black women traditionally have been socialized to have compassion for everybody except
themselves, to present themselves as fearless in their defense of their men
and children, and to show no weaknesses.

Another consequence of the interaction of racism and sexism is the larger proportion of African American women as compared to African American men who enter careers (Woody, 1992). Early editions of *Ebony* magazine
("Marriage," 1947) included regular features on stories regarding potential
mates for professional Black working women. The magazine often talked
about the need for professional career women to marry men who were blue-
collar workers because of the lack of availability of professional Black men
(Whetstone, 1996). Today there is a growing number of dual-career Black
couples because of increasing opportunities for advancement and promotion for African Americans (Black Enterprise, 1996; Thomas, 1990).
Nonetheless, the proportion of Black professional career women still
remains greater than the proportion of Black professional men. One possible consequence of this imbalance in the sex ratio of "appropriate women"
to "appropriate men" is the bargaining or dyadic power between women
and men, which in turn could influence how roles are negotiated within
families. Analyses of historical trends indicates that when the sex ratio favors
women, central themes of a culture will include attempts on the part of
women to establish themselves as independent persons in their own right,
on the one hand, and a redoubling of efforts to keep a man because of their
scarcity, on the other (Guttentag & Secord, 1983).

REALITIES OF THE DUAL-CAREER FAMILY
LIFESTYLE

We next turn to four crucial areas of dual-career family life and briefly
consider key findings and key issues. All four areas involve some aspect of
multiple role involvement and range from studies of spouses' actual role
behaviors to studies of what spouses need in the way of support for their
roles. Integrated into this brief review are responses from 10 dual-career
African American couples we interviewed in preparing this chapter. The
intent in doing the interviews was to explore whether these couples' issues
were consistent with those reported in the literature. In no way are their
responses intended to be representative of the experiences of African
American dual-career families as a group.

Couples interviewed for the chapter were selected by identifying one
couple and then asking members of the couple to recommend another

couple. Couples were selected who fit the definition of dual-career families previously described by Rapoport and Rapoport (1969).

In separate interviews the partners in these 10 couples were asked
about what they perceived to be problem areas in their dual-career
lifestyle, what problems they considered unique to Black dual-career couples, and how they thought a career counselor could be helfpul to a dual-
career African American couple. Participants' responses are reported in
this and the next section of the chapter, as appropriate to the content. The
individuals who were interviewed ranged in age from 36 to 53 years. Most
couples had two children; the average age of children in the sample was
14 years old. Partners' combined incomes ranged from $60,000 to nearly
$200,000, with three of the couples earning over $100,000 annually.

In one of the few in-depth studies of African American dual-career couples, Thomas (1990) interviewed 41 dual-career professional Black couples (average age of approximately 35 years) who had been married less
than 10 years and had at least 1 child under age 5 years. Participants
described their most important problem as having too little time to spend
with family; they also noted difficulties with child care and division of
household responsibilities. Additionally, they believed they experienced
problems and concerns unique to their race and status. These included
racial discrimination, social isolation, being the first generation of professionals in their families, and instilling an appreciation of Black values in
their children while living in a White environment.

The 10 couples interviewed echoed some of the concerns reported by
Thomas (1990). Partners uniformly voiced concerns about time constraints in all areas of their lives. They also spoke of racism and the importance of instilling in the children a sense of pride in themselves and in
their race.

How Partners Combine Family Life and Occupational Work

There is some evidence that African American couples engage in less role
specialization in the home—and that parenting and household work is a
more shared experience—than do Euro-American couples. Hossain and
Roopnarine (1993), for example, examined 63 dual-earner African American mothers' and fathers' involvement in child care with their infant, as
well as involvement in household work, and the degree of support they
received for child care. Although analysis revealed gender-differentiated
patterns of involvement in caregiving and household work along traditional lines, fathers were far from being distant or uninvolved in these
activities. Father involvement in child care and household activities did
not vary as a function of whether mothers worked full time or part time.

Similar findings are reported by John and Shelton (1997) in their comparisons of Black and White employed women and men who responded to a national survey of families and households in 1987. Their findings showed significant differences in the reported mean hours involved in household work (e.g., preparing meals, food shopping, and house cleaning) by women and men (21.7 hours vs. 37.3 hours for men and women, respectively), regardless of race, but a greater level of participation by Black men than White men (21.7 hours vs. 17.8 hours, respectively). However, there was a large variation in the number of hours of housework performed by Black men. This large variation appears to reflect that Black men's housework time varies in response to individual and family variables, such as number of hours of wife's and husband's employment, and thus, is less tied to attitudinal variables about men's rights and privileges.

These data indicate possible gender-role convergence in child care and household work in African American families. Nonetheless, female partners, on average, report taking a greater share of responsibility for the care of home and children. It is possible that for African American families, these differences may, to some degree, reflect gendered ideologies in the culture rather than those held by the couple. For example, women can more readily and explicitly use family-related employee benefits such as parental leave and flextime. Moreover, individuals, female or male, feel pressured to accommodate their personal lives to the traditional occupational structures if they expect to be rewarded by employers, and the pressure may be greater on male employees to do so.

Despite women's greater responsibility, on average, for household work and parenting, it is crucial to realize that there have been significant shifts in men's roles in the past 20 years (Levant & Pollack, 1995; Wilkie, 1993). Overall, men's participation in family work has continued to increase from 1970 to the 1990s, more so in the area of parenting than in the area of household work. There is also important variation among couples, as the data cited earlier from John and Shelton (1997) indicate. Studies of dual-career families indicate three general marital patterns, which Gilbert (1993) labeled *conventional, modern,* and *role sharing.* In a *conventional dual-career family*, both partners are involved in careers, but partners agree that most of the responsibility for family work (i.e., household work and parenting) is the woman's. Basically, in this variation, the female spouse adds her career role to her traditionally held family role and her spouse helps out to the extent that doing so does not interfere with his career. Male spouses in these families are generally much more professionally ambitious than are their spouses; they earn a much higher income and see the issues of whether and how to combine a career with family life as their spouse's to deal with, not issues they need to address themselves.

In the *modern pattern*, parenting is shared by the spouses, but the woman takes more responsibility for household work than does the husband. Most characteristic of this pattern is men's motivations to be active fathers, a motivation that may or may not be strongly associated with egalitarian views. Thus, some men may engage in a modern variation of the dual-career family because they want close relations with their children, but they may still see other aspects of family work as women's work.

The third pattern—the *role-sharing dual-career family*—is the most egalitarian and best represents the pattern many couples, especially female partners, desire. In this variation, both partners actively involve themselves in household work and family life as well as their careers. Recent studies indicate that at least one third of heterosexual dual-career families fit this variation, although many who are not role sharing describe their situation as equitable (e.g., Gerson, 1993; Gilbert, 1988).

Differences among the variations of dual-career families involve variables associated with individual partners, employment practices, and social norms. The following summarizes many of the personal, relational, and environmental factors that may influence how African American couples combine occupational and family roles:

Personal Factors.

- Worldviews, cultural background, and racial identity development (e.g., stage of racial identity, degree to which partner holds an Afrocentric worldview).
- Personality (e.g., how important is a partner's need to dominate, be emotionally intimate, be number one in her or his field?).
- Attitudes and values (e.g., partner's beliefs about rearing a child, gender and power issues, relationship with and responsibility for extended family).
- Interests, abilities, stages in careers (e.g., partner's commitment to occupational work, family relations; partner's work satisfaction and career plans, is one partner peaking career-wise and the other thinking about retirement; is one partner unemployed and having difficulty finding employment).
- Racial and ethnic views or experiences of racial or sex-based discrimination.
- Acceptance in one's community or in one's field (does one feel isolated at work; does neigherhood or work setting hold racist views?).
- Strategies for self-care and for dealing with role conflict (e.g., are a variety of coping strategies employed?).

Relational–Family Factors.

- Equity and power (e.g., how are decisions made; what seems fair; how do partners come to agreements about household work, parenting money, how to deal with racism in their own lives and in the lives of their children?).
- Partners support (e.g., can partners count on each other for support in all areas, encouragement of self-care especially for female partner?).
- Shared values and expectations (e.g., do partners share life goals; philosophy regarding childrearing practices, such as the importance of instilling in children an appreciation of Black values while living in a White environment; do partners have similar cultural backgrounds and worldviews?).

Environmental–Societal Factors.

- The work situation (e.g., are work hours flexible, any sex discrimination, race discrimination?).
- Employer's views (e.g., kinds of family policy provided, general attitude about employees who involve themselves in family life).
- Child care availability and quality.
- Support systems (e.g., family, friends, colleagues, church, community).
- Family responsibilities to parents and other relatives.
- Racial and ethnic views or discrimination.

Figure 4.1 depicts the interactive nature of these three sets of factors. It is important for counselors to understand that partners' satisfaction does not necessarily differ among patterns. Rather satisfaction with a particular pattern adopted depends on these factors, especially each partner's perceptions of fairness about the arrangements they have worked out and the sources of support for their pattern.

Among the 10 couples interviewed, most seemed to generally fit the role-sharing dual-career family. The men and the women in separate interviews indicated that the financial, caretaking, and parenting roles were shared responsibilities. Two of the couples reported that the husband was obligated to be the financial head of the household. Their beliefs seemed to be based largely on biblical teachings and to a lesser extent on what had been practiced in their parental homes. Even among these two couples, however, one wife reported that her husband was the primary nurturer of the children in the household.

Characteristic of the couples was that each partner seemed to take the role sharing aspects of their lives very seriously. Interestingly, although the

Personal Factors		Family Factors		Societal Factors
Ex.: One partner's career goals	⇔	Other partner's support of career goals	⇔	Employer's attitudes/ structure of opportunity Re: race and gender
Ex.: Worldview of each partner	⇔	Worldview of family of origin	⇔	Support Systems/ Responsibility to ones' community

FIG. 4.1.   Schematic presentation of the three factors important in career counseling. *Note.* All three factors are mutually interactive. The schema in this figure depicts one of many possible sequential arrangements.

men reported substantial involvement in caring for their children, some of the wives believed that they ultimately had more responsibility for the nurturance of the children, a belief that may be tied to implicit internalized views of themselves as family caregivers (hooks, 1994). The roles that each partner assumed in the marriage appeared consistent with their beliefs about how to combine work and family.

Perceptions of Fairness: Equity Versus Equality

Spouses' perceptions of what constitutes equity directly relate to marital quality and personal well-being. Equality of power is not the issue, but rather the perceptions of equity or proportional returns in the exchange of personal and economic resources within the norms of the culture. African American women and men tend to define themselves as coproviders rather than as persons who generate a primary and a secondary income. Moreover, African American men do not typically tie their level of involvement in family with their wives' financial contributions to the family (John & Shelton, 1997). Rather, both partners attribute meaning and importance to the wife's employment. Fossett and Kiecolt (1993) reported that among African American couples, men's and women's economic status tended to vary together because factors that promote high status for women also tended to promote high status for men (e.g., full employment).

The responses from the interviews supported these findings. In fact, one couple made a conscious decision "not to fight about money," no matter who earned it. Two of the men did report that sometimes they felt pressure from others to earn more money than their wives and that not following the myth of the male earning more money sometimes caused strain with their mostly White peer group at work.

Parenting and Role Conflict

Among heterosexual dual-career couples, deciding when to have a child is typically more the question than deciding whether to have a child. The timing of the transition to parenthood has important consequences for parental behaviors, divisions of household labor, and partners' well-being. Once partners decide to parent, decisions about the child's day-to-day care are made in the context of partners' values, employers' policies, flexibility of work schedules, the availability of care, and so forth. Generally, African American couples tend to have their children earlier in their marriage (McLoyd, 1993). This may or may not be related to increased stress, depending on sources of support for parenting. Generally, role conflict and day-to-day stress associated with parenting and careers are lowest under the following conditions:

- Partners are satisfied with their child-care arrangements.
- Partners feel satisfied with child's racial identity development.
- Employers of both partners have benefit policies that are family responsive and/or hold a positive attitude toward employees participation in family life.
- Both partners actively participate in parenting.
- Partners view each other's involvement in home roles as being fair.
- Partners are relatively satisfied with their occupational work.
- Partners understand that some stress is, by necessity, associated with parenting.
- Partners openly communicate on a regular basis about ways to manage work and parenting roles.
- Partners feel supported by their peer group and family network.

All but two of the couples interviewed had children at home—most couples had two children. The children's ages ranged from 6 to 32 years. The age range for the children still at home was 6 to 18 years. Children's mean age was 14 years. When asked whether the domain of children presented difficulties for them, nearly all respondents indicated that minimal difficulties were encountered. According to them, the biggest problem was managing time and feeling that they did not have enough time in the day.

A study by Harrison and Minor (1978), which focused on how African American women in dual-earner families handled conflicts among their roles of parent, spouse, and worker, found that women used different coping strategies depending on the kind of interrole conflict they experienced. Overall, the women reported relatively high satisfaction with their ability to cope with their multiple roles. Two common strategies for coping were investigated in the study. These are *change strategies* (i.e., acting to change the source of the stress, such as renegotiating with supervisors or spouses in areas associated with conflict and stress) and *understanding strategies* (i. e., understanding the source of the stress, such as realizing that it is expected that children can be difficult at times). This study, as well as studies of Euro-American couples, indicated that change strategies are employed more often in dealing with conflict between the parent and worker roles and the worker and spouse roles; understanding strategies are used more often in dealing with conflict between the parent and worker roles.

Sources of Support

How couples combine work and family and carry out their multiple roles depends on much more than partners' personal wishes or preferences. The social context and workplace practices are especially crucial in under-standing and counseling African American dual-career couples. The resources helpful to dual-career families are conceptually similar to those previously listed in the areas of relational–family factors and environmen-tal–societal factors.

Two sources of support are particularly crucial to spouse and family well-being. The first is the central and extensive role of significant others, particularly the mutuality of spousal support and affirmation. Shared val-ues and expectations about love, work, and the importance of racial iden-tity, as well as concern for each other's well-being, increase the ability of spouses to be supportive. Also crucial for Black couples is their relation-ship with extended family and their community.

The second source is societal–institutional support as reflected by work-place policies, nonracist attitudes among colleagues and employers, and the like. More effective coping and greater satisfaction among partners with children invariably are associated with societal resources—a nonracist envi-ronment, equitable salaries for African women and men, flexibility of work schedules, suitable child care, family-supportive employers—and benefit policies consistent with this supportive attitude. Currently, a number of companies offer flexible scheduling in the form of flextime, part-time employment, job sharing, compressed work schedules, or working at home.

Companies with supportive work and family policies, good health cov-erage, and flexible work hours have significantly less employee burnout and turnover than do companies without such policies (Seyler, Monroe, & Garland, 1995). The more employers' policies that reflect a patriarchal workplace culture in which women care for families and children and men with children are uninvolved in home responsibilities, the more difficult it becomes for both partners in African American dual-career families to parent.

It is likely that because the couples interviewed did have flexibility in their schedules, the men and women reported sharing responsibilities for events like caring for an ill child or keeping the child's medical appointments as well as sharing in the day-to-day aspects of parenting. The women did feel somewhat more obligation than their male partners to be at all of the children's social events, like athletic events and artistic performances, however.

ROLE OF THE CAREER COUNSELOR

Counselors act as the carriers and enforcers of values in their work with clients. They can reinforce racial and gender stereotypes, patriarchal values, and heterosexist beliefs that limit all African American women and men interested in a dual-career family lifestyle. It is likely that perceptions and understanding of the role of work, family, and marriage are influenced by one's worldview. *Worldview* can be defined as the customs, values, and beliefs of an identified group of people. Nobles (1976) described a European worldview and an African worldview.

The European worldview focuses on the survival of the fittest, individualism, pulling one's self up by one's bootstraps. On the other hand, the African worldview values groupness and the survival of the tribe. It may be that in the European worldview it is far easier to accommodate male dominance and a hierarchical view of work, marriage, and family. In the African worldview, it may be that the roles of each member must be more flexible because the needs for survival of the group supersedes the need for survival of the individual. Such an Afrocentric perspective could help explain research findings reported earlier that Black males are more likely to accommodate the special needs of working wives than are White males (e.g., John & Shelton, 1997; Scanzoni, 1976).

Among the couples interviewed, the men seemed to be especially supportive of their wives. In one instance, the husband reported that the family was "anchored" to the wife's career and moved based on her career needs. Although he was even more credentialed than she, her salary was higher so that they could more easily help the extended family. It was typical for the couples to feel the need to help their extended families. These couples could be responding to what Cheatham (1990) described as the *Afrocentric social order* that includes an emphasis on collaboration and survival of the group.

In addition to considering worldviews, one's racial identity development can play a role in the perspective that one assumes in viewing or living in a dual-career marriage. Cross (1971) described the racial identity development of Black individuals in the United States. He maintained that individuals go through stages that may begin with a strong positive identification with White people, with a concomitant negative evaluation of Black people. In later stages, the Black individual becomes more tentative in complete acceptance of the superiority of White people to a stage of immersion into the Black culture and a rejection of all that is associated with the White culture. Finally, the individual assumes a more racially transcendent view so that although the individual is very pro Black people and culture, he or she is accepting and appreciative of White people. Atkinson, Morten, and Sue (1993) described a similar minority identity development model.

Helms (1990) and Sabnani, Ponterotto, and Borodovsky (1991) expanded Cross's theory to include White racial identity development. They maintained that White individuals go from stages of being unaware of their Whiteness to discovery, guilt, anger, and retreat into White culture, to a final transcendent view that is much more accepting of their Whiteness and the culture of other groups.

Worldviews and racial identity development likely influence any career counseling between client and counselors, regardless of whether the dyads are of the same ethnicity. Fouad and Bingham (1995) described what they label a *CACCM*, "Culturally appropriate career counseling model." Their work is an extension of the work of Ward and Bingham (1993), which proposed an alternate model of assessment of career counseling needs for African American women. The model presents an organized method for looking at a very complex matter. This section uses steps of the Fouad and Bingham (1995) model as a framework for integrating the literature from research on dual-career families with that from multicultural career counseling.

A Model for Counselors

The first step in this model is *Establishing a Culturally Appropriate Relationship*. Because dual-career couples are already involved in careers, partners may be somewhat knowledgeable about the career-counseling process and come with expectations of how counseling may be beneficial. To be effective, It is important for the counselor to be familiar with African Americans as a group and how they may view a relationship with a counselor. Sue and Sue (1990) reported that African Americans and other racial ethnic minority group members are significantly more likely to terminate counseling after one session than are Euro-Americans. It behooves the counselor to make some initial preparation for the couple before their arrival.

In addition, the counselor should be informed about dual-career families, the variations of combining work and family normative among couples, and the personal, relational, and societal factors associated with decisions about how to combine work and family (Gilbert, Hallett, & Eldridge, 1994). That information is important because the issues the couple presents are likely to be influenced by their perceptions of the roles and responsibility of each partner. Earlier in the chapter we described the modal variations: conventional dual-career, modern, and role-sharing. In the conventional dual-career family, the husband generally commands the larger salary and both spouses agree that the wife assumes the major responsibility for the household, including upkeep of the home and caring for children if there are any. In the modern dual-career family, both partners share in parenting, however, the woman is considered responsible for household work. The role-sharing, dual-career family seems more in line with an egalitarian marriage, where both careers are important and household tasks and parenting are joint responsibilities.

The career counselor must be aware of the possible types of families and must assess the family pattern of the couple seeking services. The 10 couples interviewed seemed to be role sharing. They were readily able to suggest how career counselors could be helpful to them. Their ideas ranged from helping the partners to identify career change needs to improving communication between the couple. Couples not satisfied with less egalitarian arrangements might be struggling with issues associated with gender-role expectations. Thus, the career counselor needs to know which type of dual-career couple is coming for services because type could influence expectations and perceptions of career counseling.

Furthermore, if a counselor is to establish a culturally appropriate relationship, the counselor must have some idea regarding the couple's views of relationships with each other and relationships with counselors. Relationships are very important to African American people. The early literature on counseling with Black clients even advocated establishing a friendship rather than a counseling relationship (June & Gunnings, 1985; Tucker & Gunnings, 1974). Later research suggested more boundaries in the relationship, but still the counseling relationships and groups seem to work best when they have a friendship-like quality to them (Franklin, 1999). Akbar (1991) maintained that groups are very important to healthy functioning among African American individuals. The couple and/or family is the beginning of a small group. Add the counselor, and one can begin to imagine the ramifications of establishing appropriate rapport with the couple.

An important second step is the *Identification of Career Issues*. The couple and the counselor need to come to consensus about the career issues. The three sets of factors previously summarized—Personal Factors, Relational–Family Factors, and Environmental–Societal Factors—can be quite useful to the counselor in helping the couple to identify the issues they are facing. Under personal factors, the counselor might assess for feelings of dominance in each partner as well as his or her need for and belief about intimacy, power, parenting, and competition. The counselor will also need to help the couple explore their commitment to their careers and to their partner's career.

Career problems could occur in a marriage because one partner is satisfied with a career path and looking forward to greater advancement, whereas the other partner has peaked career-wise and is looking for a change. One of the potential benefits of a dual-career family is the opportunity for a spouse not happy in her or his work to make a career change, knowing that the other spouse can provide some financial security in the meantime. Change is always difficult. The counselor could be especially helpful in these situations by clarifying the issues associated with the personal beliefs and values, and assisting the couple in developing a plan that fits their situation.

The next set of factors are relational. The assessment also needs to consider relational factors such as those associated with issues of equity and power, partner support, values, and expectations. Many of these issues include cognition's about decision making and fairness. There may be differing beliefs about what constitutes support in relational areas, including parenting and career advancement.

Environmental factors can cause enormous strain on a dual-career couple. Issues of racism and sexism erupt on the job and spill over into the home. In fact, one of the unique problems that dual-career couples reported to us is the strain of dealing with racism at the office and deciding the proper balance for its place at home. Partners seemed very concerned about burdening each other with too much negativity from the work environment. Several of the wives worried about the racism the husband might experience on the job. One wife reported that her husband had to work twice as hard just to be appreciated on his job. One husband worried that his wife had to be concerned with sexism and racism on the job. Other environmental factors include employers' attitudes toward the family and work. Inflexible work hours and work policies that are not family friendly can also také a toll on a dual-career couple.

A third step in the CACCM is *Assessing the Impact of Cultural Variables on Career Issues*. There is perhaps no other place in the model where gender issues come so clearly into view as they do in this step. In an attempt to understand the process of coming to a career decision, Fouad and Bingham (1995) described the spheres of influence of cultural variables. The authors contended that one is born with certain biological properties that may predispose one to a particular career. Those factors, however, are shaped and influenced by societal and cultural influences such as gender, family, racial and/or ethnic group and the dominant–majority group. A number of scholars (e.g., Cook, 1993; Fitzgerald, Fassinger, & Betz, 1995; Gilbert, 1985, 1988, 1993) have written about the role of gender in dual-career couples. It is crucial for counselors to understand that gender is a cultural construct, not a characteristic of individuals (Gilbert & Scher, 1999). The culture ascribes *gendered* characteristics to individuals based on assumptions and biases tied to biological sex. *Gender* is a much broader construct than biological sex and includes the psychological, social, and cultural factors that impinge on individuals who are born biologically female or male.

Fouad and Bingham (1995) maintained that gender is the primary factor after inborn traits that begins to shape an individual's career choice. In dual-career couples, the partners' views of gender will influence their perceptions of power, role sharing, parenting, decision making, and so on. Gender views may influence the couple's thinking on which careers are important and necessary for their particular gender. As we described earlier, African American women assume they will be employed regardless of their marital status and most dual-career African American families do not fit the traditional stereotype of man as the primary breadwinner. At the same time, African American partners also struggle with women's and men's views of gender roles and male power, privilege, and superiority vis-à-vis women, although the context of this struggle is dramatically different from that of Euro-American partners.

The Black women interviewed thought as a result of being Black women, their experiences made it easier for them to be a part of a dual-career couple. They were raised to be independent. They were expected to work and take care of themselves. Most of the men had a clear expectation that the women would work. One husband stated that he could not imagine himself in a relationship in which the wife did not work. In fact, in African American families, it was not unusual for the family to decide to send the daughter to school if a choice had to be made between the son and the daughter. This situation for African American women contrasts markedly to Nigerian families, for example, in which daughters often take a back seat to the career opportunities for the men in the family (Denga, 1988; Okocha & Perrone, 1992). This example very clearly illustrates that it is important for the career counselor to understand the culture of the client and that culture is not determined by skin color. Furthermore, the counselor cannot assume that he or she knows the gender role socialization of the partners in a couple. An effective evaluation of what their career issues are can help the counselor avoid stereotypic thinking.

Counselors also need to understand the importance of family, theories of worldview, and racial identity development in working with African American partners. For example, the couples interviewed reported role strain resulting from the need to contribute to the welfare of other members of their extended family. African American couples expect and accept

the fact that some of their income must go to the uplifting of the immediate and extended family as well as other members of the Black community. In working with the couple, it is important to understand how the
partners view the parts they will play in each other's extended family.

Decisions about advancement are not only influenced by the partners,
but also by the effects on others outside the marriage. One partner in the
couple may be geographically bound because of the extended family connection or the couple may decide to move members of the extended family with them when they make a decision to relocate to another city. In
instances where the extended family is a significant determinant or factor
in career decisions, the career counselor needs to suspend traditional theories of separation–individuation in evaluating the career needs of
African American couples. Of course the counselor will need to remember
to explore all issues as appropriate, but the caution here is to remain
objective when doing crosscultural dual-career couples counseling.

The final cultural variable that needs to be assessed is the dominant or
majority group in a society. In the United States, that group is White.
African American couples must face structural barriers, such as racism and
sexism, in this society. The barriers may be real or perceived. Sometimes
perception is reality to the individual. The effects of the interactions with
the dominant group may be positive or negative and may vary from one
partner to the other. Gainor and Forrest (1991) concluded that African
American women sometimes limit their career choices because of their perception of the restrictions of sexism and racism on their ability to advance
in their chosen careers. The potential or resulting pressure can place undue
strain on a couple. As couples seek to find balance between work and family life, they may find themselves trying to decide how to shield their home
lives from the sexism and racism they experience on the job. Partners may
inadvertently project the anger and frustration from these "isms" on to their
mates. An important suggestion from the couples interviewed was that a
career counselor could help African American couples see and understand
these external pressures in a way that makes it more possible for the couple
to keep them in perspective and out of their marriages.

The last step of the model to be considered is *Setting Culturally Appropriate Goals and Interventions*. These steps are particularly important for
dual-career couples because it is likely that each partner already has a
career. The couple is not likely to need traditional career interventions.
Their needs often center around balance, time, and perhaps career
change. They may have questions about managing all the needs that are
pressing on the relationship and on them as individuals. The couple may
need to work on setting different priorities in their lives. It could be
important for them to examine Afrocentric theories about families and
careers versus Eurocentric ideas. Akbar (1991) maintained that African

Americans suffer more pathology and confusion when they imitate more European cultural beliefs. If an African American couple spends a lot of time in more European environments, the partners may inadvertently begin to accept values at a less than conscious level. The counselor's job will be to help them explore their basic beliefs and increase their awareness of the values they are currently using to make decisions.

The traditional role for the career counselor could change when working with a couple. Sometimes, the counselor might need to be an advocate or a change agent. Perhaps the stresses on the dual-career couple stem from a system that is not flexible enough to accommodate diverse lifestyles. Some employers are beginning to change their work and leave policies so that individuals are able to adjust work hours to spend time with family and jobs in ways that better serve the needs of the family. The Family Medical Leave Act has made it easier for some couples to take time off to care for family members. Because some African Americans have even more family pressures because of the role of the extended family, it would be helpful if a counselor could help employers understand the dynamics of diverse family structures. In other situations it might be important for the counselor to help the couple to become empowered in ways so that the partners are better advocates for the changes they need to ease the career pressures that are impacting on the relationship and the family.

Summary of Key Issues for Counselors

Although the research literature on career counseling with dual-career African American couples is quite limited, the findings from the available research, together with the responses from the 10 couples interviewed, suggest that these couples face many of the same issues as dual-career couples who are Euro-American. The lives of the African American couples, however, are further complicated by the specter of racism and the historical structure of work opportunities in this country. One of the husbands interviewed provided a poignant insight into the complexity and seriousness of the concerns of this population. He said, "We grow up with expectations that we are going to be somewhat like our fathers and somewhat like our race. I need someone to show me how to be."

It is not at all clear that the present training offered to career counselors prepares them to offer the kind of help needed by this father. The challenge to the profession remains the same as that expressed throughout the multicultural literature—our theories, training, assessments, and interventions must be broad enough to encompass the diverse needs of the entire population in this country.

The following list may aid counselors as they prepare to work with African American dual-career couples:

- There is a historical expectation that African American women will work.
- There are historical limitations placed on Black men in contrast to the privileged position accorded to White men.
- African American individuals may hold an Afrocentric worldview, a Eurocentric worldview or some combination of the two, therefore, it is important to suspend culture-bound judgments.
- Gender-role socialization varies within race and across economic status.
- Racism is a constant in the career lives of African Americans.
- The racial identity of the client and the counselor may influence the quality and effectiveness of a counseling intervention.
- Sensitivity and understanding increases as the counselor becomes familiar with African Americans as a group.
- Familiarity with the multicultural literature is basic.
- Knowledge of the dual-career counseling literature is essential.
- Personal, relational, and environmental factors are important in understanding the variability among dual-career relationships.
- Application of culturally appropriate assessment and intervention strategies is a must.

Finally, the counselor must remember that sometimes the most important work that a career counselor can do is to become an advocate for social change, be it in combating racism and sexism or promoting workplace polices that are family friendly. If the counselor cannot become an advocate, then perhaps the counselor can help clients become empowered to be their own best advocates for societal and workplace changes.

REFERENCES

Akbar, N. (1991). *Chains and images of psychological slavery.* Jersey City, NJ: New Mind Productions.

Atkinson, D. R., Morten, G., & Sue, D. W. (1993). *Counseling American minorities* (4th ed.). Dubuque, IA: Brown.

Barnett, R. C., & Rivers, C. (1996). She works/he works: How two-income families are happier, healthier, and better off. New York: HarperCollins.

Black Enterprise. (1996). *Careers and Business Opportunies Issue, 26,* 72–74.

Blee, K. M., & Tickamyer, A. R. (1995). Racial attitudes in men's attitudes about women's gender roles. *Journal of Marriage and the Family, 57,* 21–30.

Cheatham, H. (1990). Afrocentricity and career development of African Americans. *The Career Development Quarterly, 38,* 334–346.

Cook, P. E. (1993). The gendered context of life: Implications for women's and men's career-life plans. *The Career Development Quarterly, 41,* 227–237.

Cross, W. E. (1971). Negro-to-Black conversion experience: Toward a psychology of Black liberation. *Black World, 20,* 13–27.

Denga, D. I. (1988). Influence of traditional factors on career choice among Nigerian secondary school youth. *Journal of Multicultural Counseling and Development, 16,* 1–15.

Fitzgerald, L. F., Fassinger, R. E., & Betz, N. E. (1995). Theoretical advances in the study of women's career development. In W. B. Walsh & S. H. Osipow (Eds.), *Handbook of vocational psychology: Theory, research, and practice* (2nd ed., pp. 67–110). Mahwah, NJ: Lawrence Erlbaum Associates.

Fossett, M. A., & Kiecolt, K. J. (1993). Male availability and family structure among African Americans in U. S. metropolitan areas. *Journal of Marriage and the Family, 55,* 288–302.

Fouad, N. A., & Bingham, R. P. (1995). Career counseling with racial and ethnic minorities. In W. B. Walsh & S. H. Osipow (Eds.), *Handbook of vocational psychology: Theory, research and practice* (2nd ed., pp. 331–366). Mahwah, NJ: Lawrence Erlbaum Associates.

Franklin, A. J. (1999). Invisibility syndrome and racial identity development in psychotherapy and counseling African American men. *The Counseling Psychologist, 27,* 761–793.

Gainor, K. A., & Forrest, L. (1991). African American women's self-concept: Implications for career decisions and career counseling. *Career Development Quarterly, 39,* 261–272.

Ganong, L. H., Coleman, M., Thompson, A., & Watkins, C. G. (1996). African American and European American college students' expectations for self and for future partners. *Journal of Family Issues, 17,* 758–775.

Gerson, K. (1993). *No man's land: Men's changing commitments to family and work.* New York: Basic Books.

Gilbert, L. A. (1985). *Men in dual-career families: Current realities and future prospects.* Hillsdale, NJ: Lawrence Erlbaum Associates.

Gilbert, L. A. (1988). *Sharing it all: The rewards and struggles of two-career families.* New York: Plenum.

Gilbert, L. A. (1993). *Two careers/One family: The promise of gender equality.* Beverly Hills, CA: Sage.

Gilbert, L. A., Hallet, M. B., & Eldridge, N. (1994). In W. B. Walsh & S. H. Osipow (Eds.), *Career counseling for women* (pp. 135–160). Hillsdale, NJ: Lawrence Erlbaum Associates.

Gilbert, L. A., & Scher, M. (1999). *Gender, sex, and counseling.* Boston: Allyn & Bacon.

Greene, B. (1994). African-American women. In L. Comas-Diaz & B. Greene (Eds.), *Women of color: Integrating ethnic and gender identities in psychotherapy.* New York: Guilford.

Guttentag, M., & Secord, P. F. (1983). *Too many women? The sex ratio question.* Beverly Hills, CA: Sage.

Harrison, A. O., & Minor, J. H. (1978). Interrole conflict, coping strategies, and satisfaction among black working wives. *Journal of Marriage and the Family, 40,* 799–805.

Helms, J. E. (1990). *Black and White racial identity: Theory, research, and practice.* New York: Greenwood.

Herr, E. L., & Cramer, S. H. (1992). *Career guidance and counseling through the life span: Systematic approaches* (4th ed.). New York: HarperCollins.

hooks, b. (1981). *Ain't I a woman: Black women and feminism.* Boston: South End Press.

hooks, b. (1994). *Sisters of the yam.* Boston: South End Press.

Hossain, Z., & Roopnarine, J. L. (1993). Division of household labor and child care in dual-earner African-American families with infants. *Sex Roles, 29,* 571–583.

Hunter, A. G., & Davis, J. E. (1992). Constructing gender: An exploration of Afro-American men's conceptualization of manhood. *Gender and Society, 6,* 464–479.

John, D., & Shelton, B. A. (1997). The production of gender among Black and White women and man: The case of household labor. *Sex Roles, 36,* 171–193.

Jones, J. (1987). Black women, work, and the family under slavery. In N. Gerstel & H. G. Gross (Eds.), *Families and work* (pp. 84–110). Philadelphia: Temple University Press.

June, J. N., & Gunnings, T. (Eds.). (1985). The Black male: Critical counseling developmental, and therapeutic issues. Part 1. *Journal of Non-White Concerns in Personnel and Guidance, 13*(2), 43–87.

Levant, R. F., & Pollack, W. S. (Ed.). (1995). *A new psychology of men.* New York: Basic Books.

Lorde, A. (1984). Sexism: An American disease in blackface. In *Sister outsider.* Freedom, CA: The Crossing Press.

Marriage: 800,000 Negro girls will never get to altar, expects predict. (1947). *Ebony, 4,* 21.

McLoyd, V. C. (1993). Employment among African-American mothers in dual-earner families: Antecedents and consequences of family life and child development. In J. Frankel (Ed.), *The employed mother and the family context* (pp. 180–226). New York: Springer.

Nobles, W. W. (1976). Extended self: Rethinking the Negro self-concept. *Journal of Black Psychology, 2,* 15–24.

Okocha, A., & Perrone, P. (1992). Career salience among Nigerian dual-career women. *Career Development Quarterly, 31,* 84–93.

Orbuch, T. L., & Custer, L. (1995). The social context of married women's work and its impact on Black husbands and White husbands. *Journal of Marriage and the Family, 57,* 333–345.

Rapoport, R. L., & Rapoport, R. N. (1969). The dual-career family. *Human Relations, 22,* 3–30.

Sabnani, H. B., Ponterotto, J. G., & Borodovsky, L. G. (1991). White racial identity development and cross-cultural training: A stage model. *The Counseling Psychologist, 19,* 76–102.

Scanzoni, J. (1976). Sex roles, economic factors and marital solidarity in Black and White marriages. *Journal of Marriage and the Family, 37,* 130–144.

Seyler, D. L., Monroe, P. A., & Garland, J. C. (1995). Balancing work and family: The role of employer-supported child care benefits. *Journal of Family Issues, 16,* 170–193.

Staples, R., & Johnson, L. B. (1993). *Black families at the crossroads.* San Francisco: Jossey-Bass.

Sue, D. W., & Sue, D. (1990). *Counseling the culturally different: Theory and practice* (2nd ed.). New York: Wiley.

Thomas, V. G. (1986). Career aspirations, parental support, and work values among Black adolescents. *Journal of Multicultural Counseling and Development, 14*(4), 177–185.

Thomas, V. G. (1990). Problems of dual-career Black couples: Identification and implications for family interventions. *Journal of Multicultural Counseling and Development, 18*(2), 58–67.

Tucker, R. N., & Gunnings, T. (1974). Counseling Black youths: A quest for legitimacy. *Journal of Non-White Concerns in Personnel and Guidance, 2*(4), 208–215.

Vaz, K. M. (Ed.). (1995). *Black women in America.* Thousand Oaks, CA: Sage.

Ward, C. M., & Bingham, R. P. (1993). Career assessment of ethnic minority women. *Journal of Career Assessment, 1,* 246–257.

Whetstone, M. L. (1996). Why professional women should consider blue collar men. *Ebony, 51,* 25–26.

Wilkie, J. R. (1993). Changes in U. S. men's attitudes toward the family provider role, 1972–1989. *Gender and Society, 7,* 261–279.

Woody, B. (1992). *Black women in the workplace: Impacts of structural change in the economy.* New York: Greenwood.

Wyche, K. F. (1993). Psychology and African-American women: Findings from applied research. *Applied and Preventive Psychology, 2,* 115–121.

Chapter 5

Addressing the Career Transition Issues of African American Women: Vocational and Personal Considerations

Madonna G. Constantine
Teachers College, Columbia University

Vernita F. Parker
Booz•Allen & Hamilton, Inc.

Over the past several years, there have been significant changes in the organizational structures and operational procedures of the U.S. workforce (Zunker, 1998). In particular, issues such as unemployment, corporate downsizing, and job retirement have contributed to significant career transitions among many American workers. Willful and unforced changes in employment status, such as retirement and intentional career shifts, are known as *voluntary career transitions. Involuntary career transitions* are forced changes in job status due to phenomena such as unemployment and corporate downsizing.

It is important that career transition theories address the specific cultural, environmental, and personality factors of individuals who are in the process of changing careers (Black & Loughead, 1990). To date, however, much of the literature on career transitions has been written generally and applied across racial and ethnic groups. Moreover, few writings specifically focused on the unique social and personal factors that may affect both voluntary and involuntary career transitions of African Americans, particularly African American women (Bell, 1990; Evans & Herr, 1991; Richie, 1992; Thomas & Alderfer, 1989). Currently, African American females who are 16 years of age and older comprise 18% of the current U.S. workforce (U.S. Bureau of Labor Statistics, 1997). Thus, their representation in the American workforce is significant. As such, there is a need for information about how these women may respond to career transitions at various points in their professional lives.

Recently, the use of social constructionist principles has been identified as a culturally sensitive means of addressing the career development issues of a variety of individuals in career transition (Constantine & Erickson, 1998). *Social constructionism* posits that individuals actively construct the meanings of their perceptions and experiences, subsequently defining their own realities (Hare-Mustin & Marecek, 1988; Neimeyer, 1995). According to social constructionism, there are multiple truths and realities that have been developed from people's belief systems, cultural group memberships, and previous experiences (Bordo, 1990; Richardson, 1993; Sexton, 1997). For example, in relation to career counseling, McAuliffe (1993) used Kegan's (1982) constructivist framework to attend to the personal and occupational meanings that people interpret at various points in their lives and underscored the utility of such an approach navigating career transitions. Hence, constructivist principles may be helpful to vocational counselors in aiding African American women to facilitate career transition because of their ability to take into account cultural and systemic factors that impact these women's career development.

In this chapter, career transition concerns of African American women are identified and how these issues may vary based on voluntary or involuntary transition status are discussed. In addition, the utility of social constructionist principles in working with African American women experiencing career transitions is explicated. A case example illustrating social constructionist vocational interventions that may be used to address career transition issues in African American women is also presented.

AFRICAN AMERICAN WOMEN IN CAREER TRANSITION

Greater longevity in the American workforce, brought about in part by nonmandatory retirement, increases the likelihood of career change for many African American women (Herr & Cramer, 1996; Richie, 1992; Sinick, 1984). Although career transitions may have both positive and negative effects on these women, the positive impacts of such changes appear to outweigh the negative ones when change is indicated (Black & Loughead, 1990). West and Nicholson (1989) reported that common outcomes of career transitions are personal growth, satisfaction, improved general well-being, innovation, and greater economic gains. Emotionally, however, career transitions may cause significant stress and upheaval (Black & Loughead, 1990). Failure to cope successfully with career transitions affects a small number of workers, but fortunately, the negative consequences of such transitions tend to be short lived (Black & Loughead, 1990; Brett, 1982; Latack, 1984).

Krumboltz (1990) identified three examples of career beliefs that may cause difficulties in career transitions: inability to relocate, lack of requisite skills to perform a new job, and fear of taking risks. For African American women, these beliefs may be particularly crucial to consider in the context of exploring career transition issues. For example, some African American women may have difficulty relocating because of a personal value related to the importance of maintaining close family connections. In addition, harboring beliefs and concerns about lacking necessary job skills and having fears pertaining to taking career-related risks may be associated with issues such as lowered outcome expectations and career efficacy in some African American women (Hackett & Byars, 1996).

With regard to African American women, factors such as discrimination and gender-role socialization clearly affect their perceived occupational options and choices. Compared to White men and women, African American women are more likely to be employed in lower status and poorly paid occupations, and these types of jobs usually do not represent stepping stones to career advancement (Swinton, 1992). Additionally, research has shown that African American female professionals earn only 60% of the average salary of their White male peers (Federal Glass Ceiling Commission, 1995). Eccles (1994) postulated that gender roles are likely to impact the educational and vocational choices of women, partly through their influences on individuals' perceptions of their realistic options and their expectations of success and efficacy in such options. For example, Greenhaus, Parasuraman, and Wormley (1990) identified two types of occupational discrimination that affect the career development of racial and ethnic minorities: *access discrimination* and *treatment discrimination*. *Access discrimination* operates when people of color are prevented from entering certain jobs, careers, or organizations because of their racial or ethnic group membership. *Treatment discrimination* occurs when people of color receive fewer resources, rewards, or opportunities in their employment settings than they deserve based on job-related criteria. Because African American women may be affected by issues of sexism and racism as they pertain to perceived career options, they may tend to avoid career fields that they perceive as potentially discriminating against them because they are African American or because they are women (Evans & Herr, 1991; Hackett & Byars, 1996). In particular, African American women's perception of racism and sexism in the workforce may impact their belief about their ability to succeed in a career; subsequently, they may pursue vocational counseling with restricted identified career options and may possess lower self-efficacy than other women or than African American male clients (Richie, 1992). Additionally, the job ceiling phenomenon for African Americans and women in the United States may contribute to some African American women's reticence to pursue certain careers (Phelps & Constantine, chap. 8, this vol.). It is important that African American women distinguish between actual barriers (e.g., organizational decline, slow organizational growth, race and sex discrimination, etc.) and perceived barriers (e.g., role confusion, poor career identity, etc.) that affect their ability to reach their career goals (Zunker, 1998). It is also critical that counselors understand the relations among African American women's social, academic, and career self-concepts, in addition to self-esteem and self-efficacy, and how these factors impact their career decision-making process (Simpson, 1996).

Gainor and Forrest (1991) used Brown-Collins and Sussewell's (1986) model of African American women's self-concept to discuss implications for the career development and counseling of these women. The model explained self-concept as developing from a combination of multiple self-referents: the *psychophysiological referent*, the *African American referent*, and the *myself referent*. According to Gainor and Forrest (1991):

> the multiple self-referent model provides a framework for examining not only the personal experiences of Black women, but also their historical experiences in this country, the influences of the Black community and White American culture, as well as the interactive effects of racism and sexism. (p. 271)

The self-concept and career decisions of African American women are due partly to the self-referent that is dominant, and to the nature of interaction between the different self-referents. Counselors' knowledge of the various self-referents and how they developed and are integrated within African American women can be an important part of the intervention process.

Bell (1990) discussed the bicultural life experiences of African American career women who led their lives within the Black community, while being employed in a predominantly White workplace; she also identified the possibility of an identity conflict occurring if these two worlds were incompatible. Career counselors must be sensitive to the increased role conflict often experienced by African American women in balancing work responsibilities and family obligations (Burlew & Johnson, 1992). In studying the contextual impacts of social supports at home and in the workplace, Bailey, Wolfe, and Wolfe (1996) found a transfer effect of support for White men and women (i.e., workplace supports helped to alleviate stress at home, and support at home helped them to deal with professional stressors). They found no transfer effect for African American women and concluded that this phenomenon was partly due to the fact that many African American women may keep their personal and professional lives as separate entities. One conclusion they reached from their data was that it is important for African American women to have support systems both at home and at work to increase their satisfaction and psychological well-being. Simpson (1996) also underscored the importance of family and cultural values and exposure to positive role models in strongly impacting the career-development process of African American women.

Zunker (1998) asserted that coping skills help individuals in transition to react more rationally in response to changing situations and he believed that such skills are particularly useful in aiding adults in the process of career transition. He outlined a counseling program consisting of seven strategies that may be useful for African American women in career transition. Each of these components consists of suggested techniques and tasks that may help individuals to transition more smoothly. They are as follows:

1. *Experience identification* involves a process by which counselors and clients assess clients' work, educational, and leisure experiences and link them to interests, work expectations and requirements, and other factors related to potential occupational choices.

2. *Interest identification* is intended to broaden and stimulate individuals' exploration of career options and is often achieved through the use of standardized test instruments such as interest inventories.

3. *Skills identification* refers to the delineation of skills developed from previous work, educational, and leisure activities.

4. *Values clarification* focuses on individuals' needs and values in relation to work, leisure, family, and peer group.

5. *Education and training* aids individuals in determining information that may be important to their career exploration.

6. *Occupational planning* also assists individuals in identifying educational and training information that may be relevant to their career search.

7. *The development of a life-learning plan* is designed to help individuals enhance their decision-making abilities, plan strategies to stay abreast of technological changes, upgrade their skills, and reduce their chances of becoming obsolete.

Voluntary Career Transitions

Voluntary career transitions occur when individuals either retire or proactively seek a new career in order to improve their current vocational situation. There are a range of affective reactions that African American women may experience when they decide to voluntarily change their career status. For example, although some African American women may experience feelings of anticipation, empowerment, and hopefulness related to a voluntary career change, accompanying feelings of uncertainty, anxiety, fear, and other distressing emotions may also exist (Black & Loughead, 1990). Moreover, the issues of African American women who are experiencing mid-life career transitions may differ from those of new workforce entrants. Thus, vocational counseling programs should address the impact of work and life experiences and how they may contribute to the formulation or reformulation of individuals' skills, interests, and goals (Zunker, 1998).

New Workforce Entrants. For many young African American women entering the workforce for the first time, the commencement of a new career is in part a socialization process where they learn to work effectively as a member of an organization (Zunker, 1998). Early career decisions are a time of exploration when these women make a choice to pursue either traditional or nontraditional careers (London & Greller, 1991). This exploration may include facing potential salary disparities, lack of advancement, and role conflict between work and family if the choice is made to pursue a nontraditional career (Burlew & Johnson, 1992). Burlew (1982) found that although many African American college women pursued degrees in nontraditional areas, they had some doubts about succeeding in the fields they had chosen. Helms and Piper (1994) introduced the concept of *racial salience*, the extent to which individuals believe that their race affected their career options, to help define the role that race plays in making vocational decisions (p. 129). According to Evans and Herr (1991), the career aspirations and subsequent development of African American women may be directly affected by their perceptions of opportunities in various career fields. African American women may actually avoid career paths that may present barriers due to their race or gender. When moving into a new or initial work setting, African American female new entrants may also have to contend with the perception that they do not have the skills or experience necessary to perform certain jobs due to their age (Eby & Buch, 1995), lack of experience, or even their racial group membership. Because they may be perceived as belonging to Generation X (e.g., slackers, living only for the moment, having diffuse career goals, lacking organizational loyalty, etc.), young African American female employees may be expected to disprove negative stereotypes in their workplaces associated with their race, gender, and age. Thus, these women may be impacted by many prfessional and personal issues that significantly affect their career transition process.

Mid-Career Individuals. Some researchers (e.g., London & Greller, 1991; Zunker, 1998) explored the impact of mid-life issues on career development and several factors, such as menopause and empty-nest syndrome, have been identified as affecting many individuals at mid-life. However, there is no universal agreement as to how reaching mid-life affects career-related behavior (Zunker, 1998), particularly in African American women. For example, mid-career may represent a time when some African American women plateau in their career advancement and when many of these women reevaluate their choices, goals, and desires on both a personal and career level (Gallos, 1989; Lieblich, 1986; Roberts & Newton, 1987). Gallos (1989) reported that many mid-career women choose to devote more time developing intimate relationships instead of centering primarily on career-related pursuits. Similarly, Roberts and Newton (1987) found that the mid-life activities of many career women centered on relational issues. On the other hand, some mid-career African American women may find that on reexamination, their career no longer fits their altered self-concepts or priorities, and they may opt for a career change (London & Greller, 1991). Hence, some mid-career African American women, who wish to take advantage of the increased accessibility of higher education, are going back to school and earning college degrees as a means of furthering their career development (London & Greller, 1991).

Many mid-career women are over 40 years of age. According to Newman (1995), individuals in their 40s and 50s are one of the fastest growing segments of the population affected by career transitions. Furthermore, she asserted that, like many other workers experiencing career transitions, individuals over 40 years of age often must deal with the possible loss of job security, colleagues, and fear of failure that accompany a change in employment. In addition, they face some issues that may not be as relevant to younger workers, including a potential decrease in financial security and the loss of an established career identity (Newman, 1995). More seasoned workers may also experience longer periods of unemployment and may be less likely to be retrained at another job (Hepworth, 1980). Although these issues may stand in the way of established workers finding new employment, African American women career changers may wish to emphasize the positive aspects of their situation, such as having stability, life experience, and a solid work ethic (Newman, 1995). Isaacson (1985) suggested that individuals who voluntarily change careers during mid-life frequently require more than just vocational counseling in order to augment their opportunities in their new positions. Often, they may need retraining or even personal counseling to help them adapt to their new circumstances.

Retiring Women. A major transition for most older adults who wish to end their working life is retirement (Hornstein & Wapner, 1985; Jensen-Scott, 1993; Kragie, Gerstein, & Lichtman, 1989). Their decision to retire is often based on financial and quality-of-life considerations and voluntary retirement is a highly individual decision (Zunker, 1998). Adjustment to retirement may be diverse and complex and may encompass several types of ambivalent feelings related to this decision (e.g., relief, sadness, boredom, freedom, etc.). Retiring African American women often find that their major focus shifts from career to activities and priorities outside of work (Zunker, 1998). According to London and Greller (1991), the level of work performance of older workers is not necessarily the determining factor in whether they continue at their jobs. What seems to matter more is whether these individuals desire retirement, how they are viewed by others, and how these two factors interact.

There is evidence to indicate that older workers are perceived more negatively and are discriminated against more than their younger counterparts, and these phenomena may be particularly true for African American women. Such attitudes and behaviors may be manifested in fewer training opportunities or promotions for these women, but what also must be considered is how these attitudes may affect these workers' own sense of esteem, ability, and accomplishment (London & Greller, 1991). According to Carter and Cook (1995) and George (1990), role theory may be a beneficial framework for examining issues related to retirement adjustment. Role theory asserts that certain self-defined and socially-prescribed roles are central to self identity, and these roles are derived from personal associations, work-role activities, and leisure interests; hence, retirement, in part, may be viewed as a transition involving role expansion and redefinition (Carter & Cook, 1995). Furthermore, Carter and Cook (1995) stated that the degree to which retirement positively or negatively impacts individuals depends on the degree of importance they place on their roles and on whether they are able to replace work roles with other roles they find fulfilling. Ogilvie (1987) found that employees who obtained a high sense of self-identity from their particular occupation experienced retirement as aversive due to the subsequent loss of identity they experienced. Because of racial and gender discrimination, African American women may possess well-developed social roles (e.g., church or club affiliation) as a means of dealing with work-related stressors and, consequently, these social supports may alleviate potentially negative feelings associated with work retirement.

Involuntary Career Transitions

Zunker (1998) summarized a variety of factors contributing to involuntary career transitions in the workplace. First, he asserted that workers who do not keep up with the professional training demands and changing technologies of their field may become less useful and necessary over time. Further, he noted that with the rapid changes and advances in today's industries, obsolescence may not be necessarily related to age, but more to individual factors such as ability and motivation. Organizational downsizing and job displacement are issues faced by numerous African American women, particularly white-collar workers (Eby & Buch, 1995).

In 1988, the Worker Adjustment and Retraining Notification (WARN) Act was instituted to give workers adequate time to prepare for job loss. In essence, this legislation mandates employers with at least 100 workers to provide employees with at least 60 days advance notice of shutdowns affecting at least 50 workers and of layoffs lasting over 6 months and impacting at least one third of employees at the site (Morton, 1992). Advanced warning allows employees to adjust to the shock of no longer being employed and to commence the search for a new job before becoming officially unemployed (Latack & Dozier, 1986). In addition, prolonged unemployment may lead to feelings of resignation and cynicism as manifested in loss of motivation, infrequent job seeking, and social withdrawal (Latack & Dozier, 1986).

Eby and Buch (1995) examined Latack and Dozier's (1986) model of job loss and explored how men and women adapt to this phenomenon. The Latack and Dozier model identified three factors potentially related to adaptation to job loss and subsequent career growth: *individual characteristics* (i.e., age of worker, level of job satisfaction, stage of career, and activity level), *the environment* (i.e., financial situation, quality of social supports, and level of family adaptability and support), and the *transition process* (i.e., length of unemployment, means of dealing with grief and anger, and how the dismissal was handled). Eby and Buch (1995) found that although the model did not account for all of the factors involved in career growth following job loss, it helped to identify different factors that seemed to be involved in successful career transitions of men and women. In their sample, high family flexibility followed by financial resources were most predictive of career growth in women, whereas men were influenced most by finances, their acceptance of job loss, activity level, and previous job satisfaction. African American women who seek social support from family members, friends, and colleagues following job loss are likely to receive such support and emotional healing in return (Costa, 1995).

Important characteristics of the involuntary career transition process are the manner in which termination is communicated, resolution of anger and grief, and length of unemployment (Latack & Dozier, 1986). For instance, if African American women are terminated in a manner that is consistent with a *professional approach* (i.e., if they are provided explanations, information, and feedback about the termination), then termination decisions may actually lead to career growth in that dismissed employees may maintain self-esteem and feel a sense of control over their circumstances (Latack & Dozier, 1986). Eby and Buch (1995) asserted that job loss may eventually be reframed in a positive fashion if there are opportunities for these women to consider new alternatives, redirect their goals and priorities, or even leave an unsatisfying job. However, before career exploration and goal identification occur following an involuntary career transition, it is important that vocational counselors assist African American women in grieving the loss of their position and in regaining a balanced perspective in resolving the loss (Bejian & Salomone, 1995).

THE ROLE OF SOCIAL CONSTRUCTIONIST APPROACHES IN FACILITATING AFRICAN AMERICAN WOMEN'S CAREER TRANSITIONS

The use of social constructionist principles in vocational counseling may be beneficial in gaining an understanding of African American women's lives and experiences by asking about the meanings they may associate with their career transitions. In particular, *social constructionist principles* emphasize the influences of issues such as culture, language, and socialization on clients' construction of their current vocational situation (Constantine & Erickson, 1998; Neimeyer, 1995; Richardson, 1993; Savickas, 1993, 1995). Vocational counseling interventions within a social constructionist framework are responsive to the individual needs of African American women and are based on the ways that these clients understand their situations and transitions. Hence, because interventions are determined by the specific information counselors gain about these women and by how they perceive the nature and extent of their issues, it is increasingly likely that African American women's vocational concerns will be responded to in an appropriate and comprehensive manner. Social constructionist vocational counselors form a partnership with their African American female clients, working together as a team with the mutual objective of identifying relevant career options. Together, these clients and their counselors look for alternative perspectives and possible solutions to clients' vocational difficulties related to their career transitions.

The following case example illustrates the application of social constructionist principles in addressing the career transition issues of an African American female client:

> Stephanie (a pseudonym), a 39-year-old, married, African American female, had been employed as a medical transcriptionist at a private local hospital for the past 12 years. Last week, Stephanie received notice from her employer that her position was being terminated in 6 months due to "fiscal cutbacks." Hence, she sought vocational counseling to address her anxiety about being unemployed and "the possibility of pursuing other more desirable career interests after [her] current position ends." Stephanie lived with Phil, her husband of 9 years, and their two preschool-aged children. Phil had been employed as a mechanical engineer for over 15 years.

With regard to her vocational concerns, Stephanie verbalized her sadness and anger about being terminated from her present position, but also acknowledged feeling somewhat excited about the possibility of starting a new career. Although her current job afforded her family some financial security, she stated that she did not feel particularly challenged in this job. Stephanie indicated that her ideal occupation was to be self-employed as an independent medical transcriptionist to hospitals and other health agencies in need of such services. She believed that such a position would enable her to work out of her home and to have flexible work hours in order to care for her children. Stephanie claimed that Phil was supportive of her desire to become "an entrepreneur."

Stephanie's vocational counselor spent much of their first two counseling sessions establishing rapport, orienting Stephanie to the notion that their relationship was collaborative in nature and that Stephanie was the expert on her own life, and gaining a deeper understanding of the important issues of Stephanie's life with which she was currently dealing. In these sessions, using an occupational sociogram, Stephanie also identified the interrelationships and relative strengths between the significant others in her life and her preferred occupational interests. Additionally, Stephanie mapped out her personal career genealogy from high school to the present in order to explore the historical influences of her multiple cultural memberships (e.g., African American, female, etc.), systems (e.g., marital, familial, work, etc.), and events on her life at various points and the extent to which these influences impacted her current vocational development. By completing these exercises, Stephanie began to gain an increased understanding of the importance of being aware of her ever-changing needs and values in relation to her occupational options and preferences. By the end of the second session, after discussing the usefulness and limitations of standardized vocational assessment instruments, Stephanie also completed a battery of tests that consisted of interest and values inventories and personality measures intended to supplement existing information about her present vocational situation. As a result of the work achieved in the first two sessions, Stephanie stated that she had begun to recognize the influences of certain systemic and contextual influences on her current vocational situation and future career options.

Over the next few vocational counseling sessions, Stephanie and her counselor continued to examine relevant social, cultural, and systemic influences in her life. They used this information to contextualize the results of her standardized tests, working collaboratively to understand Stephanie's profiles on these vocational measures. During these sessions, Stephanie discussed in depth her fears and anxieties related to the possibility that she might not be able to support her family if she was not successful as an entrepreneur. She stated that although Phil's current job enabled them to live modestly without her having to work, she would feel "very guilty" about potentially not contributing more financially to their household income. Stephanie discussed her feelings with Phil, who reiterated his support of her potential decision to become a self-employed medical transcriptionist contractor.

The decision to terminate counseling was made jointly by Stephanie and her counselor once they determined that her primary goal for vocational counseling had been achieved. In preparing for termination, Stephanie's counselor asked her to identify what had been meaningful for her about the vocational counseling experience; any new perspectives she had gained from her explorations in counseling; how she felt differently about herself as a result of counseling; and resources she might draw on in the future to resolve her current and future career-related issues. By the end of counseling, Stephanie reported that she was feeling much better about her career prospects, and decided that she would pursue her goal of being self-employed.

CONCLUSIONS

Career transitions may pose difficulties for many African American women, regardless of whether or not these transitions are voluntary or involuntary. Hence, it is critical that career transition concerns of African American women are addressed in an appropriate manner. In a vocational counseling context, the use of social constructionist approaches may be a viable means of helping them to deal with issues that may arise in the process of career transition. Future writings should identify the unique vocational and personal issues that may impact the career transitions of African American women across the developmental lifespan. The use of qualitative and quantitative research methods to ascertain the aforementioned information would greatly advance the existing career development literature related to African American women.

ACKNOWLEDGMENT

We thank Robyn Liebman for her assistance with this chapter.

REFERENCES

Bailey, D., Wolfe, D., & Wolfe, C. R. (1996). The contextual impact of social support across race and gender: Implications for African-American women in the workplace. *Journal of Black Studies, 26*, 287–307.

Bejian, D. V., & Salomone, P. R. (1995). Understanding midlife career renewal: Implications for counseling. *Career Development Quarterly, 44*, 52–63.

Bell, E. L. (1990). The bicultural life experience of career-oriented black women. *Journal of Organizational Behavior, 11*, 459–477.

Black, D. R., & Loughead, T. A. (1990). Job change in perspective. *Journal of Career Development, 17*, 3–9.

Bordo, S. (1990). Feminism, postmodernism, and gender-scepticism. In L. J. Nicholson (Ed.), *Feminism/postmodernism* (pp. 133–156). London: Routledge Kegan & Paul.

Brett, J. M. (1982). Job transfer and well-being. *Journal of Applied Psychology, 67*, 450–463.

Brown-Collins, A. R., & Sussewell, D. R. (1986). The Afro-American women's emerging selves. *Journal of Black Psychology, 13*, 1–11.

Burlew, A. K., & Johnson, J. L. (1992). Role conflict and career advancement among African-American women in nontraditional professions. *Career Development Quarterly, 40*, 302–312.

Burlew, K. H. (1982). The experiences of Black females in traditional and nontraditional professions. *Psychology of Women Quarterly, 6*, 312–326.

Carter, M. A. T., & Cook, K. (1995). Adaptation to retirement: Role changes and psychological resources. *Career Development Quarterly, 44*, 67–81.

Constantine, M. G., & Erickson, C. D. (1998). Examining social constructions in vocational counselling: Implications for multicultural counselling competency. *Counselling Psychology Quarterly, 11*, 189–199.

Costa, P. (1995, January 29–February 4). What men can learn from women job hunters. *National Business Employment Weekly*, 7–8.

Eby, L. T., & Buch, K. (1995). Job loss as career growth: Responses to involuntary career transitions. *Career Development Quarterly, 44*, 26–42.

Eccles, J. S. (1994). Understanding women's educational and occupational choices. *Psychology of Women Quarterly, 18*, 585–609.

Evans, K. M., & Herr, E. L. (1991). The influence of racism and sexism in the career development of African-American women. *Journal of Multicultural Counseling and Development, 19*, 130–135.

Federal Glass Ceiling Commission. (1995). *Good for business: Making full use of the nation's human capital: The environmental scan: A fact-finding report of the Federal Glass Ceiling Commission*. Washington, DC: U.S. Government Printing Office.

Gainor, K. A., & Forrest, L. (1991). African American women's self-concept: Implications for career decisions and career counseling. *Career Development Quarterly, 39*, 261–272.

Gallos, J. (1989). Exploring women's development. In M. Arthur, D. Hall, & B. Lawrence (Eds.), *Handbook of career theory* (pp. 110–132). New York: Cambridge University Press.

George, L. K. (1990). Social structure, social processes, and social-psychological states. In R. H. Binstock & L. K. George (Eds.), *Handbook of aging and the social sciences* (3rd ed., pp. 205–226). Orlando, FL: Academic Press.

Greenhaus, J. H., Parasuraman, S., & Wormley, W. M. (1990). Effects of race on organizational experiences, job performance evaluations, and career outcomes. *Academy of Management Journal, 33*, 64–86.

Hackett, G., & Byars, A. M. (1996). Social cognitive theory and the career development of African American women. *Career Development Quarterly, 44*, 322–341.

Hare-Mustin, R. T., & Marecek, J. (1988). The meaning of difference: Gender theory, postmodernism, and psychology. *American Psychologist, 43*, 355–364.

Helms, J. E., & Piper, R. E. (1994). Implications of racial identity theory for vocational psychology. *Journal of Vocational Behavior, 44*, 124–138.

Hepworth, S. J. (1980). Moderating factors of the psychological impact of unemployment. *Journal of Occupational Psychology, 53*, 139–145.

Herr, E. L., & Cramer, S. H. (1996). *Career guidance and counseling through the lifespan: Systematic approaches* (5th ed.). New York: HarperCollins.

Hornstein, G. A., & Wapner, S. (1985). Modes of experiencing and adapting to retirement. *International Journal on Aging and Human Development, 21*, 291–315.

Isaacson, L. (1985). *Basics of career counseling*. Boston: Allyn & Bacon.

Jensen-Scott, R. L. (1993). Counseling to promote retirement adjustment. *Career Development Quarterly, 41*, 257–267.

Kegan, R. (1982). *The evolving self*. Cambridge, MA: Harvard University Press.

Kragie, E., Gerstein, M., & Lichtman, M. (1989). Do Americans plan for retirement?: Some recent trends. *Career Development Quarterly, 37,* 232–239.

Krumboltz, J. D. (1990). Representing the process of changing jobs: A reaction to the conceptual framework for job change. *Journal of Career Development, 17,* 25–29.

Latack, C. (1984). Career transitions within organizations: An exploratory study of work, non-work and coping strategies. *Organizational Behavior and Human Performance, 34,* 296–332.

Latack, J. C., & Dozier, J. B. (1986). After the ax falls: Job loss as a career transition. *Academy of Management Review, 11,* 375–392.

Lieblich, A. (1986). Successful career women at mid-life: Crises and transitions. *International Journal of Aging and Human Development, 23,* 301–312.

London, M., & Greller, M. M. (1991). Demographic trends and vocational behavior: A twenty year retrospective and agenda for the 1990s. *Journal of Vocational Behavior, 38,* 125–164.

McAuliffe, G. (1993). Constructive development and career transition: Implications for counseling. *Journal of Counseling & Development, 72,* 23–28.

Morton, T. (1992). *The survivor's guide to unemployment.* Colorado Springs, CO: Piñon Press.

Neimeyer, R. A. (1995). Constructivist psychotherapies: Features, foundations, and future directions. In R. A. Neimeyer & M. J. Mahoney (Eds.), *Constructivism in psychotherapy* (pp. 11–38). Washington, DC: American Psychological Association.

Newman, B. K. (1995). Career change for those over 40: Critical issues and insights. *Career Development Quarterly, 44,* 64–66.

Ogilvie, D. M. (1987). Life satisfaction and identity structure in late middle-aged men and women. *Psychology and Aging, 2,* 217–224.

Richardson, M. S. (1993). Work in people's lives: A location for counseling psychologists. *Journal of Counseling Psychology, 40,* 425–433.

Richie, B. S. (1992). Coping with work: Interventions with African-American women. *Women and Therapy, 12,* 97–111.

Roberts, P., & Newton, P. C. (1987). Levinsonian studies of women's adult development. *Psychology and Aging, 2,* 154–163.

Savickas, M. L. (1993). Career counseling in the postmodern era. *Journal of Cognitive Psychotherapy: An International Quarterly, 7,* 205–215.

Savickas, M. L. (1995). Constructivist counseling for career indecision. *Career Development Quarterly, 43,* 363–373.

Sexton, T. L. (1997). Constructivist thinking within the history of ideas: The challenge of a new paradigm. In T. L. Sexton & B. L. Griffin (Eds.), *Constructivist thinking in counseling practice, research, and training* (pp. 3–18). New York: Teachers College Press.

Simpson, G. (1996). Factors influencing the choice of law as a career by Black women. *Journal of Career Development, 22,* 197–209.

Sinick, D. (1984). Problems of work and retirement for an aging population. In N. C. Gysbers & Associates (Eds.), *Designing careers* (pp. 532–557). San Francisco: Jossey-Bass.

Swinton, D. H. (1992). The economic status of African Americans: Limited ownership and persistent in equality. In B. J. Tidwell (Ed.), *The state of Black America 1992* (pp. 61–117). New York: National Urban League.

Thomas, D. A., & Alderfer, C. P. (1989). The influence of race on career dynamics: Theory and research on minority career experiences. In M. B. Arthur, D. T. Hall, & B. S. Lawrence (Eds.), *Handbook of career theory* (pp. 133–158). New York: Cambridge University Press.

U.S. Bureau of Labor Statistics (1997, January). *Employment and earnings.* Washington, DC: Author.

West, M. A., & Nicholson, N. (1989). The outcomes of job change. *Journal of Vocational Behavior, 34,* 335–349.

Zunker, V. G. (1998). *Career counseling: Applied concepts of life planning* (5th ed.). Pacific Grove, CA: Brooks/Cole.

Chapter 6

Rights-of-Way: Affirmative Career Counseling With African American Women

Angela M. Byars
University of Wisconsin–Madison

> *The woman who survives intact and happy must be at once tender and tough. She must have convinced herself, or be in the unending process of convincing herself, that she, her values, and her choices are important. In a time and world where males hold sway and control, the pressure upon women to yield their rights-of-way is tremendous. And it is under those very circumstances that the woman's toughness must be in evidence.*
> —Maya Angelou (1993), "In All Ways A Woman"

The practice of yielding the right-of-way is most evident at a four-way intersection. In order for traffic to flow smoothly through an intersection, a common understanding must be reached such that every vehicle can proceed without delay, impediment, or accident. The common understanding is that the right-of-way is yielded to vehicles arriving at the intersection first and then to those on the left. Whether one has arrived first or last, all vehicles eventually continue through this crossroad. This image of an intersection highlights the interrelated nature of not only individual drivers, their goals and direction, but also the collective negotiation required to navigate through this crossroad. That is, how one is able to advance through the intersection is dependent on the cooperation of the other drivers as well.

The critical decisions about intersections are when, where, and how to proceed through them. Similar to Angelou's (1993) assertion, many social and structural factors obstruct women's rights-of-way such that their abil-

ity to proceed through various intersections of life is slowed or completely blocked. One such critical intersection in women's lives is career choice.
Yet, little is known about effective processes and outcomes in career counseling with women from visible racial and ethnic groups, in general, and
African American women, in particular.

Historically, the practice of career counseling has sought to effectively
match people to jobs without emphasizing clients' personal understanding
of their relation to work. More than 25 years ago, Stubbins (1973) asserted:

> [T]he vocational psychologist operates in a world that economics and polit-
> ical science have long since discarded—a perspective that ignores the fact
> that the Black individual's world has already taught him or her that socio-
> economic status, racial origin, and power are more determinative than apti-
> tude or interest. (p. 24)

Recently, Sue, Parham, and Santiago (1998) outlined several challenges
facing the increasing number of visible racial and ethnic groups compris-
ing the labor market. They maintained that individuals from such groups
historically faced discrimination and prejudice that resulted in unequal
access to and poor opportunities in employment and job training. It follows, then, that effective career intervention with African American
women must attend to the multiple social dimensions of their lives, such
as race and gender, as well as occupational barriers they may face.

Constant shifts in the nature and organization of work demand adaptability from individuals to competently deal with a changing world of work.
One's job duties, as well as when and where a given job is performed, can
be modified as organizations restructure to remain competitive in the labor
market. These shifts further challenged the traditional goal of a job match
or discrete career choice as a primary outcome of career counseling. Krumboltz and Coon (1995) posited that career counseling must also facilitate
clients' construction of "an identity that incorporates career rather than the
creating of a career identity distinct from the person as a whole" (p. 402).
Relatedly, Gysbers, Heppner, and Johnston (1998) advocated for a life-
career perspective to counseling that fosters clients' career consciousness or
"ability to visualize and plan their life careers" (p. 9). Career consciousness
takes a holistic view of a person, integrating her personal life philosophy as
well as her background, values, educational experiences, and emotions. The
holistic development of the African American woman career client suggests
that interventions promote deliberate examination and understanding of
their career development.

The purpose of this chapter is to review career development issues of
African American women and their implications for career intervention.
There are more than 30 million African Americans in the United States,

women accounting for over one half of this group (U.S. Bureau of the Census, 1992). African American women represent a significant segment of the U.S. population and labor force, yet little is known about their career development. The intent of this chapter is not to be exhaustive, but rather to provide a possible guiding framework for understanding and intervening in the career development of African American women.

The chapter is divided into three sections. The first section highlights some of the typical experiences of African American women that significantly shape their orientation toward work. Specifically, a synopsis of current and historical contexts for African American women's work patterns and multiple social identities is presented. In the second section, social cognitive career theory (Lent, Brown, & Hackett, 1994) is briefly presented as a model for understanding the impact of African American women's experiences, culture, and history on career choice. *Social cognitive career theory* is posed as a paradigm that explicitly promotes client empowerment, viewing them as active participants in shaping their lives rather than passive recipients of environmental forces. The final section of this chapter focuses on specific career counseling strategies to enhance African American women's career development. This section examines the use of historical resistance, social agency, and communal and self-reliance in African American women within career development interventions. The intended focus is to create a counseling atmosphere supportive of client exploration and self-understanding that can lead to an informed and purposeful career process rather than solely on career outcomes (i.e., career choice).

AFRICAN AMERICAN WOMEN AND WORK: THE NATURE OF THE INTERSECTION

Increasingly, cultural variables are being incorporated into studies investigating career-related processes in African Americans. Some researchers have even advanced conceptual models of career development that are more culturally relevant to specific racial groups (c.f. Cheatham, 1990). Such advances in the field have been due, in part, to the recognition that distinct sociocultural experiences of various racial and ethnic populations are potentially powerful influences on the career development of group members. For instance, African Americans have a unique history and an ongoing experience with racism and discrimination (Bennett, 1982; Essed, 1991; Feagin, 1991). African American women comprise diverse perspectives and realities, thus, the experiences and cognitive processes discussed are subject to within-group variation. Variables like social class, racial salience, age, and ability status complexly interact with race and ethnicity, moderating these cultural influences on career-related behavior.

Nonetheless, one guiding assumption in this review is that the general context of discrimination and oppression is shared across all subgroups of African American women. It is important, then, to understand their current occupational status within an historical context.

Enslaved African Americans worked as free labor in agricultural and domestic jobs, largely on plantations in the Southeastern United States. As a result, the other dimensions of African American cultural life, such as family life, education, and religion, became difficult, if not impossible, to pursue (Gilkes, 1994). Even after the abolition of legalized slavery, many freed African Americans became displaced workers. Poor education and high illiteracy rates negatively affected vocational opportunities for African Americans. Disadvantaged economically and educationally, African Americans were relegated to menial, domestic, low-paying jobs. Racial prejudice, discrimination, and lack of training and education kept many African American women performing jobs they had known as slaves: cooking, cleaning, and washing (Harley, 1978). Since the beginning of the 20th century, African American women's occupational history has followed several trends: concentration in low-level occupations; slow increases among professional and technical occupations; and minimal business ownership (Aldridge, 1989).

The overwhelming majority of African American women have always worked. In fact, African American women have historically had higher overall labor-force participation rates than did White women, even when married (Taeuber, 1991). The result of such a long work history is a strong work ethic in African American women (Gilkes, 1990; Greene, 1990; Jewell, 1993; Thomas, 1986). Accordingly, African American girls have been reared with the expectation to participate in the labor force. This expectation is based on three factors: economic need or their perception of future economic need, historical exposure to female work role models in the home, and relative egalitarian relationships between the sexes within the Black community (Smith, 1981).

The consequences of African American women's strong work ethic on their occupational and educational attainment is unclear. The scant social science research on African American women's educational and occupational status provides a fertile ground for myths to flourish about their success (Higginbotham, 1994). For example, African American women are slightly more likely to graduate from high school on time than are their male counterparts (81.8% vs. 76.3%, respectively; *African American Education Data Book*, 1998). African American women are also more likely to attain bachelor's degrees than African American men (U.S. Department of Education, 1998a). Yet, the range of academic disciplines in which African American women earn bachelor's degrees is quite narrow; over one half of them earn degrees in business, the social sciences, and education (U.S. Department of Education, 1998b). Although similar trends for concentration of majors in these academic disciplines exist for all college students, African American women continue to be overrepresented in these fields, even at the graduate level (Carter & Wilson, 1989).

Furthermore, the range of occupations in which African American women are employed is severely limited. Although most working women are still employed in traditional female occupations (e.g., primary and secondary schoolteachers, social workers, and nurses), African American women, in particular, are overrepresented in these fields.

McRae (1990) asserted that the overrepresentation of African American women in traditional occupations may result from the emotions, beliefs, and environmental factors affecting their career decision making. That is, internalized, negative stereotypes may lead some African American women to believe that certain jobs are meant for them. For example, occupational stereotypes of African American women as being skilled in career fields that include helping others and unskilled in technical and scientific career fields might lead them to engage in self-limiting behavior—such as enrolling in fewer preparatory math and science courses or seeking little career information about math- and science-related fields—thus, perpetuating occupational differences. Perceived opportunities (or lack thereof) and occupational stereotypes may foster self-segregation into traditional fields for African American women. Furthermore, that African American women have often been labeled as "aggressive, domineering, and hard-nosed" limits their attractiveness as potential employees and subsequently, has isolated them in the labor market (Gilkes, 1990). Even with advanced degrees, African American women struggle with racial discrimination and informal barriers to occupational advancement (Higginbotham, 1994).

Discrimination by race and gender in the labor market are realistic barriers for African American women. For example, Greenhaus, Parasuraman, and Wormley (1990) examined the effects of race on organizational experiences and outcomes of both African American and White managers. African American women comprised the majority of the total sample for African American managers in this study. Results indicated that the race of African American managers was directly related to lower ratings of their job performance by their White supervisors. Race was also related to African American managers' perceptions of organizational acceptance and job discretion. That is, African American managers felt less integrated (acceptance) and perceived themselves to have less job power (discretion) than their White counterparts. The authors highlighted how racial dynamics can adversely affect and restrict the occupational experiences of African Americans. Specifically, the access to enter organizations and their treatment within them was questioned for African American managers. Racial and gender discrimination might also contribute to occupational segregation.

Occupational segregation by race or gender addresses the pivotal issue of whether individuals from specific groups are employed in different occupations than are White men. Bielby and Baron (1986) conducted a study on the extent of gender segregation in the labor force in several hundred California establishments and firms between 1959 and 1979. Findings indicated that 96% of all women and men would have to change their jobs for there to be an equal distribution of women and men in the labor force across occupations (i.e., gender segregation index of .96). Sokoloff (1992), in a more recent study, found equally stark findings for occupational segregation by race. Results from this study showed that African American men and women in the same professions as White men and women are generally not employed in the same types of organizations and when they are, they have different job titles and reward systems.

Despite the empirical documentation that racism and sexism continue to thwart access to a range of careers, assumptions that African American women have equal access to occupational goals persist. Sokoloff (1992) contrasted the glass-ceiling concept as applied to White women to the *lucite ceiling* for African Americans. Unlike glass, lucite is opaque and not easily broken. As such, some White women break through the glass ceiling into high-level positions in various occupations, yet African American women are restricted to middle-level professions and have diminished chances of breaking through to the top. This inability to break through is often a result of the intersection of racial and gender segregation.

In spite of the devastating influence of slavery, African Americans "have made significant progress in their educational and career development" (Smith, 1983, p. 171). Many of the moderate gains that African American women have made in occupations and in education have been facilitated by the passage of several federal laws and regulations, including Title VII of the Civil Rights Act in 1964 and Title IX of the Education Amendment of 1972. However, failure to completely enforce these laws has undermined the full realization of their intended benefits (Malcolm, Hall, & Brown, 1976). As indicated by the empirical research previously reviewed, the occupational status of educated African American women remains troublesome, often due to negative reactions to their race and gender (Sokoloff, 1992). It is important, then, to examine potential processes by which African American women understand the impact of structural inequalities and discrimination on their lives.

Racial Identity: The Driver's View or Cultural Lens

Erikson (1966/1976) defined identity as a subjective sense of sameness and continuity. He acknowledged that, although individuals have multiple social identities (e.g., gender, class, race, and ethnicity), these collective identities overlap one another and form a personality configuration. Identities have both stable and situationally specific (or dynamic) properties. The degree to which any of the multiple identities influence behavior or are manifested is a function of how *salient* (or personally relevant) a given identity is to a person at a particular moment in time. Racial salience is an example of this dynamic property of identity. The concept of racial salience is important to understand the variance and diversity within one socially defined racial group. It deters one from thinking of members from one racial group as being all alike.

The social identity of race can also be powerful in determining cultural adaptations for African Americans. Parham and Austin (1994) asserted that:

> [I]n the context of social oppression, African Americans are believed to adapt by psychologically constructing for themselves a set of assumptions and beliefs about: who they are; how they feel about themselves, other African people, White people, and people from other cultural groups; what opportunities are available to them in life; and what strategies must be employed to meet their needs individually and collectively. (p. 140)

The process of increased awareness and understanding of oneself as a racial being, often in the context of racial oppression, is the focus of racial identity theory.

Helms (1996) defined *racial identity* as the psychological, internalized consequences of socialization in a racially oppressive environment and the characteristics of the self that develop in response to either benefitting or suffering under such oppression. Cross (1971) originally posed a formal theory of racial identity development for African Americans. Parham and Helms (1985) later operationalized his racial identity theory into a model with four ego statuses and related attitudes that reflect various levels of identity relative to racial salience. The model moves from low racial salience and consciousness (*Preencounter Status*), indicative of a non-Black identity, to an integrated Black identity with a balance of racial salience and consciousness to other social identities (*Internalization Status*). In sum, racial identity theory addresses the psychosocial consequences of membership in a group that shares a common racial heritage and is marginalized on the basis of race. Racial identity theory acknowledges that racial status is socially defined and imposed, with implications for differential access to institutions and resources based on that status (Helms & Piper, 1994). The concept of racial identity underscores the need to examine and understand African American clients' worldview and how their racial self is incorporated into their personal frames of reference. As noted, racial identity consists of a dynamic transaction between people's behavioral, cognitive, and affective attitudes and their environment and thus, may have powerful consequences for African American women's career behavior.

In a study that examined racial identity and specific career behavior, Manese and Fretz (1984) found that racial identity attitudes were significant predictors of the level of vocational identity foreclosure for African American undergraduate women. Specifically, findings showed that students with *Preencounter* and *Internalization* racial attitudes were more likely to consider fewer occupations as career options, and *Immersion–Emersion* racial attitudes were significantly predictive of enhanced career exploration attitudes. In another sample of African American undergraduate women, Byars (1997) found that racial identity attitudes were significantly related to perceived confidence (i.e., self-efficacy) for completing undergraduate and graduate education and coping with barriers to academic and career goals (i.e., coping efficacy). Results indicated that women who endorsed *Preencounter* racial attitudes were less confident in achieving a bachelor's degree, whereas those who endorsed *Encounter* racial attitudes were less confident in completing graduate education. Those women who endorsed *Encounter* racial attitudes were also less confident in coping with academic and career barriers, whereas those with *Internalization* attitudes were more confident on this variable.

Related to coping with challenges to one's career goals, Bell (1990) found that career-oriented African American women perceived themselves to live in two separate cultural contexts, one White and the other Black. Yet, the women in this sample reported high levels of personal satisfaction, often employing bicultural strategies (effective management of two cultural contexts—African American and White culture—while retaining one's personal and cultural identity) to navigate between the two contexts. The presumed stress resulting from consciousness of being Black in a White environment and negotiating that experience was successfully managed for this sample via bicultural behavior. These results highlight the importance of promoting Black racial identity development as a healthy psychological process outside of reactions solely to oppressive and discriminatory experiences (Smith, 1989).

These findings collectively suggest that racial identity theory is a theoretical construct that may be useful in explaining the process whereby vocational products, such as interests, choice, and values, come about (Helms & Piper, 1994). It follows from the research literature that individuals with healthy attitudes related to their racial group membership may: perceive and consider a wider range of vocational opportunities; feel more confident in their ability to overcome any hindrances that might prevent them from attaining their career goals; and have more positive expectations regarding career- and academic-related outcomes. In depth applications of racial identity theory to career development and counseling with African Americans have been reviewed by Bowman (1995), Helms and Piper (1994), and Parham and Austin (1994) to which the reader is directed for further examination.

Although racial identity appears to be a useful construct for understanding the potential impact of race on African American women's lives, race is only one instance of several cultural contexts that significantly shape how they derive meaning from life events (Smith, 1989). Myriad cultural identities for African American women can have varied outcomes for their life experience.

Multiple Oppressions: The Vehicle on the Left

In the driving analogy, the vehicle on the left represents the driver to whom the right-of-way is yielded. Socially constructed messages that denigrate and impede equal access of African American women to pursue their career goals may impair their ability to navigate the intersection. As previously illustrated, structural conditions resulting from the social constructions of gender and race continue to influence and constrain occupational choices and mobility. Under the stress of such conditions, African American women might succumb to the social messages that their unique values and worldviews are unimportant. These are examples of what Angelou (1993) referred to as pressures on women to yield their rights-of-way.

Beale (1972) initially proposed the term *double jeopardy* to describe the discriminations of racism and sexism that simultaneously oppress African American women. *Economic oppression*, identified as a third type of discrimination often faced by African American women, is a third jeopardy (Davis, 1981). More recently, King (1988) argued that concepts such as double and triple jeopardy oversimplify the relations among these forms of discriminations and further the interpretation that the effects of these variables are merely additive. That is, variables of race, gender, and class are interpreted as having direct, separate, and independent effects on the status of African American women. King, instead, proposed the term *multiple jeopardy*, highlighting the interdependent and dynamic processes among multiple forms of discrimination. The effects of racism, sexism, and classism are viewed instead as multiplicative, with no one variable superseding the other. This view of race, gender, and class as interdependent variables acknowledges them as partially distinct social hierarchies that uniquely position people to the distribution of power, privilege, and prestige (Ransford & Miller, 1983). Consistent with King's proposition, Zinn and Dill (1994) suggested that how women of color experience race, gender, and class is dependent on the intersection of these variables with all forms of discrimination and inequalities.

The experience of multiple forms of oppression also yields multiple forms of resistance to such oppression and multiple lens through which to view one's world, a type of multiple consciousness about the social and institutional dynamics producing the oppression. As long as African American women experienced multiple oppressions, they also resisted them (King, 1988). Relatedly, Robinson (1983) wrote the following of African American women's legacy of strength:

> We have been forced by society, oppression, our position, and our tradition to be responsible for the economic, social, and physical survival of our families and communities, regardless of socioeconomic status, age, geographic location, or educational attainment. Our adaptability to varied roles, while transcending societal barriers, illustrates significant coping abilities. (p. 136)

This excerpt highlights the historical resistance and social agency of African American women. It illustrates how multiple jeopardy can lead to multiple consciousness, often yielding to multiple forms of resistance. For African American women to avoid yielding their self-determination to the presence of other drivers, they must exercise the right to determine themselves first in their own voice. Despite this acknowledged rich tradition of self and community reliance, many career theories fail to incorporate these influences and potential sources of support into their examination of African American women's career development.

Issues in Current Career Theories:
Traditional Routes for Career Intersections

A general goal of career counseling is the therapeutic facilitation of clients' systematic identification and exploration of career-related factors and the subsequent implementation of a career choice. As previously discussed, cultural variables, such as social identities of race and gender, are potentially significant influences on the lives and behavior of African American women. How African American women's multiple social identities shape and influence their attitudes, skills, and understanding about the career development process and career options is needed. In spite of this need, many (traditional) career development theories and their respective approaches to career intervention do not attend to these cultural issues (Leong & Brown, 1995).

One paradigm within career counseling theories and methods is that there exists a right job for each person. Another paradigm includes the view that people implement or incorporate an identity or self-concept into their work. Still another paradigm asserts that people derive meaning from their work. Clearly, several factors contribute to an individual's choice of and motivation to work. Crites (1969) suggested that in order for occupational choice to occur, three conditions must exist: freedom to choose, options from which to choose, and the motivation to make a choice. These conditions are necessary, but not sufficient. Yet, many of the traditional career-counseling theories and techniques do not account for the social constraints on these three conditions for African American women. What impact does the valuing of these particular paradigms have on the profession's effectiveness with African American women and understanding of their career-related processes?

Analogous to the image of the intersection, many career interventions focus on directing when and how clients proceed through the intersection. Directive intervention, however, often excludes fostering in clients the tools to negotiate the intersection. Additionally, directive intervention techniques silence and disaffirm the unique voices and narratives of African American women. Many interventions are constructed such that no framework guides the understanding and processes of African Americans' experiences. For example, many career assessment interventions categorize and codify particular vocational patterns (e.g., Strong Interest Inventory, Campbell Interests and Skills Survey, Kuder Occupational Interest Survey) without avenues for contextualizing the results (i.e., qualitative data). It is thus incumbent on the career professional to seek out the information that contextualizes the resulting quantitative data. In reviewing the vocational interests literature, Bowman (1995) cautioned use of traditional interest assessment without considering potential test and cultural biases that may result in misinformation about visible racial and ethnic minority clients. This notion is underscored for African American women given that some data demonstrate discrepancies between their expressed and measured interests. As Bingham and Ward (chap. 3, this vol.) noted, career professionals must be culturally aware and competent in order to explore cultural contexts with clients and then apply and interpret such information.

The focus on career-related outcomes, like career choice and career decision, may influence career professionals to overlook valuable client experiences and worldviews. Emphasis on these career outcomes communicates a value on the endpoint of career interventions and inappropriately sets the criteria for assessing the effectiveness of the interventions. This emphasis renders clients as objects rather than participants in the counseling process. As an object, African American women are relegated to passive recipients of the interventions. That is, counseling might progress with standard procedures of interview and assessment, however, cultural variables are annexed to the prevailing career paradigm. The emphasis is on decision or choice on completion of counseling. Conversely, as participants, African American women are the principle focus in the counseling process, wherein their unique narratives are validated and form the basis of career interventions. Emphasis in this process is on the client's personal understanding and integration of experiences regarding her career behavior. To create a setting for clients to participate in the counseling process, career interventions need to accept and integrate different narratives and resist the propensity to rearticulate a specific narrative into the prevailing paradigm. Interventions must also be constructed such that narratives form the basis for counseling.

Next, an overview of social cognitive career theory (SCCT) is provided. SCCT offers one approach in addressing dynamic sociocultural variables in African American women's career behavior rather than viewing these variables in an ad-hoc fashion or as an implicit context. The reader is referred to previously published in-depth reviews on SCCT (Lent & Brown, 1996; Lent et al., 1994).

SOCIAL COGNITIVE CAREER THEORY: AN ANALYSIS OF CAREER INTERSECTIONS

Theoretical Foundation

Social cognitive theory (Bandura, 1986, 1997) posits that people's judgments about and confidence in their capabilities to perform necessary actions to achieve desired outcomes is important. These judgments, or self-efficacy beliefs, are significant guiding aspects of psychosocial functioning (Bandura, 1986, 1997). That is, what is important about people's experiences is not only the actual events themselves, but also the meaning that is attached to those experiences. Successful experiences strengthen self-efficacy beliefs, whereas failures tend to weaken them. Strong, realistic personal self-efficacy estimates also facilitate individuals' initiation of and persistence in performing a given task, which in turn, increases the likelihood of success.

The initiation of and persistence in performing a task is also related to personal beliefs about the consequences of a given course of action. Bandura (1986, 1997) termed such beliefs as *outcome expectations*. Self-efficacy beliefs, in conjunction with outcome expectations, guide behavior. However, self-efficacy, the central construct in social cognitive theory, is considered to be the more influential factor on individuals' behavior.

Bandura (1986, 1997) postulated that self-efficacy beliefs are formed and altered via four fundamental sources of information: personal accomplishments, vicarious learning, physiological and affective states, and verbal persuasion. *Outcome expectations* are shaped by direct and vicarious experiences as people learn about the consequences of directly engaging in some behavior or by observing others.

SCCT

Recently, Lent et al. (1994) expanded Bandura's (1986, 1997) work to propose a social cognitive model of career choice and development, referred to as *SCCT*. Central to the SCCT model is *career self-efficacy*, or the expectations about one's confidence to successfully negotiate various career-related tasks and pursuits. There are two organizing components in SCCT that encompass cultural dynamics. The first component addresses the early experiences that help to shape and influence career self-efficacy and outcome expectations. Specifically, Lent et al. (1994) outlined how individuals' background variables interact with and influence the nature and variety of learning experiences to which they are exposed. These background variables may consist of personal characteristics (e.g., race, sex, or physical ability status) or contextual factors (e.g., familial influences and SES). The second component in SCCT is related to the continual effects of contextual factors that are external to the person. Such factors include labor market status, racism, sexism, and perceived barriers.

Lent and Brown (1996) stated that cultural variables influence career self-efficacy and outcome expectations indirectly through their influence on learning experiences that, then, shape those beliefs. Learning experiences and socialization processes both shape and inform self-efficacy beliefs and outcome expectations related to career and academic pursuits. Career and academic self-efficacy beliefs, as well as outcome expectations, in turn, influence the development of vocational interests, goals, choices, and actions. Perceived self-efficacy, then, is a mediator through which socialization processes and past experience influence educational and career choices (Bandura, 1997). Initial support has been found for the predictiveness of career and academic self-efficacy to career choice and academic achievement for African American women (Byars, 1997).

The influence of contextual variables and socialization on career self-efficacy may vary for African American women as a function of how well they cope with potential challenges to their academic and career pursuits. Coping efficacy is another variable that may influence the relationships between career interests, contextual factors, and career choice.

Coping Efficacy

Coping efficacy is a cognitive estimate of one's perceived ability to cognitively control and manage environmental threats (Bandura, 1986). Coping efficacy affects emotional reactions as well as behavior, especially related to anxiety and stress reactions to unfamiliar or potentially aversive situations. Perceived coping efficacy can lower arousal before, during, and after a difficult experience. Related to vocational behavior, Hackett and Betz (1989) found that perceived self-inefficacy, which influences coping efficacy, predicted avoidance of academic activities. Hackett and Byars (1996) emphasized the potential value of developing effective strategies to cope with discrimination and social barriers that may limit the career behavior of African American women.

Generative Capability

Pursuit of a career necessitates that African American women create plans to organize, guide, and sustain their own behavior to realize their career goals. The ability to set goals is facilitated by a powerful human capability; symbolic representation (thought). Symbolic representation occurs via several basic capabilities: symbolizing capability, forethought capability, vicarious capability, self-regulatory capability, and self-reflective capability (Bandura, 1986). By drawing on capacities of symbolic thought, people can generate innovative courses of action. Predictive knowledge about what is likely to occur if particular events happen elicits anticipatory mechanisms that foster planfulness and adaptation (Bandura, 1997). The ability to envision the outcomes of various courses of action can also promote internal motivation. Cognitive models guide the execution of skilled action and serve as internal standards for corrective adjustments in behavioral proficiency. Cognitive guidance is especially vital when skill development is in a beginning or intermediate phase (Bandura, 1997), like pursuit of an unfamiliar occupation.

In sum, foresight capacity of likely outcomes of prospective behavior contributes to persistence toward a goal via symbolic motivators. People can govern their actions based on knowledge gained vicariously about the likely outcomes and risks of several courses of action. Via abstract modeling and vicarious learning, people extract the rules underlying specific behavior for generating behavior that goes beyond what they have seen or heard. Vicarious rewards and vicarious punishments can increase or decrease the likelihood of observers behaving in ways similar to those they have observed. As such, vicarious learning results in the conversion of modeled activities into representational guides for future action.

Goals are integral parts of SCCT. Concepts, such as career plans, daydreams, and aspirations, are essentially goal variants (Lent et al., 1994). Thus, attending to African American women's self-regulatory behavior (e.g., goals) fosters examination of their career-related self-efficacy, outcome expectations, and contextual factors that shape these variables.

SCCT is a model that may explicate how cultural variables significantly shape African American women's learning experiences. Such variables are, in effect, environments themselves that influence the types of experiences to which they are exposed. SCCT is a useful model in which to explore meaningful dimensions of race and ethnicity related to career choice. Integrating social cognitive constructs into career interventions with African American women may help counselors to be informed and effective in implementing culturally appropriate strategies and measuring career progress, interests and choices for this group.

SPECIFIC CAREER COUNSELING STRATEGIES: ALTERNATE ROUTES FOR NAVIGATING CAREER INTERSECTIONS

It is critical to explore both the personal and social resources that an African American woman brings from her experiences and her reference-group community (e.g. racial or gender group affiliation). Culturally relevant interventions must not only attend to the specific concepts and variables germane to African American women, but also affirm them as active creators of their life and careers. Affirmative career counseling moves the client beyond a survival modality that focuses on resisting oppressive forces in her life. This modality focuses on conditions and people outside of the client's sphere of influence of control. Additionally, the focus is on counteracting and reacting to oppression, and thus the client's energy centers on what is being done to her (implicit victimization) and identifying strategies to assuage the deleterious effects of such oppression. These strategies are often temporary solutions to ongoing dynamics (Brookins & Robinson, 1995). Conversely, a liberation or empowerment modality promotes self-worth and the locus of personal power is within the individual. In this way, African American women are supported to validate and positively assert who they are as a function of self-knowledge.

This approach is consistent with Borgen's (1995) articulation of narrative assessment. Narrative assessment is directed at drawing a picture of the individual's psychic space. Consistent with SCCT, clients use this information to define themselves and to construct a narrative about themselves that shapes a future life story. In this fashion, data are unearthed to tell the client's current story to date and then to begin narrating how she wants her future life story to be told. By incorporating both qualitative and quantitative data and constant dialogue, the client and counselor together tell the "idiographic story of the client's psychological life" (p. 437). Emphasis is on a collaborative relationship where the client's knowledge of herself is valued, acknowledged, and utilized. That is, narrative assessment approaches actively engage clients in telling their own career stories, which can be empowering and affirming for African American women as they are encouraged to tell their career story with all of their sociocultural influences.

The following offers strategies that might compliment a larger culturally relevant career counseling approach or model. These strategies are intended to provide both the counselor and client with contextual information to use in the career-development process. The reader is referred to Bingham and Ward's chapter (chap. 3) in this book and to Fouad and Bingham (1995) for examples of a formal model termed, *CACCM*. Additionally, Betz (1992) and Betz and Hackett (1997) proposed some applications of career self-efficacy theory to counseling: assessment of career-related self-efficacy expectations, gender role and racial socialization, and restrictive or facilitative experiential opportunities that might limit a client's confidence, interests, and breadth of career consideration. Emphasis is on the restoration of options that may have been prematurely foreclosed due to social and cultural variables like racism and sexism (Betz, 1989). The following strategies are consistent with this aim.

Remembering as Resistance

B. M. Greene (1997) highlighted the significance of remembering as resistance in her review of several writings by women of color. In her analysis, she argued that for African American women, there is power in remembering the legacy of struggle and resistance across the group's collective history. The power lies in recalling both the struggle and the forms of resistance. However, all too often, most emphasis is placed on the struggles to the ignorance of the resistances. African American women are often admonished to "Remember from whence you've come" and as such, recall the social, political, and cultural challenges that their group has historically faced. Yet, the concrete strategies and means employed to resist multiple forms of oppression are not remembered.

What is particularly powerful about memory is that it is a visual representation of an experience. As previously noted, people do not need a direct, personal experience with a given scenario or behavior in order to learn from it. Through vicarious learning, they can observe someone else in a given situation and extract rules, beliefs, and assumptions from their observation about a given behavior. This remembering-as-resistance approach references Collins' (1989) use of an inductive system of logic, accessing folk wisdom and survival-based wisdom from African American women ancestors. It follows, then, that remembering as resistance might facilitate African American women's capacity to extract and apply strategies for coping with various challenges from African American women who have gone before them. Incorporation of remembering-as-resistance strategies might be particularly facilitated by bibliotherapy.

Bibliotherapy

Throughout such works as, *The Bluest Eye*, and *Beloved*, Toni Morrison addressed the themes of place and displacement for African American women: the struggle and triumph of women to find their niche, location, essence, and position in their world and their fight against those forces that seek to displace, dislodge, or dislocate them from such a place, be it abuse, racism, or self-hate. Alice Walker's books (e.g., *The Color Purple*) examined such themes as the inevitability of struggle and the indomitability of the human spirit. She emphasized how African American women can survive whole, via forgiveness and acceptance. Walker also dealt with the theme of invisibility for African American women, invisibility resulting from oppression, abuse, and ignorance from others. Both Walker and Morrison examined the larger issue of being a womanist: A woman can be and assert herself only if she has other sisters around her to support and share in her struggle. This is a shared focus with another author, Gloria Naylor.

In Naylor's books, she illustrates how race continues to be the most powerful factor that renders Black people powerless in the United States. Another theme that Naylor addressed in her books, *The Women of Brewster Place, Linden Hills*, and *Mama Day*, is the danger of assimilation. We ultimately have to be accepted within ourselves and not look to external sources of validation. The acceptance that comes from assimilation is fleeting; it is a Brewster Place, a dead end street leading nowhere. Ultimately, the women of Brewster Place had to find acceptance within themselves because they were cut off from the rest of the city. Johnson (1927), in his book, *The Autobiography of an Ex-Colored Man*, poignantly captured this notion of the danger of assimilation, suggesting that assimilation costs individuals an aspect of themselves. After the main character successfully assimilates into the White culture and society by passing as a White man, he finally reflects, ". . . I cannot repress the thought that, after all, I have chosen the lesser part, that I have sold my birthright for a mess of pottage" (Johnson, 1927, p. 211).

Utilization of literature about African American women's experiences might prove to be a useful resource in articulating clients' obstacles as well as their strengths. Indeed, Robinson (1983) stated that "[t]he psychological reality of Black women, expressed in poetry, blues lyrics, and novels, contains more sociohistorical data than is currently to be found in any psychology text" (p. 143). The potentially deleterious effects of contextual factors (e.g., racism and sexism) might be mitigated by identifying and encouraging use of effective coping strategies regarding anticipated barriers to career pursuits. Frameworks in which the counselor and African American women clients might discuss various cultural and contextual influences on their career process may emerge from stories read. Additionally, the client and counselor may identify and examine potential coping strategies for dealing with oppressive factors as exemplified by African American women characters in the stories. Counselors should read and be conversant about the readings prior to assigning them to clients. Counselors need to be aware of themes in the book and how they might uniquely relate to the life themes and experiences of each individual client. Boyd-Franklin (1991) summarized recurrent themes that often emerge in psychotherapy with African American women, many of which parallel themes identified in the aforementioned readings, and may be a useful reference in clinically processing such topics.

Possible Selves

Markus and Nurius (1986) introduced the concept of *possible selves* that "represent individuals' idea of what they might become, what they would like to become, and what they are afraid of becoming, and thus provide a conceptual link between cognition and motivation" (p. 954). Possible selves function both as incentives for future behavior and as evaluative contexts in which to view the current self. This concept advances an agentic view of the self when possible selves are elaborate and specific enough to guide an individual toward her desired future. Within a social cognitive framework, Markus & Nurius' concept of *possible selves* is viewed as distal life goals and subgoals required to realize distal aspirations. Self-appraisal capabilities (e.g., self-efficacy) combine with aspirations to shape life courses (Bandura, 1997). In this manner, people strive to realize their envisioned self (i.e., goals) via self-regulatory mechanisms to guide and motivate their efforts toward their desired end.

The generative aspect of self-referent thought, of which self-efficacy is an example, is rooted in the ability of such thought to activate cognitive, motivational, and affectional processes that govern the translation of knowledge and abilities into effective courses of action (Bandura, 1997). As such, possible selves serve as internal motivators for future behavior and evaluative standards for self-regulation.

Effective career assessment with African American women examines the experiences, skills, and aspirations that have contributed to their current career status. Additionally, the substance of their future career-related desires must be assessed in relation to the larger view of their future, possible selves. That is, how is their current career behavior related to their general future goals? Assessing desired possible selves also provides a gauge for the counselor of the client's level of motivation and the degree of elaboration (specificity) entailed in her plans for achieving future goals. Exploration of possible vocational selves may provide the African American woman client and her counselor with insight into unexplored career interests. For example, discussing desired future goals might highlight interest areas that have been ignored or stifled due to low self-efficacy perceptions of the likelihood of pursuing or succeeding in such interest areas. The counselor might then intervene to examine the foundational bases for these perceptions. Conversely, undesired selves, or unwanted futures and outcomes, are likely to provide knowledge about how and what courses of action to avoid in not fulfilling these outcomes.

Affirmation of Self

Wyche's (1993) examination of the applied psychology literature on African American women illustrates the limited understanding of their behavior and the subsequential tendency to characterize it as aberrant. African American women have been theoretically invisible in research and, therefore, there are gaps in counselors' understanding of African American womanhood. The constant employment of race-comparative frameworks and the use of the race–sex analogy (racial vs. sexual victimization) often pits them against White women and African American men, respectively. The result is that frequently African American women's lives are defined either by or in reference to these groups. While identifying strategies to resist oppressive factors and envision possible selves, the African American woman client must also be supported in her self-definition and self-determination, instead of constructing an identity based on what or who she is not. That is, the possible self must be promoted.

The effort to reconcile and coordinate their reality, talents, and dreams may produce several outcomes for African Americans. Washington (1981, as cited in Robinson, 1983) presented three potential types of women dealing with such demands: the *suspended woman*, characterized by severely limited perceived options, wrestling with external and internal pressure; the *assimilated woman*, who attempts to assimilate into the dominant culture and is, thus, alienated from her roots and culture; and the *emergent woman*, who possesses a new awareness of and confronts the issues of her reality. The latter type represents an African American woman who is beginning to affirm her own experience.

One activity directed at affirmation of self in African American women is the creation of a personal manifesto. A *manifesto* is a formal declaration of principles and intentions. It communicates plainly the guiding beliefs and motives of an individual or organization. African American women clients might benefit from the formal articulation of a personal manifesto in developing a creed for their life. The tenets of the personal manifesto might include some components of the possible self, declaring who she is and what she is becoming. The purpose of this activity is to encourage the African American woman client to declare and confirm who she is.

As discussed previously, clarity and elaborate articulation of future goals, or possible selves, contribute to the effective execution of subgoals needed to realize distal aspirations. In this sense, affirmation of self might also contribute to the motivation required to initiate behavior and persistence toward reaching desired outcomes. Examination of the clarity regarding who the client wants to be will likely yield information about the degree of confidence she possesses in achieving that possible self. Lent and Brown (1996) noted that strong self-efficacy generates interests, enhances positive attributions, and may also produce positive outcome expectations. Thus, African American women who feel affirmed in their sense of self might also feel more confident in their career-related pursuits, entertain a wider range of career options, and expect more positive outcomes from their career behavior.

Summary

These counseling strategies are consistent with the notion of *career consciousness*, a life career perspective that fosters clients' ability to visualize and plan their life careers in such a way that careers are located within the larger identity of the whole person. They promote the articulation of African American women's narratives in their own voice, while acknowledging potentially oppressive external factors. As Hackett and Byars (1996) argued, the experience and effects of racism must be explicitly addressed along with career-related self-efficacy and outcome expectations. By increasing client-generated knowledge, in contrast to counselor-given knowledge, counselors can foster internal motivation in African American women (Hendricks, 1994). In combination with other career interventions, these strategies aim to facilitate unexplored interests and strengthen self-efficacy beliefs related to career pursuits. The need to build relevant skills and bolster efficacy beliefs should not be ignored. Instructive modeling is key in promoting acquisition of new skills, as well as guided skill perfection to learn how to translate new skills into applied action. This process involves both coping models and abstract models. Once new skills have been acquired and an understanding of how to apply such skills is gained, one must be provided with an opportunity to actually implement and transfer the skills via self-directed success experiences.

CONCLUSION: REDEFINING THE INTERSECTION

Collins (1989) stated that groups who are unequal in power are also unequal in their access to necessary resources to "implement their perspectives outside their particular group" (p. 749). She argued, however, that oppressed groups can be stimulated to resist their domination by using self-defined standpoints. This is the essence of an affirmative career-counseling approach. African American women must be supported in identifying and articulating their worldview through their own voice in order to create and plan their life careers.

The knowledge-validation process articulated by Collins (1989) offers a context in which to facilitate the development of self-defined standpoints for African American women. Because all social thought reflects the interests and standpoints of its creator, knowledge claims about a given community "must be evaluated by a community of experts whose members represent the standpoints of the groups from which they originate" and that "community of experts must maintain its credibility as defined by the larger group in which it is situated and from which it draws its basic, taken-for-granted knowledge" (p. 752). For African American women, this process emphasizes connectedness rather than separation (i.e., impersonal procedures for establishing truth) in the evolution of knowledge claims usually developed via dialogues with other community members (Collins, 1989). The point is: Every idea has an owner and the owner's identity matters.

It is not enough that vocational psychology continues to explore new variables that might give rise to differential patterns of career behavior across groups and then incorporate these new data into existing epistemology. Such practices are often addressing the degree of cultural validity for a given theory or model and are natural outcomes of race comparative frameworks. Leong and Brown (1995) argued that, in addition to cultural validity issues, researchers must attend to the cultural specificity of career theories as well. This position is echoed by Collins (1989) who posited that the knowledge-validation process referred to in the preceding paragraph facilitates the rearticulation of a "preexisting Black women's standpoint" and "recentering the language of existing academic discourse to accommodate these knowledge claims" rather than merely integrating "Black female folk culture" into the substantiated body of academic knowledge (p. 762).

Many of the values of the dominant culture insidiously devalue African American women (Greene, 1997). Career theories and interventions often reflect these values. Effective career counseling necessitates the attention to and validation of their unique cultural experiences. African American women must be and be affirmed "in all ways a woman."

REFERENCES

African American education data book. (1998). Fairfax, VA: Frederick D. Patterson Research Institute.

Aldridge, D. (1989). African American women in the economic marketplace: A continuing struggle. *Journal of Black Studies, 20,* 129–154.

Angelou, M. (1993). *Wouldn't take nothing for my journey now* (pp. 5–7). New York: Random House.

Bandura, A. (1986). *Social foundations of thought and action: A social cognitive theory.* Englewood Cliffs, NJ: Prentice-Hall.

Bandura, A. (1997). *Self-efficacy: The exercise of control.* New York: Freeman.

Beale, F. (1972). Double jeopardy: To be Black and female. In T. Cade (Ed.), *The Black woman: An anthology* (pp. 90–100). New York: New American Library.

Bell, E. L. (1990). The bicultural life experience of career-oriented Black women. *Journal of Organizational Behavior, 11,* 459–477.

Bennett, L. (1982). *Before the mayflower.* New York: Penguin.

Betz, N. E. (1989). Implications of the null environment hypothesis for women's career development and for counseling psychology. *The Counseling Psychologist, 17,* 136–144.

Betz, N. E. (1992). Counseling uses of career self-efficacy theory. *Career Development Quarterly, 41,* 22–26.

Betz, N. E., & Hackett, G. (1997). Applications of self-efficacy theory to the career assessment of women. *Journal of Career Assessment, 5,* 383–402.

Bielby, W. T., & Baron, J. N. (1986). Men and women at work: Sex segregation and statistical discrimination. *American Journal of Sociology, 91,* 759–799.

Borgen, F. H. (1995). Leading edges of vocational psychology: Diversity and vitality. In W. B. Walsh & S. H. Osipow (Eds.), *Handbook of vocational psychology: Theory, research, and practice* (2nd ed., pp. 427–441). Mahwah, NJ: Lawrence Erlbaum Associates.

Bowman, S. L. (1995). Career intervention strategies and assessment issues for African Americans. In F. T. L. Leong (Ed.), *Career development and vocational behavior of racial and ethnic minorities* (pp. 137–164). Mahwah, NJ: Lawrence Erlbaum Associates.

Boyd-Franklin, N. (1991). Recurrent themes in the treatment of African American women in group psychotherapy. *Women and Therapy, 11,* 25–40.

Brookins, C. C., & Robinson, T. L. (1995). Rites of passage as resistance to oppression. *Western Journal of Black Studies, 19,* 172–180.

Byars, A. M. (1997). *Cultural influences on the career self-efficacy of African American college women.* Unpublished doctoral dissertation, Arizona State University, Tempe, AZ.

Carter, D. J., & Wilson, R. (1989). *Minorities in higher education,* Eighth Annual Status Report. Washington, DC: American Council on Education.

Cheatham, H. E. (1990). Africentricity and career development of African-Americans. *Career Development Quarterly, 38,* 334–346.

Collins, P. H. (1989). The social construction of Black feminist thought. *Signs: Journal of Women in Culture and Society, 14,* 745–773.

Crites, J. O. (1969). *Vocational psychology: The study of vocational behavior and development.* New York: McGraw-Hill.

Cross, W. E., Jr. (1971). Negro to Black conversion experience: Toward a psychology of Black liberation. *Black World, 20,* 13–27.

Davis, A. (1981). *Women, race, and class.* New York: Random House.

Erikson, E. (1976). The concept of identity in race relations: Notes and queries. In A. Dashefsky (Ed.), *Ethnic identity in society* (pp. 59–71). Chicago: Rand McNally. Reprinted from *Daedalus, 95,* 1996, 145–171.

Essed, P. (1991). *Understanding everyday racism: An interdisciplinary approach.* Newbury Park, CA: Sage.

Feagin, J. R. (1991). The continuing significance of race: Anti-Black discrimination in public places. *American Sociological Review, 56,* 101–116.

Fouad, N. A., & Bingham, R. P. (1995). Career counseling with racial and ethnic minorities. In W. B. Walsh & S. H. Osipow (Eds.), *Handbook of vocational psychology: Theory, research, and practice* (2nd ed., pp. 331–365). Mahwah, NJ: Lawrence Erlbaum Associates.

Gilkes, C. T. (1990). Liberated to work like dogs!: Labeling Black women and their work. In H. Y. Grossman & N. L. Chester (Eds.), *The experience and meaning of work in women's lives* (pp. 165–188). Hillsdale, NJ: Lawrence Erlbaum Associates.

Gilkes, C. T. (1994). "If it wasn't for the women . . .": African American women, community work, and social change. In M. B. Zinn & B. T. Dill (Eds.), *Women of color in U.S. society* (pp. 229–246). Philadelphia: Temple University Press.

Greene, B. A. (1990). Sturdy bridges: The role of African American mothers in the socialization of African American children. *Women and Therapy, 10*, 205–225.

Greene, B. A. (1997). Psychotherapy with African American women: Integrating feminist and psychodynamic models. *Smith College Studies in Social Work, 67*, 299–322.

Greene, B. M. (1997). Remembering as resistance in the literature of women of color. In L. Brannon & B. M. Greene (Eds.), *Rethinking american literature* (pp. 97–114). Urbana, IL: National Council of Teachers of English.

Greenhaus, J. H., Parasuraman, S., & Wormley, W. M. (1990). Effects of race on organizational experiences, job performance evaluations, and career outcomes. *Academy of Management Journal, 33*, 64–86.

Gysbers, N. C., Heppner, M. J., & Johnston, J. A. (1998). *Career counseling: Process, issues, and techniques*. Boston: Allyn & Bacon.

Hackett, G., & Betz, N. E. (1989). An exploration of the mathematics self-efficacy/mathematics performance correspondence. *Journal of Research in Mathematics Education, 20*, 261–273.

Hackett, G., & Byars, A. M. (1996). Social cognitive theory and the career development of African American women. *Career Development Quarterly, 44*, 322–340.

Harley, S. (1978). Northern Black female workers: Jacksonian era. In S. Harley & R. Terborg-Penn (Eds.), *The Afro-American woman: Struggles and images* (pp. 5–16). Port Washington, NY: Kennikat Press.

Helms, J. E. (1996). Toward a methodology for measuring and assessing racial as distinguished from ethnic identity. In G. R. Sodowsky & J. C. Impara (Eds.), *Multicultural assessment in counseling and clinical psychology* (pp. 143–192). Lincoln, NE: Buros Institute of Mental Measurements.

Helms, J. E., & Piper, R. E. (1994). Implications of racial identity theory for vocational psychology. *Journal of Vocational Behavior, 44*, 124–38.

Hendricks, F. M. (1994). Career counseling with African American college students. *Journal of Career Development, 21*, 117–126.

Higginbotham, E. (1994). Black professional women: Job ceilings and employment sectors. In M. B. Zinn & B. T. Dill (Eds.), *Women of color in U.S. society* (pp. 113–137). Philadelphia: Temple University Press.

Jewell, K. S. (1993). *From mammy to Miss America and beyond: Cultural images and the shaping of the U.S. social policy*. New York: Routledge & Kegan Paul.

Johnson, J. W. (1927). *The autobiography of an ex-colored man*. New York: Vintage Books.

King, D. K. (1988). Multiple jeopardy, multiple consciousness: The context of a Black feminist ideology. *Signs: Journal of Women in Culture and Society, 14*, 42–72.

Krumboltz, J. D., & Coon, D. W. (1995). Current professional issues in vocational psychology. In W. B. Walsh & S. H. Osipow (Eds.), *Handbook of vocational psychology: Theory, research, and practice* (2nd ed., pp. 391–426). Mahwah, NJ: Lawrence Erlbaum Associates.

Lent, R. W., & Brown, S. D. (1996). Social cognitive approach to career development: An overview. *Career Development Quarterly, 44*, 310–321.

Lent, R. W., Brown, S. D., & Hackett, G. (1994). Toward a unified social cognitive theory of career/academic interest, choice, and performance [Monograph]. *Journal of Vocational Behavior, 45*, 79–122.

Leong, F. T. L., & Brown, M. T. (1995). Theoretical issues in cross-cultural career development: Cultural validity and cultural specificity. In W. B. Walsh & S. H. Osipow (Eds.),

Handbook of vocational psychology: Theory, research, and practice (2nd ed., pp. 391–426). Mahwah, NJ: Lawrence Erlbaum Associates.

Malcolm, S. M., Hall, P. Q., & Brown, J. W. (1976). *The double bind: The price of being minority women in science*. Washington, DC: American Association for the Advancement of Science Report.

Manese, J. E., & Fretz, B. R. (1984, August). *Relationship between Black students' racial identity attitudes and vocational exploration*. Paper presented at the annual meeting of the American Psychological Association, Toronto.

Markus, H., & Nurius, P. (1986). Possible selves. *American Psychologist, 41*, 954–969.

McRae, M. B. (1990). Sex-role socialization and perception of opportunity structure: Impact on educational and occupational decisions of Black females. *Educational Considerations, 18*, 16–18.

Morrison, T. (1970). *The bluest eye*. New York: Holt, Rinehart and Winston.

Morrison, T. (1987). *Beloved*. New York: Knopf: Distributed by Random House.

Naylor, G. (1982). *The women of Brewster Place*. New York: Viking Press.

Naylor, G. (1985). *Linden Hills*. New York: Ticknor & Fields.

Naylor, G. (1988). *Mama Day*. New York: Ticknor & Fields.

Parham, T. A., & Austin, N. L. (1994). Career development and African Americans: A contextual reappraisal using the nigrescence construct. *Journal of Vocational Behavior, 44*, 139–154.

Parham, T. A., & Helms, J. E. (1985). Relation of racial identity attitudes to self-actualization and affective states of Black students. *Journal of Counseling Psychology, 32*, 431–440.

Ransford, H. E., & Miller, J. (1983). Race, sex, and feminist outlooks. *American Sociological Review, 48*, 46–59.

Robinson, C. R. (1983). Black women: A tradition of self-reliant strength. *Women and Therapy, 2*, 135–144.

Smith, E. J. (1981). The career development of young Black females: The forgotten group. *Youth and Society, 12*, 277–312.

Smith, E. J. (1983). Issues in racial minorities' career behavior. In W. B. Walsh & S. H. Osipow (Eds.), *Handbook of vocational psychology* (Vol. 1, pp. 161–222). Hillsdale, NJ: Lawrence Erlbaum Associates.

Smith, E. J. (1989). Black racial identity development: Issues and concerns. *The Counseling Psychologist, 17*, 277–288.

Sokoloff, N. J. (1992). *Black women and White women in the professions: Occupational segregation by race and gender, 1960–1980*. New York: Routledge & Kegan Paul.

Stubbins, J. (1973). Social context of college counseling. In C. Warnath (Ed.), *New directions for college counselors* (pp. 21–46). San Francisco: Jossey-Bass.

Sue, D. W., Parham, T. A., & Santiago, G. B. (1998). The changing face of work in the United States: Implications for individual, institutional, and societal survival. *Cultural Diversity and Mental Health, 4*, 153–164.

Taeuber, C. M. (Ed.). (1991). *Statistical handbook of women in America*. Phoenix, AZ: Oryx Press.

Thomas, V. G. (1986). Career aspirations, parental support and work values among Black female adolescents. *Journal of Multicultural Counseling and Development, 14*, 177–185.

U.S. Bureau of the Census (1992). *Statistical Abstract of the United States* (112th ed.). Washington, DC: U.S. Department of Commerce.

U.S. Department of Education (1998a). Table 8.—Years of school completed by persons age 25 and over and 25 to 29, by race/ethnicity and sex: 1910 to 1996. In *Digest of education statistics*. Washington, DC: National Center for Education Statistics.

U.S. Department of Education (1998b). Table 266.—Bachelor's degrees conferred by institutions of higher education, by racial/ethnic group, major field of study, and sex of student: 1994–95. In *Digest of education statistics*. Washington, DC: National Center for Education Statistics.

Walker, A. (1982). *The color purple*. New York: Harcourt Brace Jovanovich.

Wyche, K. F. (1993). Psychology and African American women: Findings from applied research. *Applied and Preventive Psychology, 2*, 115–121.

Zinn, M. B., & Dill, B. T. (1994). *Women of color in U.S. society*. Philadelphia: Temple University Press.

Career Counseling With African Americans in Nontraditional Career Fields

Angela M. Hargrow
University of North Carolina

Fredericka Hendricks
Loyola Marymount University

It has been predicted that in the 21st century, one third of the U.S. workforce will be comprised of racial ethnic minorities (Bingham & Ward, 1994). The workforce of the future is expected to open new doors to women and minority groups (Shields & Shields, 1993). It is estimated that 26% of the new workforce will be minorities. During the past 10 years, the largest job sources for African American men and women have been in blue-collar, service-sector occupations. These occupations have been considered *traditional* in that the percentage of African Americans represented in that occupational field is at or above their percentage level in the general population. A *nontraditional* career field is one in which there is an underrepresentation of individuals on the basis of race and/or gender (this is defined in depth later in the chapter). For instance, nursing is an example of a nontraditional career field for African American men.

The labor statistics show that African American women typically occupy positions as secretaries, nursing aids, cooks, cashiers, retail-sales workers, elementary school teachers, cleaners, and janitors. Except for elementary schoolteachers, these occupations require little training or skills, offer low pay, demand little work experience, and offer less chances for advancement. In 1996, the largest sources of jobs for African American men were in fields such as correctional officers, security guards, cooks, motor vehicle operators (e.g., bus drivers, truck drivers, etc.), janitors, laborers, grounds keepers, and mechanics (U.S. Department of Labor, 1997).

In 1990, women held 2.5% of the most well-paying jobs such as professors, scientists, engineers, lawyers, physicians, registered nurses, and managers in marketing, public relations, and advertising. Sadly, African American women only made up 6.6% of these women (U.S. Department of Labor, 1996). Examining labor statistics in 1996, it was found that women held 49% of the managerial and professional jobs, yet, African American women only comprised 9% of these women (U.S. Department of Labor, 1997). Again, using 1996 labor data, it was found that men held 51% of the most well-paying jobs in the United States and African American men only comprised 5.8% of these men (U.S. Department of Labor, 1997).

Bowman (1993) suggested that many African Americans perceive that a given occupation is open or closed to them. Self-selection into or out of occupations is often based on racial stereotypes and information about discrimination in the workplace (Betz, 1994). Researchers (Betz, 1990; Bowman, 1993; Parham & Austin, 1994) believed that African Americans select occupations with which they are familiar and to which they have had exposure from members of their community. These occupations are usually of a working-class or service nature (Bowman, 1995).

The research on African Americans in nontraditional fields is scarce. To date, most of the research focused on White women, with a spattering of attention given to the experiences of White men in nontraditional fields. However, researchers have been remiss in examining African American men and women in nontraditional occupations. In particular, there is a paucity of information pertaining to African American men in nontraditional career fields. Therefore, we must alert the readers of this chapter to the fact that much of the information presented in this chapter is based on the research of African American women in nontraditional fields, the experiences of African American men and women the authors have seen in career counseling, the authors' personal experiences as African American women, and when possible, we extrapolated from the small body of literature available on African American males in nontraditional career fields.

In this chapter, the process of career counseling with African Americans in nontraditional occupations is examined. This chapter is organized into four sections. First, a brief historical overview of African American career choice and what it means to be an African American man or woman in a nontraditional career field is provided. Also in this section, factors that may impact nontraditional occupational choices are explored. Second, specific career-counseling issues that pertain to being an African American in a nontraditional field are examined. Third, career-counseling strategies and interventions to consider when counseling African Americans in (or for) nontraditional career fields are described. Fourth, the reader is provided with a list of resources and professional organizations that may be useful when working with African American clients in non-traditional occupations.

HISTORICAL OVERVIEW OF TRADITIONAL CAREER FIELDS

Defining what it means to be in a traditional or nontraditional occupation for African Americans can be somewhat of a unique issue, given American's history of slave labor and indenturement. Therefore, it is important to briefly review historical antecedents that have had an impact on the career choices of African Americans in the United States. In particular, the lack of access to the educational system for African Americans prior to the Civil War and the subsequent impact of educational opportunities made available after the Civil War for career advancement is examined.

In 1740, teaching slaves to read and write was made illegal in most Southern states (Noble, 1956). After several slave revolts by literate African Americans, every Southern state prohibited the education of African Americans, free or slave (Perkins, 1988). African Americans in the postbellum years were interested in the elevation of the race. The philosophy of race uplift by means of education became important after emancipation. In 1870, the Fifteenth Amendment granted franchise to African American men and the first gender split between the race appeared. During the 1880s, a conservative view of the African American woman's role appeared. African American publications began to emphasize the woman's domestic duties and her role as wife and mother. In 1890, only 30 Black women attained a bachelor's degree (Bowles & DeCosta, 1971). Between 1865 and 1900 several Black colleges were established in the South. Religious ideology and philanthropic enthusiasm were critical factors in the promotion of higher education for African Americans during this time period. Most Negro education was characterized by a belief in the moral and intellectual inferiority of African American people. As a result of these beliefs, many advocates of African American education emphasized the fields of teaching and ministry as a way for African Americans to gain respectability and religiosity.

The enactment of Black codes[1] in the South directly affected the educational policy and career choices of African Americans. A liberal education trend for African Americans was diverted by the founder of the

---

[1]*Black codes* were state laws created in the Southern United States to control the activities of African Americans after the American Civil War. These codes varied in severity and often restricted the civil rights of African Americans. One such code allowed African Americans to only work as farmers or domestic servants (*World Book*, 1997).

Hampton Institute, General S. C. Armstrong. Armstrong was considered an expert in the area of Negro education. He believed that Black men and women were educable, but inferior (Simpson, 1984). Armstrong was a proponent of industrial education for African Americans. He maintained that "Negroes should be trained in a manner consistent with their position in American life" (Bullock, 1970, p. 77). Booker T. Washington propelled Armstrong's concept of industrial education to the forefront of African American educational policy. Washington became the first major fundraiser for Black colleges. Philanthropic funds were given to those institutions that supported Washington's ideological position on education for African Americans (Simpson, 1984). Washington believed that African Americans should enter social service professions that would cater to the needs of the Black community (Bullock, 1970).

W. E. DuBois, on the other hand, advocated a liberal education as a means of uplifting the race. Black women generally supported DuBois' argument. African American women who attended college, typically studied homemaking or prepared to become teachers (Noble, 1956). Today, African Americans are found to be heavily concentrated in social service professions. Kimball (1971) found that African Americans tend to choose social-service occupations more often than do Whites. Perhaps this is a carryover effect from both Washington and DuBois' educational ideologies—serve the community as well as uplift the race.

The 1960s social and political climate advanced occupational training and provided opportunities for women and minorities via education. It was during this period that the federal government enacted several laws to combat discriminatory procedures and practices in higher education: The 1964 Civil Rights Act, which prohibited discrimination based on color, race, religion, or national origin, was enacted. In 1965, the Higher Education Act established the Educational Opportunity Grant and the Guaranteed Student Loan Program, which helped many minority students through the educational pipeline. The 1965 affirmative action Executive Order 11246, the 1967 Executive Order 11375, which prohibited discrimination based on sex, and Title IX of the 1972 Education Act amendments, which prohibited sexual discrimination in any program assisted by the Federal government, would be instrumental in helping to protect African Americans seeking to enter nontraditional occupations.

Since the time of slavery, African Americans traditionally worked in service-related fields. By the late 1800s, education became important to uplifting the African American race. Schools and colleges were educating African Americans in social-service occupations such as teaching, medicine, and social work. The political climate of the 1960s ushered in new educational and occupational opportunities for women and men. The federal laws enacted during this time allowed many people to seek career opportunities in areas previously denied to them. These changes opened doors for African Americans to consider nontraditional fields as new avenues for occupational growth.

Defining What It Means to Be an African American in a Nontraditional Field

Occupations that have less than 30% of the same-sex workers are considered nontraditional for gender categories (Chusmir, 1990). Occupations where African American women constitute less than 25% of the total employed are considered nontraditional career fields (U.S. Department of Labor, 1996). There is a total of 126,708 million people who are over the age of 16 and who work in the United States. African Americans constitute 10.7% (13,542 million) of the total workforce (U.S. Department of Labor, 1997). Therefore, *nontraditional fields* for African Americans are defined as those fields where African Americans make up less than 30% of the total African American workforce (in that field). Historically, nontraditional fields for African Americans have been in the areas of science, math, and engineering. These are fields that have required education beyond high school diplomas.

In 1995, professional African American women were employed mostly as registered nurses, elementary schoolteachers, social workers, accountants and auditors, and prekindergarten or kindergarten teachers (U.S. Department of Labor, 1996). However, the greatest number of women (i.e., 2.7 million) worked in technical, sales and administrative support occupations. There was almost twice the number of African American women in administrative support jobs as there were in technical and sales jobs combined (U.S. Department of Labor, 1996). Most service occupations are dominated by women and are considered traditional jobs for women. A total of 1.7 million African American women worked in service occupations in 1995.

The exception to these service positions are protective service occupations that include police and detectives, guards, and firefighters. These three service occupations are considered nontraditional occupations for African American women because they constitute 25% or less of the total employed (U.S. Department of Labor, 1996). Burlew (1982) considered *nontraditional fields* to be those that are usually defined as masculine. She identified lawyers, doctors, nonhealth technical professions, engineers, and physical and social sciences as nontraditional fields for African American women. Other nontraditional occupations for African America women include the occupational groups of precision production, craft, and repair, as well as farming, forestry, and fishing (U.S. Department of Labor, 1996).

In 1996, African American men were mostly employed in service occupations such as security guards, janitors, cooks, and motor vehicle operators (U.S. Department of Labor, 1997). African American males held less than 1% of jobs in the managerial and professional specialty occupations in 1996. No clear data exists on which specific occupations represent nontraditional fields for African American men. The top four nontraditional occupations for men include social work, nursing, elementary school teaching, and office work (Chusmir, 1990). Men held less than 32% of the aforementioned positions, whereas African American men makeup 23% or less of these men (U.S. Department of Labor, 1997). This is in sharp contrast to White males who held 51% of jobs in these occupations. Other nontraditional occupations for men include librarians, child-care workers, service workers, hair dressers, and retail-store clerks (Chusmir, 1990; Williams, 1992).

The literature documented several factors (e.g., family and educational background, personal characteristics, and support for professional growth) that may affect the choice of a nontraditional occupation (Burlew, 1982; Chusmir, 1983; Chusmir, 1990; Murrell, Frieze, & Frost, 1991; Padavic, 1991; Thomas, 1983; Van Buren, Kelly, & Hall, 1993). However, there has been little attempt to investigate how these factors work together to influence the choice of nontraditional careers for African American men and women. Jones (1991) outlined an interactive model for therapists that aids in understanding the psychological functioning of the African American psychotherapy client. His model consists of four factors that may influence how the individual operates in the world: *Reactions to Racial Oppression*, *Influence of African-American Culture*, *Influence of Majority Culture*, and *Personal Experiences and Endowments*.

It is believed that a similar class of variables also impacts the African American career client and should be recognized and explored by the career counselor. Therefore, Jones' (1991) original model has been expanded and modified to reflect the concerns of an African American in a nontraditional career field: *Racial–Sexual Discrimination in the Work Environment, Influence of African American Culture, Influence of Institutional–Organizational Culture, Personal Career Experiences*. Under each main factor, (except for the Racial–Sexual Discrimination factor, which is discussed separately later in the chapter) we listed examples of variables that may be subsumed under that factor (see Fig. 7.1). For an example, under *Influence of Institutional–Organizational Culture*, variables to consider are barriers and internal support structures. Barriers that may hinder occupational growth are examined in a later section of this chapter.

Support for professional growth plays a critical role in the choice and maintenance of a nontraditional career field. Therefore, another variable under *Influence of Institutional–Organizational Culture* has to do with men-

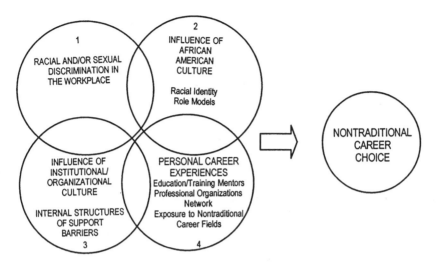

FIG. 7.1.   Interactive model of factors influencing the choice of a nontraditional career.

toring. Research on men in female professions suggested that men are often mentored and encouraged to pursue their nontraditional career by other males in positions of power in that field (i.e., Deans of graduate programs, graduate professors, supervisors, etc.; Williams, 1992). Often, women in nontraditional careers are mentored by men because so few woman exist as role models.

Variables related to the *Influence of African American Culture* include racial identity, role modeling, and exposure to nontraditional careers. Savenye (1990) found positive attitudes by ninth graders were related to their exposure to men and women in nontraditional career fields. Mau, Domnick, and Ellworth (1995) suggested that role models are important to facilitating nontraditional career choices for females. Malcolm (cf., Burlew, 1982) reported that African American women in nontraditional fields emphasized the importance of role models in their development. Relatedly, Sandberg et al. (1987) found that women who aspired to nontraditional careers received a high level of support from parents. A framework for men who make nontraditional career choices created by Chusmir (1990) took into account familial and societal influences.

Education, which is a variable to consider under *Personal Career Experiences* has been a critical factor in the career development of women. Specifically related to nontraditional career fields, Rubenfeld and Gilroy (1991) found that women in their study, who had attended all female high schools, showed more interest in nontraditional career fields than did women who attended coeducational high schools. In a study by Burlew

(1982), African American college women, who aspired to careers that were dominated by males, were found more likely to have mothers who worked outside the home and were more educated. Additionally, women in the study held less traditional sex-role beliefs, had personal work experience, and expressed a great deal of confidence in their career plans. In their study of African American college women, Murrell et al. (1991) found that the women who aspired to careers in male-dominated professions maintained higher educational and career expectations than did women planning careers in female-dominated professions.

As depicted in the model, various factors interact with each other in a dynamic manner to influence the choice of a nontraditional occupation. At any given point in time, one factor may influence an individual's choice more heavily than another. This model allows the career counselor to explore each factor separately as well as collectively. It also allows the unique history of the individual to be examined. Jones (1991) reminded counselors to remember that there are "substantial individual differences with respect to the relative degrees of influence of each of the four factors" (p. 585). Therein lies the beauty of the model; no one factor is responsible for the individual's nontraditional career choice. In this chapter, all the possible variables that influence individuals choosing a nontraditional occupation have not yet been exhausted. Thus far, the most researched variables and issues have been discussed and briefly highlighted; these have been found to impact the choice of a nontraditional career.

ISSUES IN CAREER COUNSELING WITH AFRICAN AMERICANS IN NONTRADITIONAL FIELDS

Career Issues Concerning Being One of Only a Few in the Field

Several issues are particularly relevant when counseling African Americans in nontraditional fields. The first issue is related to being one of only a few in a field. Many people who enter nontraditional fields often see themselves as tokens, feel very isolated, and experience role conflicts. The next areas of concern have to do with the stress from living biculturally and managing workplace barriers. Counselors who have a clear understanding of these issues can be helpful to persons considering nontraditional fields or those who are currently employed in nontraditional occupations.

Kanter defined *token individuals* as those persons who are treated as representations of their particular categories (i.e., women, African Americans) rather than as individuals (cf., Heikes, 1991). She found tokenism was associated with several conditions. First, is pressure to perform as the result of high visibility, which causes either overachievement or underachievement. The second condition results in group polarization because members of the dominant group perceive characteristics of the token to be very salient even if those characteristics do not impact job performance.

The final condition Kanter (Heikes, 1991) attributes to tokenism states that individual characteristics of the token are perceived to represent the dominant group's existing stereotypes. When the dominant group adopts these stereotypes, the only behaviors that are acceptable are those that fit the stereotype. These beliefs often result in role entrapment for the token individual. One example of tokenism is being placed in a symbolic role. A *symbolic role* is a role in which employers use race or gender to demonstrate to outsiders that they have a diverse workplace. African Americans in nontraditional fields may be placed in symbolic roles that exclude them from exercising any real power or making critical decisions (Graham, 1995).

Men who hold token status often describe experiences that differ significantly from women who hold token statuses (Heikes, 1991). Several men in a study conducted by Williams (1992) perceived their token status in several nontraditional fields (e.g., nursing, librarians, social workers, and elementary teachers) to be an advantage in hiring and promotions. Many others saw their token status as a disadvantage because it caused them to be tracked into practice areas within their professions. This tracking effect tends to push men into specialty areas that are thought to be more appropriate areas for men. At the same time, these areas are often the jobs that are higher paying and considered more prestigious. Williams (1992) contrasted this with the glass-ceiling effect for women and calls it the glass escalator for men. However, racism may cause African American men to have a short ride on the glass escalator.

Isolation is one of the major concerns for African Americans in nontraditional career fields. Researchers found that a sense of *isolation*—or being the only one—can effect job performance, morale, and self-confidence (Hendricks, 1996; Malcolm et al., 1976; Roche, 1979). Peterson (1990) found that isolation is one of the more salient concerns for African American women faculty. As can be expected, lack of support and mentorship increase feelings of isolation for African American women (Moses, 1989; Reid, 1990; Wilson, 1989). Minority men in William's study (1992) felt least comfortable with their coworkers in social settings. They felt their female coworkers (especially, if their coworkers were White) accepted them at work, but were uncomfortable associating with them outside of work.

Some African Americans in nontraditional fields experience isolation not only within their respective fields, but also from other African American organizations. This is the case with African American Economists (Ruffins, 1996). According to the 1996 Current Population Statistics, African Americans make up 3.9% of all economists. However, only approximately

1.2% have earned a Ph.D. (Ruffins, 1996). Many of these economists feel they are often left out of gatherings designed to address the economic state of Black America. This isolation leads many African American economists to speculate on why another African American would look to earning a Ph.D. in economics (Ruffins, 1996).

African Americans can expect role conflict or strain whenever they combine family and work roles (Carey, 1990). However, most family obligations continue to be the responsibility of the woman (Carey, 1990), regardless of her employment status. Women in nontraditional fields appear to have a disadvantage in that these jobs are traditionally male dominated and geared toward a lifestyle where men are not primary caretakers (cf., Burlew & Johnson, 1992). Male-dominated occupations call for long-term commitments and have more time demands than do traditional female occupations (Hayes, 1986). Given this belief, it is commonly believed that woman experience more role strain than do men.

Murrell et al. (1991) found that due to socialization, African American female college students felt that there would be less conflict between career and family roles. However, Burlew and Johnson (1992) studied role conflict among African American females who were working in traditional and nontraditional fields. The results indicated that women in nontraditional fields experienced more marital discord that was not related to the number of children they had or whether their husband had as much education as they had. They concluded that marital discord was related to the combined effects of stress from work and home life. These findings indicate that African American women who aspire to nontraditional fields do not feel they will experience role conflict. However, when in the field, they actually experience more stress than expected as it relates to working and being married.

Men tend to experience role strain that surrounds their identity as men. Society does not expect to see a man in a traditionally female occupation. These societal expectations may cause the man to feel self-conscious because his identity as a man is constantly being questioned (Hayes, 1986). African American men may experience more role strain when working in female-dominated fields because of gender stereotypes and prejudicial attitudes about men in traditionally feminine occupations. Relatedly, because the man is in a typically female occupation, his monetary earnings may reflect this occupational status. Hence, he may not be the major breadwinner of the family, thereby leading him to question his traditional masculine role. Unfortunately, American society has socialized men (and women, to some extent) to believe that a man's masculinity is measured by the size of his paycheck (Doyle, 1989; Keen, 1991).

A different type of role conflict or strain has to do with one's responsibility to the African American community. Many African Americans value affiliation, collectivity (Cheatham, 1990), and working to better their community. Often, African Americans have interests in advancing their respective fields and also of helping the African American community. When combined, these ideals can pose problems for many African Americans who feel like their work on African American issues are not respected by Whites in power. They feel shunned by their colleagues for doing work on what is seen as irrelevant issues. They report difficulty publishing in journals that represent their field of interest (Ruffins, 1996). Academicians state that their interest in African American issues can interfere with the tenure process (Hendricks, 1996). The lack of value and consideration of African American issues leads to a conflict around one's identity as an African American and as a member of one's field.

African Americans working in nontraditional fields are like pioneers exploring new territory. As a result of these new positions, they often adapt a bicultural lifestyle where they must negotiate working in the White world and living in the African American community (Bell, 1990). African Americans who are bicultural can hold on to their African roots without totally assimilating into White culture. It is a process of keeping both lives separate. This concept is called *biculturalism* and was coined by Bell (1990) in her research with African American women. However, there is evidence that suggests that African American males also experience the split between working within the White culture and living in their respective Black communities.

Sources of Stress

The duality of biculturalism can be a source of problems for many African Americans. The women in Bell's (1990) study described feeling *marginal*, or like they were existing on the borders of both groups. Many felt like they had to work hard to maintain their allegiance to their cultural group, while working twice as hard to fit in with their White coworkers. They felt they were always on guard and that they must perform twice as well as their White counterparts. African Americans who hold more conservative views often feel shunned by more liberal African Americans for holding views that are perceived as similar to views held by their White coworkers. This often leads to personal attacks and a label as an *Uncle Tom* (Ruffins, 1996). An identity conflict can arise when African Americans have strong personal and emotional commitments to two groups that are incompatible. This happens when a person feels the pressure to suppress one of their cultural identities in order to fit in with the other cultural group. This suppression of a cultural identity causes frustration and internal role conflicts (Bell, 1990).

One way in which African Americans manage their bicultural identity is to compartmentalize their relationships (cf., Bell, 1990). This allows them to maintain their cultural identity and reduces the stress of living biculturally. *Compartmentalization* occurs when they create strict boundaries between the White and Black aspects of their lives (Bell, 1990). Problems arise when the boundaries between work life and supportive relationships that exist in the African American community, are far apart. This can cause feelings of isolation and alienation. An additional source of stress can arise from members of one's home community, who may believe that African Americans working in predominantly White settings are loosing their Blackness and assimilating into White culture. This is evident in Washington's article (Washington, 1996); he wrote about his promotion into a management position. He found that his promotion required him to give up his baggy clothes and Afrocentric t-shirts to wear a suit and tie. As a result, he began to feel uncomfortable walking through his neighborhood because the people who once said hello as he passed now looked at him with suspicion. He wrote:

> My feelings were as mixed as my neighborhood. I enjoyed my new job and my new clothes, but I felt as though I had sacrificed an essential part of myself to get them. I feared that I would become out of touch with the kind of neighborhoods I had always lived in. I wondered if it was possible to keep one foot in the boardroom and another on the street corner. (Washington, 1996, p. 88)

African American men and women may encounter various barriers related to their occupational choice. These various barriers may be related to occupational advancement, workplace culture, compensatory benefits, or professional relationships. Confronting barriers in any of these categories can be a source of stress and lead to dissatisfaction with an occupational choice. Barriers that have been reported by African American women include race discrimination, lack of financial resources, sex discrimination, marital conflict, and perceived lack of professional support (Hendricks, 1996; Herr & Cramer, 1996). Researchers found that African American women in occupations, such as medicine, law, and engineering, report more barriers related to their career choice than do African American women in more traditional professions such as teaching or social work (Herr & Cramer, 1996). There is little empirical data on barriers experienced in nontraditional fields by African American men. However, Heikes (1991) contended that masculine-type characteristics—strength, emulousness, assertiveness—exhibited by males in a female-dominated profession, such as nursing, may become barriers.

Hayes (1986) wrote, "Societal occupational discrimination can be a function of historically entrenched norms surrounding sex roles" (p. 92). African Americans in nontraditional fields experience both racial and sexual discrimination (Mansfield et al., 1991; Martin, 1994; Simpson, 1984; Swerdlow, 1989). Negative stereotypes exist for both women and men who enter nontraditional fields (Pfost & Fiore, 1990). Men may feel that women are not able to handle work that has traditionally been done by men (Mansfield et al., 1991) or that the woman who desires to work in male-dominated fields are not behaving like women are supposed to behave. Men in traditionally female occupations are often thought to be wimpy, gay, feminine, passive, or that something must be wrong with them (Hayes, 1986; Williams, 1992). These stereotypes often result in lowered self-esteem and doubt as to why someone would enter the field (Williams, 1992).

Together, workplace racism and sexism can have additive effects (Smith & Stewart, 1983). The combined effects of racism and sexism can cause African American women to experience racial and sexual harassment (Hall, 1982; Simpson, 1984), tokenism, and gender-role stereotypes (Betz, 1994). Feelings of mistrust, anger, resentment may be experienced by African Americans due to oppressive situations that allow them to be subjected to affirmative action accusations, persistent stereotypes, and negative misconceptions about their work behaviors (Jenkins, 1985).

Differential pay scales impact the choice of nontraditional careers. Nontraditional fields for women tend to be male-dominated fields, therefore, women in nontraditional fields often report better pay and opportunities for advancement (Williams, 1992). Women are often encouraged to enter nontraditional fields for higher psychological and monetary rewards as well as to increase their representation in male-dominated occupations (Hayes, 1986). However, Terberg (cited in Hammer-Higgins & Atwood, 1989) found that women managers tend to occupy positions with lower status, lower pay, and had fewer opportunities for advancement within their fields. Nontraditional jobs for men tend to be female-dominated jobs and are associated with low pay, less status, and are less valued (Chusmir, 1983, 1990; Hayes, 1986; Williams, 1992). Often, men are viewed as absurd for entering female-dominated fields because those positions are less respected (Hayes, 1986; Williams, 1992). Furthermore, African Americans have historically been paid less than White Americans. Therefore, it may be even more frustrating for African American men to chose female-dominated fields because of the promise of lower wages.

CAREER COUNSELING STRATEGIES AND INTERVENTIONS FOR AFRICAN AMERICANS IN NONTRADITIONAL FIELDS

Advising Students and Adults Considering Nontraditional Fields

As with most life choices, the decision to pursue a nontraditional occupation can be weighed in terms of costs and benefits. Naturally, there will be individual variability in satisfaction with career choice. Counselors can be very helpful to students and adults contemplating careers in nontraditional fields. As long as career counselors are aware of these possible costs to African Americans making nontraditional career choices, they will be able to present realistic information to their clients. Although there are positive consequences to a choice of a nontraditional field, it will be essential to make students and adults aware of the negative consequences (Hayes, 1986). Both men and women need to be cognizant of the barriers associated with entering nontraditional fields such as attitudes around traditional sex-role behaviors, discrimination during the job application stage, stereotypes, and differential pay and opportunities for advancement. Many of these costs were delineated in the previous section (e.g., stress, isolation, tokenism, role conflict).

Clients should be cautioned that when they make certain career and behavioral choices, there may be negative consequences or negative roles associated with those choices. For instance, Graham (1995) contended that some African American professionals in corporate America relinquished their racial identity and sacrificed personal integrity in order to be successful in the White business world. Furthermore, many of the negative consequences are related to factors that decrease job satisfaction such as low status, low pay, problems with coworkers, and homophobia (Hayes, 1986).

There are several benefits for persons seeking to enter nontraditional career fields. However, these benefits differ based on gender. Hayes (1986) listed four reasons he felt men would enter female-dominated occupations: freedom of options and dual-earner roles; pursuit of personal abilities and self-fulfillment; stability and upward mobility; and interaction with the opposite sex. African American men may value helping and giving back to the community and many nontraditional fields for men include occupations (i.e., teaching, nursing) that would allow them to satisfy those values. Reasons cited as benefits for women entering into nontraditional fields have to do with increased pay, more prestige, opportunities for advancement, and higher status (Chusmir, 1990; Murrell et al., 1991; Williams, 1992). Additionally, counselors can emphasize the continued growth of such nontraditional fields as information technology and entrepreneualism.

Equally important is for counselors to have knowledge of traditional career theory as well as career-development models that account for the African American experience (see Cheatham, 1990). This knowledge allows them to utilize both traditional and nontraditional counseling interventions and strategies. Counselors can help clients review organizational structure, policies, and hiring practices. For example, a potential African American employee may want to investigate how many African Americans were promoted, demoted, or resigned in a given year. Counselors can help clients learn about the organization's or institution's internal structures that support occupational advancement and how equitable that structure has been for African Americans. Counselors can help clients ask questions that may be important philosophically or socially to African American clients such as: Does your company promote or sponsor educational initiatives aimed at fostering the career growth and development of African Americans (i.e., corporate revenues given to the United Negro College Fund, UNCF, or minority summer programs for high school or college students)?

Counselors need to help clients identify ways of surviving unpleasant racial experiences that may occur. African American women have been found to have high aspirations, but low expectations, for fulfilling their career goals due to the perception of racism and sexism (Evans & Herr, 1991). Therefore, coconstructing viable options empowers clients to be proactive and deliberate in their choices. According to Jones (1991), maladjustment can occur when African Americans are cognitively rigid and unable to explore multiple options when reacting to racial discrimination. Counselors can work with students and adults to develop strategies for overcoming many of the barriers associated with their nontraditional career choice (Hammer-Higgins & Atwood, 1989). Students and adults can benefit from materials or discussions around sexism and how past sex-role socialization can restrict a person's options and experiences (Pfost & Fiore, 1990). Furthermore, increased exposure to persons currently working in a nontraditional field can serve as role models and/or mentors (Chusmir, 1990).

Conclusion and Future Directions

In this chapter, some of the issues counselors will need to address when they are working with African American men and women in nontraditional career fields have been identified and highlighted. The information presented in this chapter has only begun to scratch the surface of the needs and concerns of this unique population. Therefore, several areas are in need of further exploration. First, more research needs to focus on African American males in nontraditional occupations. The number of men in nontraditional fields is small. The empirical research presented in this chapter, with a few exceptions, used a limited sample group—women. Hence, we need to be cautious in the way we conceptualize the African American male in a nontraditional occupation, in order to avoid broad generalizations. Second, work needs to be done that will investigate the career planning and guidance of African American youth. Preparation for many of the nontraditional fields discussed in this chapter needs to begin in elementary school. Early exposure to nontraditional career fields through positive role models or programmed career interventions (i.e., summer math and science camps) will encourage young students to pursue and prepare for a nontraditional career. Third, several of the factors that influence the choice of a nontraditional career could be examined in depth with a broad sample of men and women. Finally, exploration into the role of mentors and support networks could help our understanding of factors that facilitate the retention of African Americans in nontraditional fields.

We hope that counselors armed with the information presented in this chapter are in a better position to help African Americans in nontraditional fields. If a counselor has an awareness of these issues, career counseling and planning will be more effective, nonrestrictive, and relevant to the needs of the African American career client.

RESOURCES AND PROFESSIONAL ORGANIZATIONS FOR AFRICAN AMERICANS IN NON-TRADITIONAL FIELDS

The following is a list of organizations and websites that pertain to African Americans. The resources are listed by broad occupational categories. Please keep in mind that websites are continually being added and new organizations formed, so this list is by no means exhaustive.

Academe
Association of Black Anthropologists
4350 N. Fairfax Drive, Ste. 640
Arlington, VA 22203
703-528-1902

Association of Black Sociologists
c/o Robert G. Newby
Dept. of Sociology
Central Michigan University
Mt. Pleasant, MI 48859
517-774-3160
ABSLST-L@cmuvm.cmich.edu

National Association of Black
   Professors
PO Box 526
Crisfield, MD 21817
410-968-2393

National Conference of Black
   Political Scientists
c/o Franklin D. Jones
Dept. of Public Affairs
Texas Southern University
Houston, TX 77045
404-656-0763

National Congress of Black Faculty
PO Box 526
Crisfield, MD 21817
410-968-2393

Aviation
National Black Coalition of Federal
   Aviation Employees
Washington Headquarters
PO Box 44392
Washington, DC 20026-4392
202-267-7911

Negro Airmen International
PO Box 1340
Tuskegee, AL 36087
205-727-0721

Organization of Black Airline Pilots
PO Box 5793
Englewood, NJ 07631
201-568-8145

Business/Finance/Banking
National Black MBA Association
180 North Michigan Avenue, Ste. 1515
Chicago, IL 60601
312-236-2622

National Association of Black
  Accountants
7249A Hanover Parkway
Greenbelt, MD 20770
301-474-6222

National Association of Minority
  Women in Business
906 Grand Avenue, Ste. 200
Kansas City, MO 64106
816-421-3335

National Association of Negro
  Business and Professional
  Women's Clubs
1806 New Hampshire Avenue, NW
Washington, DC 20009
202-483-4206

National Association of Urban
  Bankers
1010 Wayne Avenue, Ste. 1210
Silver Spring, MD 20910
301-589-2141

National Bankers Association
1802 T. Street, NW
Washington, DC 20009
202-588-5432

Entrepreneur
National Association of Black
  Women Entrepreneurs Inc.
PO Box 1375
Detroit, MI 48231
810-356-3686

Association of Black Women
  Entrepreneurs
Box 49368
Los Angeles, CA 90049
213-624-8639

National Council of Negro Women
  Inc.
633 Pennsylvania Avenue, NW
Washington, DC 20004
202-737-0120

National Association of Women
  Business Owners

1100 Wayne Ave., Suite 830
Silver Spring, MD 20910
301-608-2590

National Association for Female
  Executives
30 Irving Place, 5th Floor
New York, NY 10003
212-477-2200

The Small Business Resource Center
http://www.webcom.com/seaquest/sbrc/
welcome.htmlEntrprenet
http://www.enterprise.org

Engineering
National Society of Blacks in
  Engineering (NSBE)
1454 Duke Street
Alexandria, VA 22313-5588
703-549-2207
http://www.nsbe.org/

National Association of Black
  Consulting Engineers
1979 Beaumont Drive
Baton Rouge, LA 70806
504-927-7240

National Organization for the
  Professional Advancement of Black
  Chemists and Chemical Engineers
c/o Dept. of Chemistry
525 Howard Street
Washington, DC 20059
202-269-4129

Fire Fighters
International Association of Black
  Professional Fire Fighters
8700 Central Avenue, Ste. 206
Landover, MD 20785
301-808-0804

Police Officers
National Organization of Black Law
  Enforcement Executives
908 Pennsylvania Ave., S.E.
Washington, DC 20003
202-546-8811

National Black Police Association
1919 Pennsylvania Avenue, N.W.
Washington, DC 20006
202-457-0568

General Science Areas
National Association of Black
  Geologists and Geophysicists
PO Box 720157
Houston, TX 77272

National Society of Black Physicists
1601 East Market Street
101 Martena Hall
Greensboro, NC 27411
919-334-7646

The Faces of Science: African
  Americans in the Sciences
http://www.lib.lsu.edu/lib/chem/
  display/faces.html

Journalism/Publishing/Writing
Black Women in Publishing
10 East 87th Street
New York, NY 10128
212-427-8100

International Black Writers
PO Box 1030
Chicago, IL 60690
708-331-6421

International Black Writers and
  Artists
PO Box 43576
Los Angeles, CA 90043
213-964-3721

National Association of Black
  Journalists
PO Box 17212
Washington, DC 20041
703-648-1270

National Association of African
  American Sportswriters and
  Broadcasters
21 Bedford Street
Wyandanch, NY 11798
516-491-7774

Law
National Association of Black Women
  Attorneys
724 Ninth Street, NW, Ste. 206
Washington, DC 20001
202-637-3570

National Conference of Black
  Lawyers
2 West 125th Street
New York, NY 10027
212-864-4000

Psychology/Psychiatry/Social Work
Association of Black Psychologists
PO Box 55999
Washington, DC 20040-5999
202-722-0808
http:/www.abpsi.org

Black Psychiatrists of America
c/o Dr. Issac Slaughter
2730 Adeline Street
Oakland, CA 94607
510-465-1800

National Association of Black Social
Workers
642 Beckwith Court, S.W.
Atlanta, Georgia 30314
404-584-7967

Medicine
Association of Black Cardiologists
225 Peachtree Street, Ste. 1420
Atlanta, GA 30303
404-582-8777

Miscellaneous Categories
Black Stuntmen's Association
8949 West 24th Street
Los Angeles, CA 90034
213-870-9020

Black Women's Network
PO Box 12072
Milwaukee, WI 53212
414-562-4500

Association of Black Foundation
Executives
1828 L. Street, NW
Washington, DC 20036
202-466-6512

International Black Toy Manufac-
turer's Association
PO Box 348
Springfield Gardens, NY 11413

National Association of Blacks
Within Government
1820 Eleventh Street, NW

Washington, DC 20001-5015
202-667-3280

National Consortium for Black
Professional Development
PO Box 18308
Louisville, KY 40218-0308
502-896-2838

Nontraditional Employment for
Women
243 W. 20th Street
New York, NY 10011
212-727-6252

REFERENCES

Bell, E. L. (1990). The bicultural life experience of career-oriented black women. *Journal of Organizational Behavior, 11*, 459–477.

Betz, N. E. (1990, June). *What stops women and minorities from choosing and completing majors in science and engineering.* Paper presented at a seminar for the Federation of Behavioral, Psychological and Cognitive Sciences, Washington, DC.

Betz, N. E. (1994). Basic issues and concepts in career counseling for women. In W. P. Walsh & S. M. Osipow (Eds.), *Career counseling for women* (pp. 1–41). Mahwah, NJ: Lawrence Erlbaum Associates.

Bingham, R. P., & Ward, C. M. (1994). Career counseling with ethnic-minority women. In W. P. Walsh & S. M. Osipow (Eds.), *Career counseling for women* (pp. 165–195). Mahwah, NJ: Lawrence Erlbaum Associates.

Blackwell, L. E. (1981). *Mainstreaming outsiders: The production of black professionals.* New York: General Hall.

Bowles, F., & DeCosta, F. A. (1971). *Two worlds: A profile of negro higher education.* New York: McGraw-Hill.

Bowman, S. L. (1993). Career intervention strategies for ethnic minorities. *Career Development Quarterly, 42*, 14–25.

Bullock, H. A. (1970). *A history of Negro education in the South.* New York: Praeger.

Burlew, A. K. (1982). The experiences of black female sin traditional and nontraditional professions. *Psychology of Women Quarterly, 6*(3), 312–326.

Burlew, A. K., & Johnson, J. L. (1992). Role conflict and career advancement among african american women in nontraditional professions. *The Career Development Quarterly, 40*, 302–312.

Carey, P. M. (1990). Beyond superwoman: On being a successful black women administrator. *Initiatives, 53*, 15–18.

Cheatham, H. E. (1990). Afrocentricity and the career development of african americans. *Career Development Quarterly, 38*, 334–346.

Chusmir, L. H. (1983). Characteristics and Predictive dimensions of women who make nontraditional vocational choices. *The Personnel and Guidance Journal, 62*(1), 43–47.

Chusmir, L. H. (1990). Men who make nontraditional career choices. *Journal of Counseling & Development, 69*, 11–16.

Doyle, J. A. (1989). *The male experience.* Dubuque, IA: Brown.

Evans, K. M., & Herr, E. L. (1991). The influence of racism and sexism in the career development of african american women. *Journal of Multicultural Counseling and Development, 19,* 130–135.

Graham, L. O. (1995). "Head nigger in charge": Roles that Black professionals play in the corporate world. *Business and Society Review, 94,* 43–50.

Hall, M. R. (1982). The classroom climate: A chilly one for women. Washington, DC: Association of American Colleges.

Hammer-Higgins, P., & Atwood, V. A. (1989). The management game: An educational intervention for counseling women with nontraditional career goals. *The Career Development Quarterly, 38,* 6–22.

Hayes, R. (1986). Men's decisions to enter or avoid nontraditional occupations. *The Career Development Quarterly,* 89–101.

Heikes, E. J. (1991). When men are the minority: The case of men in nursing. *The Sociological Quarterly, 32*(3), 389–401.

Hendricks, F. M. (1996). *Career experiences of Black women faculty at research I universities.* Unpublished doctoral dissertation, University of Missouri-Columbia.

Herr, E. L., & Cramer, S. H. (1996). *Career guidance and counseling through the lifespan.* New York: Harper Collins.

Jenkins, Y. M. (1985). The integration of psychotherapy-vocational interventions: Relevance for black women. *Psychotherapy, 22*(2), 394–397.

Jones, A. C. (1991). Psychological functioning in african americans: A conceptual guide for use in psychotherapy. In R. L. Jones (Ed.), *Black Psychology* (pp. 577–589). New York: Harper & Row.

Keen, S. (1991). *Fire in the belly: On being a man.* New York: Bantam.

Kimball, R. (1971). *Black and White vocational interests on Holland's self-directed search.* Baltimore: Maryland University Cultural Study Center.

Malcolm, S. M. (1990). Reclaiming our past. *Journal of Negro Education, 59,* 246–259.

Mansfield, P. K., Koch, P. B., Henderson, J., Vicary, J. R., Cohn, M., & Young, E. W. (1991). The job climate for women in traditionally male blue-collar occupations. *Sex Roles, 25*(1–2), 63–79.

Mau, W., Domnick, M., & Ellsworth, R. A. (1995). Characteristics of female students who aspire to science and engineering or homemaking occupations. *The Career Development Quarterly, 43,* 323–337.

Moses, Y. T. (1989). *Black women in academe: Issues and strategies.* Washington, DC: Project on the Status and Education for Women, Association of American Colleges.

Murrell, A. J., Frieze, I. H., & Frost, J. L. (1991). Aspiring to careers in male and female dominated professions. *Psychology of Women Quarterly, 15,* 103–126.

Noble, J. (1956). *The negro woman's college education.* New York: Teachers College Press, Columbia University.

Padavic, I. (1991). Attractions of male blue-collar jobs for Black and White women: Economic need, exposure, and attitudes. *Social Science Quarterly, 72,* 33–49.

Parham, T. A., & Austin, L. N. (1994). Career development and african americans: A contextual reappraisal using the nigrescence construct. *Journal of Vocational Behavior, 44,* 139–154.

Perkins, L. (1988). The education of black women in the nineteenth century. *Initiatives, 53,* 32–52.

Peterson, S. (1990). Challenges for Black women faculty. *Initiatives, 53,* 33–36.

Pfost, K. S., & Fiore, M. (1990). Pursuit of nontraditional occupations: fear of success or fear of not being chosen? *Sex Roles, 23*(½), 15–25.

Reid, P. T. (1990). African-american women in academia: Paradoxes and barriers. In S. Lie and V. O'Leary (Eds.), *Storming the tower: Women in the academic world* (pp. 148–162). East Brunswick, NJ: Nichol/GP Publishing.

Roche, G. R. (1979). Much ado about mentors. *Harvard Business Review, 57*, 14–18.

Rubenfeld, M., & Gilroy, F. (1991). Relationship between college women's occupational interests and a single-sex environment. *Career Development Quarterly, 40*, 64–70.

Ruffins, P. (1996). Black economists. *Black Issues in Higher Education*, 18–25.

Sandberg, D. E., Ehrhardt, A. A., Mellins, C. A., Ince, S. E., & Meyer-Bahlburg, H. F. L. (1987). The influence of individual and family characteristics upon career aspirations of girls during childhood and adolescence. *Sex Roles, 16*, 649–668.

Savenye, W. C. (1990). Role models and student attitudes toward nontraditional careers. *Educational Technology Research Development, 38*(3), 5–13.

Shields, C., & Shields, L. C. (1993). *Work sister work*. New York: Birch Lane Press.

Simpson, G. (1984). The daughters of Charlotte Ray: The career development process during the exploratory and establishment stages of black women attorneys. *Sex Roles, 11*, 113–139.

Smith, A., & Stewart, A. J. (1983). Approaches to studying racism and sexism in black women's lives. *Journal of Social Issues, 39*(3), 1–15.

Swerdlow, M. (1989). Men's accommodations to women entering a nontraditional occupation: A case of rapid transit operatives. *Gender & Society, 3*(3), 373–387.

Thomas, V. G. (1983). Perceived traditionality and nontraditionality of career aspirations of Black college women. *Perceptual and Motor Skills, 57*, 979–982.

U.S. Department of Labor, Women's Bureau. (1996). *Black women in the labor force*. Washington, DC: U.S. Government Printing Office.

U.S. Department of Labor, Bureau of Labor Statistics. (1997). *Employment and Earning*. Washington, DC: U.S. Government Printing Office.

Van Buren, J. B., Kelly, K. R., & Hall, A. S. (1993). Modeling nontraditional career choices: Effects of gender and school location on response to a brief videotape. *Journal of Counseling and Development, 72*(1), 101–104.

Washington, J. (1996). A hip hop brother in suit and tie. *Emerge*, 88.

Williams, C. L. (1992). The glass escalator: Hidden advantages for men in the female professions. *Social Problems, 39*(3), 253–276.

Wilson, R. (1989). Women of color in academic administration: Trends, progress, and barriers. *Sex Roles, 21*, 85–97.

World Book. (1997). Black Codes. Available: http://www.worldbook.com/blackhistory/bh055. html (1997, November 12.)

Chapter 8

Hitting the Roof: The Impact of the Glass-Ceiling Effect on the Career Development of African Americans

Rosemary E. Phelps
University of Georgia

Madonna G. Constantine
Teachers College, Columbia University

The term *glass ceiling* was popularized in the 1980s to describe an invisible and seemingly impenetrable barrier that impedes women from attaining top company positions, regardless of their professional accomplishments and qualifications (Federal Glass Ceiling Commission, 1995a; Morrison & von Glinow, 1990). Since its original usage over 10 years ago, this phrase has been expanded to include the range of issues, policies, and practices that keep qualified women and racial and ethnic minorities (i.e., African Americans, American Indians, Asian and Pacific Islander Americans, and Hispanic Americans) from advancing to higher level positions of responsibility and authority in corporate America (Redwood, 1996; Zachariasiewicz, 1993). To date, the majority of the glass-ceiling literature focused on obstacles faced by White women in the workplace. However, although all groups affected by the glass ceiling may perceive it to be a serious impediment, the issues are not the same for White women as they are for women and men of various racial and ethnic minority backgrounds (Federal Glass Ceiling Commission, 1995a). In fact, issues related to the glass ceiling tend to differ widely by specific racial and ethnic minority group, and there is also within-group diversity in each of these groups.

With regard to African Americans, the literature base in the area of the glass ceiling is sparse as compared to writings on White women; moreover, much of the previous research on African American professionals and the glass ceiling has focused primarily on the experiences of African American men (Morrison & von Glinow, 1990). Much of the existing literature related to the glass ceiling in African Americans addressed contextual variables in corporate America that may contribute to the presence and maintenance of the glass ceiling. However, there is a need for increased information about the impact of the glass ceiling on the career mobility of African American professionals. As such, this chapter was written with the primary purpose of delineating the glass ceiling's effects on the career development of African American women and men in the workforce. More specifically, this chapter presents a brief historical and contemporary overview of the glass ceiling, discusses barriers to career advancement for African Americans, and addresses issues related to the glass ceiling's impact on African Americans employed in major occupational settings such as business and industry, higher education, and government. In addition, both organizational interventions and career counseling considerations are discussed to address the impact of the glass ceiling on this workforce population.

HISTORICAL AND CONTEMPORARY OVERVIEW OF THE GLASS CEILING

The term *glass ceiling* was first coined in a 1986 article in the *Wall Street Journal* that focused on the struggles women were experiencing with regard to obtaining mid- and senior-level executive positions in business, government, and other institutions in the American workplace (Adams, 1993; Zachariasiewicz, 1993). More specifically, the phrase referred to a perceived transparent barrier between women and the executive suite that prevented them from achieving the uppermost positions of power in American corporations (Federal Glass Ceiling Commission, 1995a). Due to increasing concern regarding the prevalence of the glass ceiling in women and people of color, the U.S. Department of Labor compiled and publicized a 1991 report illuminating the nature and extent of this phenomenon. As a result of this report, the Glass Ceiling Act was introduced in 1991, and was later enacted with small modifications as Title II of the Civil Rights Act of 1991.

The Department of Labor's 1991 report also served as a catalyst for the development of a 21-member Federal Glass Ceiling Commission that was charged with the mission of preparing a fact-finding report that described the opportunities for, and artificial barriers to, the career advancement of people of color and women to senior-level positions in the private sector and a report focusing on recommendations to address the dismantling of identified artificial barriers to the career advancement of women and people of color (Federal Glass Ceiling Commission, 1995a, 1995b). With only minimal progress having been made in addressing this form of institutional discrimination, many individuals, particularly people of color in the workplace, tend to agree that a glass ceiling continues to exist in most aspects of corporate America.

BARRIERS TO CAREER ADVANCEMENT FOR AFRICAN AMERICANS

According to data from the 1990 Bureau of the Census, African Americans comprise over 12% of U.S. population. Yet, in relation to their proportion in the general population, African American men and women are less than half as likely to be employed in top-level executive and administrative positions in most industries; they are also employed in less than 2.5% of the upper level jobs found in the private sector (Federal Glass Ceiling Commission, 1995a). Presently, ethnic and racial minorities, women, or both are estimated to constitute 57% of the American workforce, and this figure is projected to increase to 62% by the year 2005; racial and ethnic minorities alone make up over 21% of the workforce (Bureau of Labor Statistics, 1992). In sharp contrast, 97% of the senior managers of Fortune-1000 industrial and Fortune-500 service industries are White, and 95% to 97% are male (Federal Glass Ceiling Commission, 1995a). Hence, these statistics seem to indicate the extent to which top-level corporate positions have failed to reflect the diversity of the current American workforce, and they clearly support the popular perception that the glass ceiling disproportionately affects African Americans and other people of color.

In recent years, a variety of theories have been postulated by researchers to explain the glass-ceiling phenomenon with regard to African Americans and other racial and ethnic minority individuals. Morrison and von Glinow (1990) categorized these perspectives into the following primary groups:

1. Racial differences serve as detriments to people of color such that these personal "deficiencies" are responsible for their differential treatment in higher levels of corporate America. These theories suggest that there are variables inherent to people of color that account for their lower job status.
2. Discrimination by Whites based on societal prejudices and biases is the main reason for career-advancement inequities with regard to people of color.
3. Institutional policies and practices contribute to the discriminatory treatment of people of color in organizations.

Morrison and von Glinow (1990) asserted that elements of each of these groups of theories may be related to the glass-ceiling phenomenon for African Americans and other people of color.

The aforementioned theories notwithstanding, some individuals believe that the primary underlying reason for the glass ceiling's existence is perceived to be a loss or lack of control by many White male managers due to increasing numbers of ethnic and racial minorities within corporate America (Federal Glass Ceiling Commission, 1995a). Some White managers may feel that every position given to a person of color represents a lost opportunity and a direct threat to their own chances for career advancement. Thus, even if a White male company president, for example, seems to support an informal corporate policy related to the advancement of racial and ethnic minority employees in top-level positions, he may not choose to actively enforce the policy if there is no specific monitoring or accountability system related to instituting this policy.

Nonetheless, the barriers to racial and ethnic minorities in the workplace extend beyond career-advancement issues. Previous research has indicated that even when employed in high-level positions, people of color lag behind significantly in compensation when compared to their White male counterparts (Morrison & von Glinow, 1990). More specifically, African American men with professional degrees tend to earn only $.79 for every $1.00 earned by White men with the same credentials, and African American women earn only 60% of the average salary of their White male peers (Federal Glass Ceiling Commission, 1995a). African American women, a group that is frequently overlooked in the glass-ceiling literature, also tend to feel that they are affected in the workplace by the double burden of race and sex. Many of these women have perceived the glass ceiling to resemble a concrete or brick wall that isolates them and prevents them from learning about the organization due to lack of exposure to the organizational mainstream (Federal Glass Ceiling Commission, 1995a).

THE GLASS CEILING IN BUSINESS AND INDUSTRY, HIGHER EDUCATION, AND GOVERNMENT

Business and Industry

When people of color enter the corporate job market, they are often placed in staff or highly specific technical positions, rather than the managerial positions that are stepping stones to top-level positions; much of the blame for this phenomenon falls on the corporations themselves because although high-level executives seem to support inclusive hiring and promotion policies, there tends to be inconsistent follow-through in practice (Federal Glass Ceiling Commission, 1995a). Adams (1993) reported that although people in business and industry do not deny the existence of discrimination, ethnic and racial minority employees have not been in the kinds of work positions in which they are currently employed as long as their White male counterparts.

Higher Education

In illuminating the extent to which the glass ceiling exists for African Americans in academia, Adams (1993) delineated several alarming facts. First, he asserted that although racial and ethnic minorities make up approximately 21% of college student enrollment and receive over 14% of the doctoral degrees, only 3% of college professors and nearly 6% of college presidents are African American; of these college presidents, one half serve at historically Black colleges or universities. Ramey (1995), in her survey of African American women college administrators, reported that the most frequently cited barriers to career advancement were racism and sexism; additional barriers identified by the respondents included family issues, perceptions of incompetence, lack of authority, limited networking opportunities, and isolation. Many of the women in Ramey's (1995) study believed that their ability to successfully negotiate and advance within the higher education system was often due to support systems in the form of leadership programs and mentoring relationships.

Government

There is not a great deal of data on the glass ceiling with regard to African Americans employed in government institutions. However, executive and administrative advancement opportunities for African Americans tend to be more plentiful in government and nonprofit sectors than in private business (Federal Glass Ceiling Commission, 1995a). In addition, although not referring specifically to African Americans, Adams (1993) reported that racial and ethnic minority women employed in government positions possessed fewer opportunities for career promotion than did their White counterparts, even with equal qualifications.

Organizational Interventions to Address the Glass Ceiling

The glass ceiling has been documented in numerous ways, including empirical studies (e.g., Morrison, Schreiber, & Price, 1995; *Women of Color in Corporate Management: A Statistical Picture*, 1997), governmental reports (e.g., Bell & Nkomo, 1994), and personal accounts by women and racial and ethnic minority group members (e.g., Griffiths, 1996). Although the glass ceiling is a recognized phenomenon for African Americans in business and industry, government, and education, eradication of the phenomenon is far from complete. Organizational interventions are vital in the full eradication of the glass ceiling.

Organizational interventions have often been unsuccessful due to a lack of commitment by employers, the implementation of piecemeal approaches in dealing with the glass ceiling, a lack of substantive and continuous action at all levels throughout an organization, and a lack of understanding of the glass ceiling and related issues. Thomas and Ely (1996) identified two paradigms that have been historically utilized in promoting diversity: the *discrimination-and-fairness paradigm* and the *access-and-legitimacy paradigm*. With the *discrimination-and-fairness paradigm*, the rationale is based on issues related to compliance, fair treatment, recruitment and retention goals, and equal opportunity. According to Thomas and Ely (1996), the *access-and-legitimacy paradigm* is based on the "acceptance and celebration of differences," resulting in the recognition of a need for demographically similar employees when accessing and serving a more diverse clientele (p. 83). Thomas and Ely (1996) maintained that diversity efforts will continue to be less than successful until a new paradigm is implemented. This new paradigm, the *learning-and-effectiveness paradigm*, focuses on integration (not assimilation or differentiation) and involves understanding diversity "as the varied perspectives and approaches to work that members of different identity groups bring" (p. 80). It is a model in which an organization can become stronger because it is able to grow and learn from all of its employees.

The work of Thomas and Ely (1996) has clear implications when thinking about successful diversity efforts. It is apparent that a major first step in implementing successful organizational diversity initiatives will involve a reexamination of current definitions and rationales regarding diversity. A conceptual shift in the definitions and rationales regarding diversity is needed, and the role and goals of the organization in diversity efforts must be thoroughly examined. Several writers (e.g., Merenivitach & Reigle, 1979 cited in Morrison & von Glinow, 1990; Morrison & von Glinow, 1990) suggested that the effectiveness of interventions may also depend, in large part, on an organization's current diversity status. Thus, it may be useful to conceptualize organizational interventions from a developmental perspective (i. e., organizations progress through phases, different phases require different interventions). If a developmental framework is used, conducting an organizational diversity needs assessment and identifying types of interventions compatible with various diversity phases may be necessary in order to provide interventions that are most effective for a particular organization at a given point in time. In addition, successful organizational implementation requires attention to the practices and policies that maintain the status quo in an organization; accountability at all levels; and the willingness and commitment of executives and administrators to make difficult, and sometimes unpopular, decisions. For instance, glass-ceiling decisions and actions may be perceived as negatively affecting some individual employees in order to achieve a broader goal of diversity and the inclusion of African American employees.

Elimination of the glass ceiling can lead to an improved quality of life, the maximization of one's potential, increased productivity, and a satisfying and fulfilling career for employees. In turn, organizations can benefit by being more productive, effective, and competitive; having an improved image; and having employees with higher morale.

It is important to understand that the culture of an organization must change in order to eliminate the glass ceiling for African Americans and other racial and ethnic minority group members. This sounds logical and simple enough, however, to change an environment in which the power structure, principles, standard policies, basic assumptions, and workplace values are systematically exclusionary of African Americans is more difficult than it may first appear. Organizational interventions can be categorized into several major areas: employee development and training needs, mentoring and networking relationships, relational issues, and accessibility. Each of these areas is discussed in terms of eliminating the glass ceiling for African Americans.

Employee Development and Training Needs.   Education and training regarding the glass ceiling is essential for all employees. A recommendation by the U.S. Department of Labor's Glass Ceiling Commission stated that:

> organizations must establish on-going training and educational programs on race relations for all organizational members. Such training can help get to the root of many of the barriers African Americans experience . . . racism and prejudice. (Bell & Nkomo, 1994, p. 1)

The manner in which employee development is implemented can be a critical factor. An initial consideration involves communication. How is the topic communicated to employees? What words are used to describe the purpose and nature of the training? In a similar vein, the effectiveness of training is also dependent on how the training is viewed and presented. Are the glass ceiling issues being presented in terms of an intellectual and learning opportunity (something to be studied), as someone else's problem, or as a key element of the organizational identity?

Careful attention to format, structure, and perceptions generated by various types of training must also be considered. The context, setting, intent, and purpose of specific training should be carefully considered so that it is not viewed as offensive or insensitive. For example, some organizations may provide specific training for African American employees, which may be perceived as remedial in nature or as a benefit afforded only to African American employees. On the other hand, some organizations may assume that no specific training is necessary and that generalized training offered to all employees is sufficient for African American employees. Morrison and von Glinow (1990) noted a trend of providing a variety of training opportunities to address diversity issues. Such variety can promote flexibility in training opportunities, both in terms of format and content. Skill-building programs are often conducted when addressing the glass ceiling; however, other important areas include career and self-awareness, mentoring, leadership development, assessment and evaluation of programmatic interventions, conflict resolution, dealing with racism, equal access, equity, prejudice, bias, and discrimination. New training models and conceptual frameworks may be needed in order to facilitate effective employment development. Hall and Parker (1993) discussed an approach called *workplace flexibility* that empowers employees and views them in their entirety, including work–life issues and issues related to difference.

Mentoring and Networking Relationships.   Mentoring and networking relationships have been shown to be important factors in the academic and/or educational attainment, career development, and career success of individuals (Davidson & Cooper, 1992; Fagenson, 1989; Gerstein, 1985). Networking relationships involve individuals with mutual interests who provide support, information, collaboration, accessibility, and contacts for professional and personal growth. In addition, networks can help familiarize its members with policy information and increase awareness of professional career opportunities. In networking relationships, contact is often with a variety of individuals who may be of equal or higher status. Networking systems, which can be formal as well as informal, may actually be more important than mentoring relationships (American Society for Public Administration, 1992). Networks can be useful in addressing glass-ceiling issues by providing different perspectives on overcoming barriers, broadening one's awareness and knowledge of career opportunities, and providing a more expansive base of support and encouragement.

Mentoring relationships, on the other hand, evolve over time and usually involve two individuals, one of whom has less experience and/or status. Mentors provide guidance, feedback, encouragement, assistance, accessibility, insight, an introduction to the rules and norms of an organization, help in developing a professional identity, and other job-related tips that can be useful to a protégé. Mentoring can be done through formal as well as informal channels. Formal mentoring involves the establishment of a working relationship facilitated by formalized organizational policies and the organizational structure. This type of mentoring usually has official recognition by the organization and can also contribute to the career progress of the mentor (Flanders, 1994). Informal mentoring is a less structured process that does not necessarily involve the organizational structure.

Although studies indicate that mentoring relationships can have a significant impact, the specific dynamics and outcomes of these relationships for women and racial and ethnic minorities are not very clear. Research on cross-sex and crossracial mentoring relationships have provided mixed information and findings. Some findings indicate that crossrace mentoring relationships "take longer to initiate, are more likely to end in an unfriendly fashion, and provide less psychosocial support than same-race relationships" (Morrison & von Glinow, 1990, p. 203). Similar findings are also reported with cross-sex mentoring relationships. It has been found that they, too, can be problematic and include specific problems such as male mentors blocking career development, holding stereotypical views of women, and feeling threatened (Arnold & Davidson, 1990; Fagenson, 1988; Fitt & Newton, 1981; Flanders, 1994; Ford & Wells, 1985; Kram, 1985; Lie & O'Leary, 1990; Morrison & von Glinow, 1990; Thomas & Alderfer, 1989). On the other hand, some studies indicate that cross-sex (e.g., male mentor–female protégé) mentoring relationships provide the greatest benefits (Erkut & Mokros, 1984; Farylo & Paludi, 1985).

Specific issues identified in relationships in which women mentor each other include the lack of female mentors (Arnold & Davidson, 1990; Davidson & Cooper, 1992) and women's expectations of each other (O'Leary, 1988).

Mentoring may be especially important given the alienation and isolation often experienced by African Americans. It should be recognized and utilized as one tool in addressing the glass ceiling (O'Leary & Mitchell, 1990). Mentoring relationships can be helpful in addressing the glass ceiling by providing a more extensive range of knowledge about an organization and its employees, gaining access to key resources, providing access to more experiences and opportunities, and understanding power relations in an organization. Specifically, mentors can provide career advice and guidance, help a protégé identify allies, share lessons learned, serve as an advocate, provide feedback on a protégé's skills and abilities, provide information on how to overcome barriers, and provide information and support on being bicultural in an organizational environment.

Arnold and Davidson (1990) discussed the need for specific training and preparation of mentors. Who the mentor is and what that mentor can offer are important in the success of the relationship and ultimately in addressing the glass ceiling. The selection of mentors and the mentoring process warrant careful thought and consideration. In crossracial mentoring relationships, mentors must recognize and understand the political, psychological, and social barriers faced by African Americans in the organization and in society.

Relational Issues.   Relationships with colleagues are key in the satisfaction, career success, and morale of employees. Working relationships can play a major role in the achievement and success of African Americans. White colleagues who feel threatened by African Americans may hold biases, prejudices, and stereotypical views that can interfere with the success of African American colleagues. This is especially problematic if the White colleagues are in managerial or supervisory positions.

Another relational issue involves the perceived interpersonal style of African Americans by White colleagues. Often, the same words and behaviors that are spoken and exhibited by Whites are viewed negatively when spoken and performed by African Americans. This type of evaluation and misinterpretation can be difficult. It is important for organizations to understand this dynamic and not allow it to be used against African Americans.

It can be useful to examine the social psychology and industrial–organizational psychology literature (e.g., Thomas, Phillips, & Brown, 1998) when attempting to understand the dynamics of these relational issues. Both fields provide information on the importance of group identities to the self-concept and on behavior in organizations (e.g., Cox, 1994). A clear understanding of social identity theory, racial and ethnic identity theory, and culture identity theory is a must if organizations are going to be successful in addressing relational issues for African Americans.

Accessibility.   Accessibility to resources and information is an important factor in the career success of all employees. For African American employees, it is often complex because of the psychosocial and psychohistorical factors involved. Accessibility also involves issues of equity. Equity is often confused with equality. The two concepts are not interchangeable. *Equal treatment* generally means the same resources for everyone involved. However, equal treatment can continue to perpetuate inequities. To ensure accessibility, organizations must pay attention to equity issues and equitable treatment.

CAREER COUNSELING AND CAREER
DEVELOPMENT CONSIDERATIONS

The previous sections focused on organizational interventions and the glass ceiling. Although successful eradication of the glass ceiling involves organizational interventions, there are also important career-counseling and career-development issues to consider. The remainder of this chapter examines key career-counseling and career-development issues for African Americans. These issues and how they can affect the career satisfaction and career advancement of African Americans, in terms of the glass ceiling, should be clearly understood. This understanding can help individuals make more informed career choices and can help them enter organizations more knowledgeable about some of the glass-ceiling issues they may face. In addition, an understanding of these issues can serve as a foundation in implementing successful organizational diversity initiatives.

Historically, race and ethnicity have not been included as variables in many of the major career development theories and models. The career development, behavior, and patterns of African Americans and other racial and ethnic minority group members have been evaluated, in large part, based on White male behavior and development. Within recent years, there has been increased attention focused on the lack of research and the inadequacy of career-development theories for African Americans (e.g., Brown, 1995). New theories (e.g., Cheatham, 1990) are being developed that may more accurately explain the career development and career experiences of African Americans. The development of new theories relevant to African Americans is a step in the right direction. In order to fully understand the glass ceiling and its impact on African Americans, race and its consequences must be addressed without hesitation and as a primary factor in career development theories, career development research, and in the work environment.

The lack of information regarding the career development of African Americans is problematic and widespread. Other writers (e.g., Bowman, 1993) noted the dearth of information and the difficulty in finding material on African Americans and other racial and ethnic minority groups in the area of career development. This certainly held true in the writing of this chapter. Some statistics and demographic information were available, usually in government reports and documents. However, there is not an abundance of information on the glass ceiling; the major portion of that body of literature focuses on women, which generally does not include African American women. One major consequence of this lack of information is the perpetuation of stereotypes, myths, and misperceptions regarding African Americans and the glass ceiling. If progress is to be made with regard to the glass ceiling, more printed information is needed that is factual and accessible.

A lack of appropriate and relevant theories has direct implications for career counseling with African Americans. Without relevant theories and frameworks, it can be difficult to identify salient career factors, to adequately address important career issues, or to understand the role of various factors in the career processes of African Americans. For example, the role of self-concept and self-referent attitudes have long been examined in relation to career choice and career development. However, it has been noted (e.g., Gainor & Forrest, 1991; Snyder, Verderber, Langmeyer, & Myers, 1992) that these factors often have not been examined, conceptualized, or understood in the context of African Americans. That is, the sociopolitical and sociohistorical (e.g., racism, sexism, bias, and discrimination) realities and experiences of African Americans have not been considered along with their personal and individual realities. The importance of fully understanding the role of race and ethnicity in the career processes of African Americans continues to be noted.

Specific Variables for Consideration in the Career Development of African Americans

In the literature related to the career development of African Americans, several variables have been identified as important and worthy of continued research. It has been noted that these variables are important for counselors to understand in order to provide more effective counseling, for individuals to more thoroughly understand as they make career decisions and choices, for theorists to more fully integrate into career theory development, and for scholars to examine more comprehensively in research studies.

Biculturalism. Biculturalism in the work environment is a variable that is beginning to receive attention in the literature (Bell, 1990; Cox, 1994; Hall & Parker, 1993). According to Bell (1990), a *bicultural world* exists for Black women in that they must negotiate and develop their careers in a predominantly White world, while also maintaining their roles in and ties to the Black community. More exploration of the processes and consequences of living a bicultural life is needed.

Sex and Gender. The effects of sex and race have not been systematically studied with regard to African Americans and the glass ceiling. More information is needed in order to thoroughly understand the interaction of these two variables. In addition, gender issues (e.g., gender-role socialization) have not fully been examined in this regard.

SES. Another area in which interaction effects have not been examined systematically involves race and SES. One does not have to search very long to find studies in which SES has not been considered or controlled for, which makes it a confounding variable. Thus, providing an accurate interpretation of the data becomes difficult. More consideration of SES and class issues is needed.

Racial and Ethnic Identity. There is increasingly more indication that racial identity and ethnic identity are important in the lives, behavior, and psychological processes of African Americans. Industrial–organizational psychologists are placing more emphasis on the examination of group identities as they related to organizations and the impact of group identity on an individual within an organization, other members of an organization, and the organization itself (Cox, 1994; see Thomas et al., 1998). Additional research is needed to determine how group identity (e.g., racial and ethnic identity) affects issues related to the glass ceiling. More in-depth examination of these variables can also provide much-needed information on within-group variation.

Discrimination and Institutional Racism. These continue to be factors that affect the glass ceiling and career development for African Americans (see Cohn, 1997). For as long as African Americans have experienced discrimination and institutional racism in the workplace, little systematic research has been conducted to help fully understand their complexities. Continued attention and action in these areas are needed.

SUMMARY

The statistics and information presented in this chapter clearly indicate that the glass ceiling does exist and that it does have an (often negative) impact on the career development of African Americans. Contents of this chapter also provide some insights into the various obstacles and barriers associated with the glass ceiling and offer suggestions on the knowledge and actions needed to remove these barriers and obstacles. The eradication of the glass ceiling for African Americans and other racial and ethnic minority group members is not an endeavor that can be done overnight or haphazardly. Efforts must be systematic, long-term, and with the dedicated efforts of those who have a full understanding of the issues involved, including those persons who have the power to implement change within an organization on a wide scale.

It is clear that African Americans have continued to push forward despite the obstacles and barriers they experience. Adversity and difficult circumstances are not new situations for African Americans: There is the recognition that progress can be made in spite of adversity.

ACKNOWLEDGMENTS

We would like to thank Robyn Liebman and Deborah B. Altschul for their valuable assistance with this chapter.

REFERENCES

Adams, B. (1993). The glass ceiling: Are women and minorities blocked from the executive suite? *The Congressional Quarterly Researcher, 3*(40), 937–960.

American Society for Public Administration (1992). *Breaking through the glass ceiling: A career guide for women in government.* Washington, DC: National Capital Area Chapter.

Arnold, V., & Davidson, M. J. (1990). Adopt a mentor—the new way ahead for women managers? *Women in Management Review and Abstracts, 5*(1), 10–18.

Bell, E. L. (1990). The bicultural life experience of career-oriented Black women. *Journal of Organizational Behavior, 11*, 459–477.

Bell, E. L. J. E., & Nkomo, S. M. (1994). *Barriers to work place advancement experienced by African Americans.* (Monograph prepared for the Glass Ceiling Commission). Washington, DC: United States Department of Labor.

Bowman, S. L. (1993). Career intervention strategies for ethnic minorities. *The Career Development Quarterly, 42*, 14–25.

Brown, M. T. (1995). The career development of African Americans: Theoretical and empirical issues. In F. T. L. Leong (Ed.), *Career development and vocational behavior of racial and ethnic minorities* (pp. 7–36). Mahwah, NJ: Lawrence Erlbaum Associates.

Bureau of Labor Statistics. (1992, May). *Outlook 1990–2005,* 39.

Cheatham, H. E. (1990). Africentricity and career development of African Americans. *Career Development Quarterly, 38*, 334–346.

Cohn, J. (1997). The effects of racial and ethnic discrimination on the career development of minority persons. In H. S. Farmer and Associates *Women's Mental Health and Development, Volume 2: Diversity and women's career development: From adolescence to adulthood* (pp. 161–171). Thousand Oaks, CA: Sage.

Cox, T. H., Jr. (1994). *Cultural diversity in organizations: Theory, research, and practice.* San Francisco: Berrett-Kohler.

Davidson, M. J., & Cooper, C. L. (1992). *Shattering the glass ceiling: The woman manager.* London: Paul Chapman.

Erkut, S., & Mokros, J. R. (1984). *Professors as models and mentors for college students.* (Working Paper No. 65). Wellesley, MA: Wellesley College Center for Research on Women.

Fagenson, E. A. (1988). The power of a mentor. *Groups and Organization Studies, 13*, 182–194.

Fagenson, E. A. (1989). The mentor advantage: Perceived career/job experiences of proteges versus non-proteges. *Journal of Organizational Behavior, 10*, 309–320.

Farylo, J., & Paludi, M. A. (1985). Developmental discontinuities in mentor choice by male students. *Journal of Social Psychology, 125*(4), 521–522.

Federal Glass Ceiling Commission. (1995a). *Good for business: Making full use of the nation's human capital: The environmental scan: A fact-finding report of the Federal Glass Ceiling Commission.* Washington, DC: U.S. Government Printing Office.

Federal Glass Ceiling Commission. (1995b). *A solid investment: Making full use of the nation's human capital: Recommendations of the Federal Glass Ceiling Commission.* Washington, DC: U.S. Government Printing Office.

Fitt, L. W., & Newton, D. A. (1981). When the mentor is a man and the protege a woman. *Harvard Business Review,* 56–60.

Flanders, M. L. (1994). *Breakthrough: The career woman's guide to shattering the glass ceiling.* London: Paul Chapman.

Ford, D., & Wells, L., Jr. (1985). Upward mobility factors among Black public administrators. *Centerboard: Journal of the Center for Human Relations Studies, 3*(1), 38–48.

Gainor, K. A., & Forrest, L. (1991). African American women's self-concept: Implications for career decisions and career counseling. *The Career Development Quarterly, 39*, 261–272.

Gerstein, M. (1985). *Journal of Counseling and Development, 64*, 156–157.

Griffiths, S. (Ed). (1996). *Beyond the glass ceiling: Forty women whose ideas shape the modern world.* Manchester, England: Manchester University Press.

Hall, D. T., & Parker, V. A. (1993). The role of workplace flexibility in managing diversity. *Organizational Dynamics, 22,* 5–18.

Kram, K. E. (1985). Improving the mentoring process. *Training and Development Journal, 39*(4), 40–43.

Lie, S. S., & O'Leary, V. (Eds). (1990). *Storming the tower: Women in the academic world.* London: Kogan Page.

Morrison, A. M., Schreiber, C. T., & Price, K. F. (1995). *A glass ceiling survey: Benchmarking barriers and practices.* Greensboro, NC: Center for Creative Leadership.

Morrison, A. M., & von Glinow, M. A. (1990). Women and minorities in management. *American Psychologist, 45*(2), 200–208.

O'Leary, V. E. (1988). Women's relationships with women in the workplace. In B. Gutek, A. H. Stromberg, & L. Larwood (Eds.), *Women and work: An annual review, Volume 3* (pp. 189–213). Newbury Park, CA: Sage.

O'Leary, V. E., & Mitchell, J. M. (1990). Women connecting with women: Networks and mentors in the United States. In S. S. Lie & V. E. O'Leary (Eds.), *Storming the tower: Women in the academic world* (pp. 58–74). London: Kogan Page.

Ramey, F. H. (1995). Obstacles faced by African American women administrators in higher education: How they cope. *The Western Journal of Black Studies, 19,* 113–119.

Redwood, R. (1996, May/June). Giving credit where credit is due: The work of the Federal Glass Ceiling Commission. *Credit World,* 34–36.

Snyder, R. A., Verderber, K. S., Langmeyer, L., & Myers, M. (1992). A reconsideration of self- and organization-referent attitudes as "causes" of the glass ceiling effect. *Group and Organization Management, 17,* 260–278.

Thomas, D. A., & Alderfer, C. P. (1989). The influence of race on career dynamics: Theory and research on minority career experiences. In M. Arthur, D. Hall, & B. Lawrence (Eds.), *Handbook of career theory* (pp. 133–158). Cambridge, England: Cambridge University Press.

Thomas, D. A., & Ely, R. J. (1996, September–October). Making differences matter: A new paradigm for managing diversity. *Harvard Business Review,* 79–90.

Thomas, K. M., Phillips, L. D., & Brown, S. (1998). Redefining race in the workplace: Insights from ethnic identity theory. *Journal of Black Psychology, 24,* 76–92.

Women of color in corporate management: A statistical picture. (1998). A Catalyst study sponsored by The Alfred P. Sloan Foundation. New York: Catalyst.

Zachariasiewicz, R. (1993, May/June). Breaking the glass ceiling. *Credit World,* 21–23.

Chapter 9

Future Directions in Career Counseling Theory, Research, and Practice With African Americans

Donald B. Pope-Davis
University of Notre Dame

Byron K. Hargrove
Seton Hall University

Increased attention has been given to the specific career needs of African Americans during the last 10 years. However, although the attention has been long overdue, traditional career-counseling theories continue to limit their consideration of the full range of vocational behaviors, choices, and decisions among African Americans. As the largest racial and ethnic minority group in the United States to date, African Americans continue to face a number of vocational problems including disproportionately high rates of underemployment, unemployment, poverty, and educational deficits. These problems appear to be persistent and evoke even more concern as we head into the 21st century (Hoyt, 1989; Okacha, 1994). Career-counseling theories should allow practitioners to understand, predict, ameliorate, and perhaps prevent many of these vocational problems. Unfortunately, much of the theoretical development in the vocational literature on African Americans appears to be limited and in its infancy. Thus, there appear to be numerous opportunities for future directions.

This chapter examines four possible theory-building directions. They are as follows:

1. Vocational psychologists need to focus more attention on enhancing and testing traditional and emerging theoretical efforts for their cultural relevancy with African Americans. Lack of applying these models with African Americans and failing to infuse cultural variables into career-counseling models appear to be two important barriers in deciding whether

177

or not theorists should abandon previous theoretical foundations or begin developing alternate culturally relevant approaches.

2. Theorists should move away from simply comparing the career development of African Americans with Whites, while using Eurocentric-based frameworks (e.g., Smith, 1983). Instead, move toward developing a range of within-group models that are consistent with the diversity among African Americans.

3. Future directions in theory should be able to address the range of career needs (e.g., from job placement to career actualization) motivating the vocational behaviors of African Americans across diverse educational backgrounds, gender groups, and social classes.

4. Vocational psychologists should begin to acknowledge and incorporate information about vocational behavior from multiple perspectives; a multidiscipline approach may also inspire a movement toward generating culturally-relevant models of career development for African Americans.

This chapter is an attempt to clarify each of these future initiatives in the career-counseling theory literature for African Americans with the hope of enhancing research as well as practice for this population.

FROM CULTURAL SENSITIVITY TO CULTURE-SPECIFIC MODELS

It may be useful to view theory-building efforts along a continuum, extending from traditional, White middle-class, Eurocentric-based models to more culturally specific models of African American career development. Some researchers (e.g., Cheatham, 1990; Osipow & Littlejohn, 1995; Sharf, 1992) recently highlighted some conceptual themes (e.g., cultural values, racial identity, and social learning processes) that may provide directions for future theory building. The recent emergence of social cognitive models (Hackett & Lent, 1992; Lent & Brown, 1996; Lent, Brown, & Hackett, 1994) in the vocational literature may provide one promising approach toward moving career-counseling approaches along this continuum.

The social cognitive approach has been suggested as a useful approach in addressing many of the sociocultural career issues facing African Americans (Brown, 1995; Hackett & Byars, 1995; Osipow & Littlejohn, 1996; Sharf, 1992). Over the last 10 years, social cognitive factors, such as career self-efficacy, have been shown to be important determinants in academic- and career-related behaviors of late adolescents and young adults (e.g., mostly college students; Lent & Hackett, 1987). The application of career self-efficacy to women's career development has generated the most research attention. Several domain-specific lines of research have been established in the career self-efficacy literature including occupational self-efficacy, math self-efficacy, and decision-making self-efficacy (Betz, 1992). The self-efficacy construct also appears to be a viable theoretical construct because of its direct practical implications. That is, vocational programs and counseling interventions can be designed to address the four operational sources of self-efficacy beliefs: *performance accomplishments, vicarious learning, verbal encouragement,* and *physiological arousal* (e.g., Betz, 1992). Hackett and Byars (1995) recently outlined how African American women, by way of cultural socialization and contextual barriers (e.g., racism and sexism), may receive limited sources of career self-efficacy beliefs that may ultimately affect their career choices. Although a potentially promising line of inquiry in the vocational literature, there has been limited attention given to using career self-efficacy theory to understand the vocational behavior, choices, and decisions of African Americans.

A more comprehensive social cognitive approach that may be useful is Lent et al.'s (1994) emerging SCCT. Building on the self-efficacy research, Lent and his colleagues recently expanded Bandura's social cognitive model to describe segmental models of interest development, career choice, and career-related performance for individuals particularly at the career entry stage of development. As the debate over the relevancy of traditional theories continues in the vocational literature, SCCT appears to be a culturally sensitive approach in that it builds on many of the criticisms of traditional career theories.

Lent et al. (1994) argued that SCCT provides a cultural context for understanding career development. The model incorporates the interaction of personal background variables (e.g., gender, ethnicity, SES, etc.), social cognitive mechanisms (e.g., self-efficacy beliefs, outcome expectations, and goals), and distal and proximal environmental and contextual mechanisms (e.g., family support, discrimination, opportunity structures, etc.). Although traditional career-development theories only address racial, cultural, and environmental variables in a cursory fashion, SCCT attempts to describe how cultural learning experiences directly impact an individual's personal agency. Personal agency, which is reflective of both self-efficacy beliefs and outcome expectations, in turn, influences the development of career interests and career goals. Lent and his colleagues (1994) proposed that differences in learning experiences due to racial and/or gender socialization may directly impact the sources of career-specific self-efficacy beliefs and outcome expectations. They also provided pathways that describe when and where contextual or sociocultural environmental factors may moderate vocational behaviors. As an example, Evans and Herr (1991) described how African American women may often avoid certain career fields and alter their career goals in order to deal with the dual effects of real and perceived racism and sexism in the workplace. Lent and his colleagues (1994) suggested that SCCT needs to expand in order to focus more on contextual influences, outcome expectations, and individuals at different career stages.

Relative to self-efficacy mechanisms is the limited attention given to the role of outcome expectations or one's expectations about the rewards or negative consequences of a specific vocational behavior. From the social cognitive perspective, outcome expectations encompass different types of values (or valued outcomes) such as the expectation to receive money, help others, have social interaction, or work autonomously. African Americans may seek particular jobs or career paths that are consistent with their values (Hall & Post-Kammer, 1987). SCCT may help to explain how expectations for receiving valued outcomes may relate to interest development and the formation of career goals. For instance, the traditional overrepresentation of college-educated African Americans pursuing careers in education, social service, and social sciences may be a reflection of values that have been socialized within the context of their families or community (Carter & Cook, 1992; Hall & Post-Kammer, 1987). Thus, SCCT may provide a useful framework for developing interventions that enhance the self-efficacy beliefs and outcome expectations of African Americans. Despite its potential, few studies have focused on applying this model with African Americans (Hackett & Byars, 1995; Lent et al., 1994; Lent & Brown, 1996). SCCT may provide one step toward establishing a more culturally sensitive career-counseling model for African Americans.

Although the social cognitive approach may appear to be a more culturally sensitive model that can be applied to any group, future directions in theory building appears to be the need for developing culture-specific models of career development for African Americans. For example, Cheatham's (1990) proposed Africentricity model has been highlighted as a precursor to building a culture-specific model for African Americans (e.g., Brown, 1995; Hackett & Lent, 1992). According to Cheatham (1990), an understanding of both Eurocentric and Afrocentric social orders may be important in understanding some African American student vocational outcomes and behaviors (i.e., goal setting, attributes, career choices, cultural patterns, labor market knowledge, and values). Cheatham (1990) postulated that experiences in America (e.g., legacy of slavery, impact of race and color, economic deprivation, and institutional racism) for African Americans interact with the development of an Africentric social order including family structure, norms, values, attitudes, gender roles, religion, and forms of expression. The Eurocentric social order is also important in shaping the career-development patterns of African Americans students. Cheatham specifically focused on the differences in the values socialized within the Africentric social order (e.g.,. interdependence, communalism, and mutuality) and the Eurocentric social order (e.g., competition, individualism, and ethnocentrism). In addition to only focusing on African American college-student career development, this proposed approach appears to have some research limitations as noted by Brown (1995; e.g., confounding race with SES, magnifying ethnic differences, and failing to test propositions). Nonetheless, with continued development this approach could be fruitful (Brown, 1995). This model may be a promising step toward understanding culturally relevant career patterns such as the overrepresentation of African Americans in education and social science career fields (Cheatham, 1990; Hall & Post-Kammer, 1987; Todisco & Salomone, 1991). Future efforts need to establish valid research measures for both social orders, clarify relationships between these two social orders, and test how these variables may impact the career patterns and choices of African Americans. Furthermore, this precursor may serve as a benchmark for the growing trend to integrate multicultural variables with vocational variables. For instance, efforts need to be made to examine the relations among the Africentricity model and other cultural frameworks (e.g., racial identity, acculturation, and worldview) in the career-development literature. As specific African American career-development models begin to emerge, there should be an emphasis on developing more detailed within-group career development models complemented by appropriate within-group research.

WITHIN-GROUP MODELS OF CAREER BEHAVIOR

Efforts in theory building should focus on developing more complex and precise within-group models (Osipow & Littlejohn, 1996). One theme across the many models developed in the vocational psychology literature has been the dependence on college students at the career entry stage as the sample of choice to represent the life span of all African Americans. As researchers have pointed out, African Americans are made of up several SESs, social classes, regional subgroups, and ethnic groups, all of which have uniquely diverse career concerns. Thus, career theorists need to abandon their White, middle-class, Eurocentric assumptions about career development in order to begin characterizing the vocational and life experiences of diverse subgroups of African Americans. All African Americans are not the same! Some possible within-group models that need the most attention are presented in the following section.

Gender-Specific Models

Most of the theoretical and empirical advancements made within vocational psychology over the last 10 years have been exemplified by research on women's career development (Betz & Fitzgerald, 1993; Gelso & Fretz, 1992). For example, the nature of women's career choices has been examined from a number of perspectives (e.g., traditional vs. nontraditional, home vs. career orientation, and career salience dimensions; Fitzgerald, Fassinger, & Betz, 1995). There have even been causal models that were developed that incorporate more variables than male-based models of career development (e.g., Fassinger, 1990). Despite the number of sophisticated advances made in understanding women's career choices, African American women and other women of color appear to have been left out. The majority of the studies on women's career development have focused on White women. Thus, the generalizability to African American women has been apparent. In addition to proactively including African Americans in our research, future directions in theory need to account for the interaction of race, gender, and culture as they impact the career choices of African American women and men from different socioeconomic backgrounds and at varying stages across the life span (e.g., Bowman, 1993).

Racial Identity

Another within-group approach that should be developed in the vocational literature is the application of racial–cultural identity models to the career development of African Americans. Recent proposals have been published in the literature on the potential utility of racial identity in understanding career choices, workplace dynamics, and career patterns (Carter & Cook, 1992; Helms & Piper, 1994; Parham & Austin, 1994). The relevance or lack of relevance for traditional Eurocentric models of career development with some African Americans may be a reflection of the types of racial identity attitudes they hold. Carter and Cook (1992) noted a number of possible implications for African American and other racial and ethnic members based on their racial and cultural identity attitudes. The authors suggested that individuals with *Preencounter* and *Conformity* attitudes may not be aware of racial discrimination that may affect career aspirations and work satisfaction. Individuals with *Encounter* and *Dissonance* attitudes may be conflicted by and unsure about whether sociocultural factors are relevant in their career development. Individuals with *Immersion–Emersion* and *Resistance* may limit their career options to work that only helps and services other African Americans. Finally, individuals with *Internalization–Introspection* and *Awareness* attitudes may have broader career paths, but also have a realistic sense of barriers and limitations.

Whether this holds true, is unknown at this point. Based on the review by Helms and Piper (1994) on studies applying racial identity in vocational psychology, early research in this area has been scant, unsystematic, and mixed. However, Helms and Piper (1994) qualify these results by indicating that the construct of racial salience in the vocational domain needs to be measured in conjunction with racial identity. Thus, the importance of racial identity at the career entry stage or in the workplace may be moderated by whether race is salient to the individual or in the work setting (Helms & Piper, 1994).

Despite some skepticism over the direct relation between racial identity and career behaviors (e.g., Brown, 1995), more research is needed in this area before any definitive conclusions can be made. Future theory-building efforts should begin to integrate racial identity with a variety of vocational constructs (e.g., values systems, occupational stereotyping, career role models, and workforce relationships) and other similarly related cultural variables.

Acculturation

Similar to racial identity, the concept of acculturation as a within-group variable has received significant attention in the multicultural counseling literature over the past 20 years. *Acculturation* generally refers to the degree to which individuals participate in and adopt the secondary culture of the dominant White society as opposed to their primary culture of origin (Landrine & Klonoff, 1994). Level of acculturation emphasizes that African Americans may choose to adopt the dominant culture's traditions and behaviors in different ways and thus, are not a homogenous group. Given that vocational behavior is one domain that occurs within a sociocultural context, how an African American chooses to acculturate may also be reflected in his or her career development. Landrine and Klonoff (1994) recently introduced the concept of acculturation for African Americans by developing the first African American Acculturation scale (AAAS). Based on their preliminary data, the authors found support for a unique African American culture that spans across gender, social class, and level of education. Future directions in career theory may investigate the relations between acculturation and career interests, educational and career choices, amount and type of occupational information, and perceptions of career opportunities and barriers. Additionally, acculturation should be examined in relation to other similar psychological constructs such as racial identity, worldview, and Africentricity.

Acculturation may be viewed as one of many behavioral strategies used by African Americans to cope with the dominant system within the context of career development. Coleman (1994) recently described six possible behavioral strategies (i.e., assimilation, acculturation, alternation, integration, separation, and fusion) that African Americans or any other individuals may use to cope with cultural diversity in the United States. Like acculturation, the measurement of many of these behavior strategies is limited or nonexistant when it comes to African Americans. As valid and reliable measures are developed, this approach may be particularly useful in the career-counseling literature in terms of theory, research, and practice.

FROM BASIC JOB NEEDS TO CAREER ACTUALIZATION

Another important direction toward advancing career-counseling theory with African Americans is to create models that take into consideration the broad range of vocational needs. Many of the traditional theories of career development have been developed by and for a small number of White college-educated individuals who are generally in better positions to attain the American Dream. There are a number of White, middle-class assumptions behind the philosophy and practice of seeking careers. In the vocational realm, that may mean getting at least a college degree, pursuing a respectable, high-status profession, obtaining a comfortable lifestyle, and developing career networks. Consequently, access to higher education appears to be one major gatekeeping mechanism that opens or closes many career opportunities. However, there appear to be very few models that can account for the career paths of the majority of African Americans who neither participate in higher education nor pursue highly selective professions or career paths. For instance, what theories can explain the vocational behavior behind a single mother's decision to stay on welfare as opposed to finding a job versus a multitalented young student's indecision over pursuing medical school or majoring in music? How are these individuals different (or similar) in terms of their vocational needs? Given that the unemployment rate is disproportionately higher in the African American community, many African Americans may be motivated simply to find a job that meets their basic needs and the needs of their immediate family rather than pursue their personal need for a successful career. Perhaps the construct of needs, in terms of Maslow's (1964) hierarchy of needs, may be a useful framework for developing an appropriate career counseling theory.

According to Maslow, individuals are motivated to seek a range of needs from physiological needs to self-actualization needs. Theoretically, lower order needs must be met before higher order needs and values can be addressed. *Physiological needs* are needs that ensure our basic survival such as food and water. At a basic level, individuals may see their career development in terms of simply trying to obtain a paying job so that they can buy food for themselves and their families. The next level of self-motivators, according to Maslow, are *safety needs*. These may include shelter, security, law and order, and protection. In terms of vocational behavior, individuals may be motivated to obtain a job that provides a contracted salary or hourly rate and a range of benefits (i.e., health benefits and life insurance). People may also have their safety needs met if they feel physically safe at work, feel free from harassment and discrimination, or free from being laid off or fired. Therefore, career-counseling theories and interventions should be able to address and examine circumstances where meeting low-order needs may be the most important issues for some African Americans.

Maslow also indicated that there are higher order needs that must be met. The third need level in the hierarchy addresses *needs of love and belongingness*. The need for social supports and affiliations are important in within the vocational context. Individuals may be motivated for social acceptance and cooperative interpersonal relationships with coworkers, superiors, and customers. Identification with the institution or company may also be an important belongingness need. Having similar values, interests, and a shared sense of duty and purpose may promote cohesiveness and a comfortable and satisfying work environment. Thus, individuals who are dissatisfied with their work climate or academic program may be expressing a decline in this basic need.

Once the need for belongingness has been met, Maslow (1964) suggested that individuals are motivated to pursue their own *self-esteem needs*. Persons are driven to develop their own competencies and sense of self-worth. Vocationally speaking, individuals may have their self-esteem needs met after they have become knowledgeable about some topic or feel efficacious in doing a range of job tasks. Individuals may also pursue educational degrees, licenses, certifications, and special training to enhance their sense of self-esteem and prestige. The pursuit of higher education often may be an attempt to fulfill this need and open the door for reaching the highest need of self-actualization.

Maslow (1964) characterized *self-actualization* as the highest level in personal growth that many people only aspire to reach. *Self-actualizers* are able to achieve their potential, contribute to society, and know their own creative mission in life. Building on a solid sense of fulfilled work competence, individuals may begin to pursue the ideal of career actualization. Thus, the highest endpoint in career development may be the attempt to become fully career actualized. Therefore, individuals may view working as a valuable means for meeting their basic needs or allowing them to express their total creativity and potential, while contributing to the welfare of others.

African American career clients may present a variety of need deficits across the need hierarchy. Due to specific life experiences and perceived barriers, a single mother may or may not value the need to become self-actualized. She may believe that meeting her basic low-level needs may be her highest goal in terms of career development. Meanwhile, the college student who plans to pursue medical school may perceive that his self-esteem needs will be met and place him closer to becoming career actualized. Future directions in developing a model based on career needs would include clarifying the factors that may predict where individuals may be along the hierarchy. Factors such as education, SES, gender, occupational information, and perception of barriers may influence how close individuals are to becoming fully career actualized.

A MULTIDISCIPLINARY PERSPECTIVE

Career-choice behavior and patterns have long been investigated by more than just vocational psychologists and career counselors. Economists and sociologists, for example, have examined career-development issues across many groups for decades. Future directions in career-development theory should incorporate diverse perspectives on vocational behavior from other disciplines. Psychologists should begin to collaborate with sociologists, economists, and other career specialists in order to delineate the most critical person and environmental variables in the career development of African Americans.

Sociologists have incorporated the role of SES, discrimination in the workplace, and the role of family members in understanding vocational behavior much more than psychologists. For example, *status attainment theory*, which is represented by the work of Blau (1956) and others, suggests that the SES of an individual's current job can be predicted by the SES of one's first job, encouragement from parents and teachers, cognitive ability, and from the father's occupation and education level. This theory emphasizes many of the same processes that social cognitive models address (e.g., role models and verbal encouragement and learning experiences in the family). However, this approach focuses more on issues related to SES, which has often been confounded with race in many psychological theories and research studies. Knowing that such theories exist may offer some guidance and provide another perspective in evaluating existing psychological frameworks.

Economists can offer their perspective on understanding the labor market. According to the *dual-economy theory*, there are primary (or core) and secondary (or peripheral) labor markets, each entailing separate norms and advantages. For example, jobs in the primary markets are often represented by large firms, high wages, opportunity for advancement, access to advanced technology and global commerce, and high status. Peripheral markets typically offer minimum or low wages, little advancement, high turnover, and low status (see Sharf, 1992). This classification approach focuses on vocational environmental variables outside of the individual and can help counselors become aware of the different hiring practices, earning potential, and work relationships (Sharf, 1992). Other factors that are addressed outside of psychology are gender and racial discrimination in the workplace, attitudes toward participating in the labor market, the ability to cope with noncontrolled chance events (e.g., accidental theory), and the belief that early education and training are valuable and necessary investments for gaining greater long-term earnings and status (e.g., human capital theory). Thus, future theory-building efforts in the vocational psychology literature can benefit from collaborating with economists and sociologists in order to learn what person and environmental factors are important and how they may relate with existing career-counseling models. This approach may also confirm trends already in our fields as well as help promote theory integration.

SOME CONSIDERATIONS FOR STRATEGIES AND INTERVENTIONS

As theory-building efforts continue to expand our understanding of African American career development, career interventions need to stem from these theoretical conceptualizations. Many of the theories discussed in this chapter provide specific guidelines for individual, group, or programmatic interventions. Provided in the following text are some promising interventions for African Americans.

Social Cognitive Interventions

The construct of career self-efficacy may be particularly useful for setting up systematic career interventions because it is based on criteria that can be measured. According to theory, interventions that provide opportunities to have successful performance accomplishments (e.g., learning math skills, operating machinery or speaking a new language); exposure to career role models; techniques for managing anxiety or creating enthusiasm; and verbal encouragement from mentors, parents, and counselors can help to develop positive career self-efficacy beliefs among African Americans (e.g., Betz, 1992). The importance of role models as a form of learning to help African Americans is generally accepted in the career-intervention literature (Bowman, 1995; Murry & Mosidi, 1993). For example, Hall and Post-Kammer (1987) indicated that one of the main reasons that Blacks are underrepresented in the math and science careers is due to a lack of successful Black role models in those nontraditional fields. Although more theoretical and empirical attention has been given to the importance of providing role models, there has been less systematic attention given to the importance of career mentors to African Americans. Having a mentor may provide many African Americans with sources of self-efficacy, including encouragement, modeling, and direct help with work performances. In her review of the mentoring literature, Arden (1990) forecasted a growing movement in the popularity of mentoring for adults in the corporate realm and in higher education as a valuable career-development strategy. Arden specifically recommended that psychologists, career counselors, and educators need to develop intervention programs that help women and minorities become more aware of the developmental stages, advantages, and limitations of mentoring and other support–advisory relationships in their career development.

Brown and Lent (1996) recently argued that SCCT-driven career-counseling interventions may also help clients explore their self-efficacy beliefs, outcome expectations, and career barriers. Counselors using this approach attempt to examine the social cognitive beliefs of clients that lead to their foreclosed career interests and choices, challenge their client's limiting self-efficacy beliefs, and help clients learn coping strategies for their real and perceived barriers. Program interventions (e.g., Chartrand & Rose, 1996) based on this theory may also be practical for use with African Americans.

Needs-Based Interventions

Future career programs and counseling interventions need to be designed to address the diverse needs of African Americans. Specific career interventions should be developed that enable African Americans to meet their low-order job needs (e.g., food, water, shelter, and community) as well as their higher order career needs (i.e., self-esteem, self-actualization). Individuals motivated to have employment that can address their physiological and safety needs must have the appropriate interventions such as networking, basic job skills training, resume development, and advocacy. Individuals needing to have their need for belongingness fulfilled may need help in seeking role models and mentors as well as counseling support in negotiating their work climate. Interventions attempting to help persons wishing to have their need for self-esteem met may need to engage in psychoeducational programs, as well counseling, that help to raise their self-efficacy beliefs and general sense of competence. In-depth vocational assessment and counseling that values the integration of personal and career issues may be useful for helping individuals reach career actualization. Programs that provide exposure to a wide variety of work experiences and feedback may further empower African Americans to consider developing and reaching their potential in the vocational realm and other life realms. Finally, understanding African Americans' racial identity, level of acculturation, worldview, and perception of barriers may be appropriate aspects of developing interventions across all the need levels.

Culturally-Competent Career Counselors

In order to develop accurate interventions with African Americans, career counselors and vocational psychologists of all racial and/or ethnic backgrounds must develop cultural competencies so that they can appropriately address the needs of their clients. Some of the competencies that need to be developed are as follows:

- Awareness and knowledge about one's own cultural biases, assumptions, and stereotypes regarding African Americans in education and work environments and how they impact one's perceptions, attitudes, beliefs, and choice(s) of intervention.
- Awareness and knowledge about one's own biases and stereotypes about different jobs and occupations, as well as who is qualified for these positions.
- Increase one's knowledge about within-group differences (and similarities) in the African American community, which may include values, beliefs, language, SES, gender, class, and racial and cultural identity. Remember that the African American community is also comprised of immigrants whose historical and cultural identities may be different from those who were born and raised in the United States.
- Increase one's knowledge about African Americans regarding the role of the church, family, extended families, and social support systems (Wilson & Stith, 1991) and how they influence career decisions.
- Awareness and knowledge about the educational and career patterns of African Americans such as their traditional versus nontraditional career paths.
- Awareness and knowledge about the real and perceived barriers that African Americans face in society (e.g., racism, sexism, communication styles and differences, etc.).
- Awareness and knowledge about the real and perceived barriers that African Americans face in the educational system and in the workplace.

- Awareness of the attitudes African Americans and their families have toward work, education, and job hunting as well as the manner in which career or job decisions are made.
- Awareness and knowledge about the attitudes African Americans have toward seeking help for their job- or career-related concerns.
- Knowledge about the cultural relevancy of career assessments with African Americans and other groups.
- Acquire skills to employ creative and nontraditional interventions with African Americans.
- Acquire skills to implement multilevel interventions (e.g., systemic, group, and individual interventions).
- Acquire the ability and experience to integrate career-counseling theories, multicultural counseling theory, and competence (Pope-Davis & Coleman, 1997; Sue, Ivey, & Pedersen, 1996), and personal counseling theories.

CONCLUSION

As we begin the 21st century, it seems appropriate to reflect on the ways in which career-counseling theory, research, and practice can address the needs of African Americans. Although some of these reflections have been discussed in this chapter, it is only a beginning. As theories and research are applied to various aspects of African American career development, it is important to assess the impact these efforts have on the actual practice of career counseling for this population. Diversity of values, beliefs, and attitudes, as well as cultural assumptions and expectations, provide many an opportunity to create new and different paradigms in theory, research, and practice. The profession must begin to accept this challenge if it is to remain culturally relevant and sensitive to the ever-increasing diversity in our society.

REFERENCES

Arden, A. D. (1990). Mentoring and adult career development: The evolution of a theory. *The Counseling Psychologist, 18*, 275–299.

Betz, N. E. (1992). Counseling uses of career self-efficacy theory. *The Career Development Quarterly, 41*, 22–26.

Betz, N. E., & Fitzgerald, L. F. (1993). Individuality and diversity: Theory and research in counseling psychology. *Annual Review in Psychology, 44*, 343–381.

Blau, P. M. (1956). Social mobility and interpersonal relations. *American Sociological Review, 21*, 290–295.

Bowman, S. L. (1993). Career intervention strategies for ethnic minorities. *The Career Development Quarterly, 42,* 14–25.

Bowman, S. L. (1995). Career intervention strategies and assessment issues for African Americans. In F. T. Leong (Ed.), *Career development and vocational behavior of racial and ethnic minorities* (pp. 137–164). Mahwah, NJ: Lawrence Erlbaum Associates.

Brown, M. T. (1995). The career development of African Americans: Theoretical and empirical issues. In F. T. Leong (Eds.), *Career development and vocational behavior of racial and ethnic minorities* (pp. 7–36). Mahwah, NJ: Lawrence Erlbaum Associates.

Brown, S. D., & Lent, R. W. (1996). A social cognitive framework for career choice counseling. *The Career Development Quarterly, 42,* 354–366.

Carter, R. T., & Cook, D. A. (1992). A culturally relevant perspective for understanding the career paths of visible racial/ethnic group people. In Z. Leibowitz & D. Lea (Eds.), *Adult Career Development* (pp. 192–217, 2nd ed). Alexandria, VA: AACD, The National Career Development Association.

Chartrand, J. M., & Rose, M. L. (1996). Career interventions for at-risk populations: Incorporating social cognitive influences. *The Career Development Quarterly, 44,* 341–353.

Cheatham, H. E. (1990). Africentricity and career development of African Americans. *The Career Development Quarterly, 38,* 334–346.

Coleman, H. (1994). Strategies for coping with cultural diversity. *The Counseling Psychologist, 23,* 722–740.

Evans, K. M., & Herr, E. L. (1991). The influence of racism and sexism in the career development of African American women. *Journal of Multicultural Counseling and Development, 19,* 130–135.

Fassinger, R. E. (1990). Causal models of career choice in two samples of college women. *Journal of Vocational Behavior, 36,* 225–240.

Fitzgerald, L. F., Fassinger, R. E., & Betz, N. E. (1995). Theoretical advances in the study of women's career development. In W. B. Walsh & S. H. Osipow (Eds.), *Handbook of Vocational Psychology* (pp. 67–109, 2nd ed.). Hillsdale, NJ: Lawrence Erlbaum Associates.

Gelso, C. J., & Fretz, B. R. (1992). *Counseling psychology.* New York: Harcourt Brace.

Hackett, G., & Byars, A. M. (1995). Social cognitive theory and the career development of African American women. *The Career Development Quarterly, 44,* 322–367.

Hackett, G., & Lent, R. W. (1992). Theoretical advances and current inquiry in career psychology. In S. D. Brown & R. W. Lent (Eds.), *Handbook of counseling psychology* (2nd ed., pp. 419–421). New York: Wiley.

Hall, E. R., & Post-Kammer, P. (1987). Black mathematics and science majors: Why so few? *The Career Development Quarterly,* 206–219.

Helms, J. E., & Piper, R. E. (1994). Implications of racial identity theory for vocational psychology. *Journal of Vocational Behvavior, 44,* 124–138.

Hoyt, K. B. (1989). The career status of women and minority persons: A 20-year retrospective. *The Career Development Quarterly, 37,* 202–211.

Landrine, H., & Klonoff, E. (1994). The African American acculturation scale: Development, reliability, and validity. *Journal of Black Psychology, 20,* 104–127.

Lent, R., & Hackett, G. (1987). Career self-efficacy: Empirical status and future directions. *Journal of Vocational Behavior, 30,* 347–382.

Lent, R. W., & Brown, S. D. (1996). Social cognitive approach to career development: An overview. *The Career Development Quarterly, 44,* 310–321.

Lent, R. W., Brown, S. D., & Hackett, G. (1994). Toward a unified social cognitive theory of career/academic interest, choice, and performance. *Journal of Vocational Behavior [Monograph], 45,* 79–122.

Maslow, A. H. (1964). *Motivation and personality.* New York: Harper & Row.

Murry, E., & Mosidi, R. (1993). Career development counseling for African Americans: An appraisal of the obstacles and intervention strategies. *Journal of Negro Education, 62*(4), 441–447.

Okacha, A. G. (1994). Preparing racial ethnic minorities for the workforce 2000. *Journal of Multicultual Counseling and Development, 22,* 106–114.

Osipow, S. H., & Littlejohn, E. M. (1996). Toward a multicultural theory of career development: Prospects and dilemmas. In F. T. Leong (Eds.), *Career development and vocational behavior of racial and ethnic minorities* (pp. 251–261). Mahwah, NJ: Lawrence Erlbaum Associates.

Parham, T. A., & Austin, N. L. (1994). Career development and African Americans: A contextual reappraisal using the nigrescence construct. *Journal of Vocational Behavior, 44,* 139–154.

Sharf, R. (1992). *Applying career development theory to counseling.* Pacific Grove, CA: Brooks/Cole.

Smith, E. J. (1983). Issues in racial minorities' career behavior. In W. B. Walsh & S. A. Osipow (Eds.), *Handbook of vocational psychology Vol. 1. Foundations* (pp. 161–222). Hillsdale, NJ: Lawrence Erlbaum Associates.

Sue, D. W., Ivey, A. E., & Pedersen, P. D. (Eds.). (1996). *A theory of multicultural counseling and therapy.* Pacific Grove, CA: Brooks/Cole.

Todisco, M., & Salomone, P. R. (1991). Facilitating effective cross-cultural relationships: The White counselor and the Black client. *Journal of Multicultural Counseling and Development, 19,* 147–157.

Wilson, L., & Stith, S. (1991). Culturally sensitive therapy with Black clients. *Journal of Multicultural Counseling and Development, 19,* 32–43.

Author Index

Subject Index